AMERICAN DEMON

D0096793

ELIOT NESS
AND THE HUNT FOR AMERICA'S JACK THE RIPPER

DANIEL STASHOWER

NEW YORK TIMES BESTSELLING AUTHOR
OF *THE HOUR OF PERIL*

Praise for *American Demon*

"An iconic police investigator on the hunt for a grisly murderer. Put that on a double bill. I'll go make the popcorn."

—Patton Oswalt, *The New York Times*

"Mr. Stashower spins a seamless narrative of the grisly crime wave filled with vivid detail."

—*The Wall Street Journal*

"Stashower provides shrewd analysis and paints each scene with vivid, macabre details. You'll sweat reading it."

—*The Washington Post*

"Hang on for the ride. . . . [*American Demon*] places you right on the scene, describing the ghastly horrors of [America's] Jack the Ripper while also recounting how crime fighter Eliot Ness started piecing the investigation together, one puzzle piece at a time."

—*Forbes*

"[Stashower] deftly sets Ness's battles against institutional antagonists against an engagingly told, suspenseful account of the search for a notorious killer. . . . Riveting and illuminating."

—*Kirkus Reviews* (starred review)

"The combination of a baffling unsolved crime with a nuanced portrayal of an American icon adds up to another winner for this talented author."

—*Publishers Weekly* (starred review)

"This account is a gripping true-crime thriller that paints a picture of Ness that's significantly different from the version we've seen in *The Untouchables*. . . . True-crime fans will want this one on their TBR lists."

—*Booklist*

"[Stashower's] personal connection to the city breathes life into the well-researched and chilling account."

—*Library Journal*

"Nicely crafted, the book will appeal to hard-core Ness fans and true-crime freaks."

—*New York Journal of Books*

"A thrillingly bedeviling true-crime story interlaced with a nuanced character study—not of the criminal but of his flawed pursuer."
—*Shelf Awareness*

"When it comes to historical crime nonfiction, Stashower is untouchable."
—Harlan Coben, *New York Times* bestselling author of *Win*

"Dan Stashower brings both the novelist's pen and the historian's eye to throw new light on one of history's most baffling cold cases."
—Donna Andrews, *New York Times* bestselling
author of *Murder Most Fowl*

"Chilling . . . Stashower deftly fuses meticulous research with nail-biting storytelling to give this narrative history all the thrills of the best crime fiction."
—Abbott Kahler, *New York Times* bestselling
author (as Karen Abbott) of *The Ghosts of Eden Park*

"A deep and fascinating dive . . . Bringing the character and times to vivid life, Stashower once again makes an important contribution to the annals of American crime."
—Mark Olshaker,
New York Times bestselling coauthor of *Mindhunter,*
The Cases That Haunt Us, and *The Killer Across the Table*

Praise for *In the Hour of Peril*

"Hurtles across a landscape of conspirators, heroes, and politicos in hotel suites, ladies' parlors, and railway depots . . . Now we have the chance to relish the story of the clever and determined characters who were dedicated to his safety."
—*The New York Times Book Review*

"Stashower uses the train's journey as a narrative arc, allowing him to tell the broader story of prewar America and providing insight into the traits that would make Lincoln such a great leader. . . . The chugging

train also injects the book with momentum and suspense as it nears Baltimore."   —*The Washington Post*

"Reads like the best political thriller . . . a great addition for fans of great books of history."   —Associated Press

"A convincing and well-researched chronicle . . . Succeeds as both a historical inquiry and a detective story."
                                                —*Kirkus Reviews* (starred review)

"An enthralling page-turner that is sure to please true crime, thriller, and history fans."   —*Publishers Weekly*

"Riveting . . . History that reads like a race-against-the-clock thriller."
                        —Harlan Coben, #1 *New York Times* bestselling author of *Live Wire*

"Reads like a first-class detective novel. But Daniel Stashower makes it clear that this plot was anything but fiction—it was real."
                                —James M. McPherson, *New York Times* bestselling
                                author of *Abraham Lincoln: A Presidential Life*

"In this fast-paced page-turner, Daniel Stashower not only deploys the skills of a gifted veteran mystery writer but also thoughtfully analyzes the murky evidence surrounding the alleged 1861 'Baltimore plot' to assassinate Lincoln."   —Michael Burlingame, author of the
                                critically acclaimed two-volume *Abraham Lincoln: A Life*,
                                preeminent Lincoln scholar, and holder of a chair in
                                Lincoln studies in Springfield

"Reads like a modern-day assassination thriller. Stashower accurately brings to life the centuries-old conflict between presidential security and political priorities. . . . Change the dates and upgrade the weapons, and the threat is as relevant today as it was in 1861."
                        —Edwin Russell, former special agent, United States Secret Service

ALSO BY DANIEL STASHOWER

The Hour of Peril: The Secret Plot to Murder Lincoln Before the Civil War

The Beautiful Cigar Girl: Mary Rogers, Edgar Allan Poe, and the Invention of Murder

The Boy Genius and the Mogul: The Untold Story of Television

Teller of Tales: The Life of Arthur Conan Doyle

AMERICAN DEMON

Eliot Ness and the Hunt for America's Jack the Ripper

DANIEL STASHOWER

MINOTAUR
BOOKS
NEW YORK

Published in the United States by Minotaur Books, an imprint of St. Martin's Publishing Group

AMERICAN DEMON. Copyright © 2022 by Daniel Stashower. All rights reserved. Printed in the United States of America. For information, address St. Martin's Publishing Group, 120 Broadway, New York, NY 10271.

www.minotaurbooks.com

Designed by Omar Chapa

The Library of Congress has cataloged the hardcover edition as follows:

Names: Stashower, Daniel, author.
Title: American demon : Eliot Ness and the hunt for America's Jack the Ripper / Daniel Stashower.
Description: First edition. | New York : Minotaur Books, [2022] | Includes bibliographical references and index.
Identifiers: LCCN 2022009070 | ISBN 9781250041166 (hardcover) | ISBN 9781466837317 (ebook)
Subjects: LCSH: Serial murders—Ohio—Cleveland—Case studies. | Homicide investigation—Ohio—Cleveland—Case studies. | Ness, Eliot.
Classification: LCC HV6534.C55 S73 2022 | DDC 364.152/320977132—dc23/eng/20220303
LC record available at https://lccn.loc.gov/2022009070

ISBN 978-1-250-90572-7 (trade paperback)

Our books may be purchased in bulk for promotional, educational, or business use. Please contact your local bookseller or the Macmillan Corporate and Premium Sales Department at 1-800-221-7945, extension 5442, or by email at MacmillanSpecialMarkets@macmillan.com.

First Minotaur Books Trade Paperback Edition: 2023

10 9 8 7 6 5 4 3 2 1

For Fred P. Stashower (1902–1994) and David L. Stashower (1929–2018).
Something to fill that untidy gap on the second shelf.

CONTENTS

16   There Goes Eliot Ness   276
17   The American Sweeney   291

     Epilogue: Eliot-Am-Big-U-ous Ness   303
     Acknowledgments   307
     Notes   309
     Bibliography   327
     Index   331

PROLOGUE

The Last of the Good Guys

For about three years, beginning in 1936, Eliot Ness kept tabs on my grandfather Fred P. Stashower. According to information in Ness's possession, Fred P. Stashower was "an old egg-tossing vandal." This, I admit, was news to me.

Eliot Ness, who rose to fame during the Prohibition era as "the man who got Al Capone," kept tabs on a lot of people. His private papers, now preserved at Cleveland's Western Reserve Historical Society, feature a rogue's gallery of bootleggers, rumrunners, racketeers, and gangsters of all stripes. Scrapbooks from his Chicago days chronicle his storied career as the leader of "the Untouchables," the legendary team of Prohibition agents who smashed up Al Capone's illicit breweries. "Eight Agents Caught Capone," reads one clipping. "Eliot Ness, On the Spot, Escaped Death." There are also images of their famous battering-ram truck, rigged up with a heavy steel prow to crash through the doors of the "alky kitchens" that fueled Capone's multimillion-dollar empire. There's even a newspaper artist's rendering of an enraged Capone swinging a baseball bat over his head, preparing to crack open the skull of a mob turncoat.

Still, as I flipped ahead in the scrapbooks, it became clear that the Untouchables formed a surprisingly narrow slice of Ness's career. We're often told that there are no second acts in American lives, but Ness, whose career in Chicago ended at the age of twenty-eight, badly needed one. He found it, after a couple of years in the wilderness, as director of public safety in Cleveland, a position that placed him in charge of the police, fire, and building departments of America's seventh largest city. "Most of the veteran policemen were cynical and didn't believe Ness was for real," one local reporter would recall. "The politicians of both parties were sure he was an overpublicized tyro, a Boy Scout built up by the newspapers, who would soon fall on his face."

There was reason to think so. Ness was the youngest safety director in the history of any large city, and he arrived in Cleveland at a particularly turbulent moment. The city had been an industrial powerhouse in the 1920s, but all progress halted as the effects of the Great Depression took hold. "Cleveland coasted downhill at dizzying speed," a city historian would note.

Worse yet, the Depression created a vacuum in which the underworld thrived. During the Prohibition years, Cleveland became a major hub of bootleg liquor and its "sinister offshoots," including high-stakes gambling, prostitution, and racketeering. This, in turn, gave rise to a web of graft that ran through every level of the city's government and police force. Things got so bad, according to Clayton Fritchey of the *Cleveland Press*, that policemen were expected to "tip their hats when they passed a gangster on the streets."

From his first day on the job, Cleveland's new "top cop" chipped away at an entrenched system of bribes and payoffs. Ness took an aggressive, hands-on approach, insisting that he would not be a "remote director," chained to a desk at city hall. "I am going to be out," he said, "and I'll cover this town pretty well." Not only that, he promised, "I will do undercover work to obtain my own evidence and acquaint myself personally with conditions."

In truth, the odds of Ness going undercover were slim. His face appeared on the front pages of the city's newspapers almost daily, making him easily one of the most recognizable figures in town. In case anyone missed the photos, reporters were quick to embellish, often dwelling on his boyish good looks. "He is about 5 feet 11½ inches tall, weighs 172 pounds, has a mop of unruly brown hair which he futilely attempts to keep parted," the *Press* observed. "His eyes are blue and keen and his complexion ruddy. He is trim and athletic. He looks more like a collegian than an expert criminologist."

His looks were deceiving. Day after day, for months at a time, Clevelanders awoke to read of some fresh feat of derring-do from their young safety director. Ness had kicked open the doors of an after-hours gambling parlor while the city slept, or cracked down on an extortion racket, or rousted a crooked precinct captain. "There was never anybody like him," said one admirer. "He really captured the imagination of the public in his early years, and he was given a hero's worship."

But there was one stubborn blot on his otherwise flawless record. Beginning in 1934, and continuing on Ness's watch, a string of brutal murders staggered the city. The killings were utterly without precedent—so grisly and shocking that they came to be called "a real-life 'Murders in the Rue Morgue.'" Though Cleveland had seen more than its share of violent crime, being nearly as "mobbed up" as Chicago and New York, these murders were chillingly exceptional. Each of the victims had been beheaded—some, it appeared, while still alive. The remains, in most cases, were painstakingly dismembered and scattered across the city.

The horror took many forms. A pair of schoolboys would stumble over a headless torso, or a hacked-off section of an arm or a leg would be spotted floating down the Cuyahoga River, or a severed head would appear in a city dump. Each atrocity touched off a fresh cycle of fear, outrage, and calls for action, with thunderous headlines such as "The Mad Butcher Strikes Again" and "Who Is This Mad Torso Killer?" Fifty years earlier, the entire world had recoiled as a series of horrific crimes unfolded in London's Whitechapel district. Now, it seemed, an unnervingly similar note of terror had been struck in America. "Cleveland's Torso Killer," read one national headline, "Slays in Same Manner as Jack the Ripper."

There were many parallels, certainly, but also troubling inconsistencies that posed a challenge to investigators. No pattern could be seen in the tally of the dead—there were men and women, blacks and whites, straights and gays. The victims, when they could be identified at all, were found to be indigents, drifters, or prostitutes—people who would not be missed. Some were known to have been living rough in the hobo jungles of Kingsbury Run, a dried-up riverbed that cut across the city's southeast side. This gloomy no-man's-land—a patchwork of trash heaps, cooking fires, and pools of industrial sludge—served as the killer's hunting grounds.

Cleveland's detective bureau launched a massive effort, putting in hundreds of hours of overtime. When conventional methods failed to bring results, they pushed themselves to devise fresh ones. A veteran detective named Peter Merylo even set himself out as bait, disguised in hobo gear, but the killer remained elusive. Many hoped that the investigation had reached a turning point when Eliot Ness took personal charge in September of 1936, but the "scientifically-trained investigator" appeared just as flummoxed as the army of detectives under his command.

"Ten times in Cleveland a mad headsman has killed—and 10 times he has dissected with consummate skill the body of his victim," wrote a *Cleveland Press* reporter at the height of the drama. "Ten times, indicating skill at surgery or efficiency at butchery, he has baffled police so completely that today there is no tangible clew to the killer. What is he like, this ghoul who delights in cutting up the bodies of men and women, leaving legs and arms and heads and torsos to be found by small boys, bridge watchmen, chance passersby?"

As the death toll continued to climb, Ness found himself besieged. "I want to see this psycho caught," he declared, but nothing in his training or experience had prepared him to track a serial killer—the phrase itself had yet to be coined. As pressure mounted, Ness grew edgy and frustrated. Capone had been nailed on a technicality: a strict interpretation of the United States Tax Code, the most rigid and banal set of rules in existence. This time, the rule book had yet to be written. Ness faced a criminal who not only flouted the law but whose motives were only dimly understood.

Here was a problem that couldn't be solved with a steel-nosed truck.

For the past three years, I've had an Eliot Ness action figure on my desk. Also, an Eliot Ness Transogram board game and a graphic novel featuring Ness and Batman. Ness, I've come to learn, comes with a whole lot of pop culture baggage. He's a maddeningly slippery figure, and it's often difficult to separate fact from fiction. Even the year of his birth is a subject of debate.

Much of the hyperbole surrounding Ness springs from the pages of *The Untouchables*, a rock 'em, sock 'em potboiler of a memoir published in 1957, in collaboration with sportswriter Oscar Fraley. The dialogue sounds like an Edward G. Robinson gangster flick: "We walked up to these goons and that one with the shiner started for his roscoe." Ness has been roundly criticized for the book's many exaggerations and inventions, but at least some of these embroideries originated with Fraley. Among Ness's papers, there is a copy of a long memo that he sent to his collaborator, laying out the "background and incidents of the Capone case." The writing is awkward and scattershot, but over the course of a dense twenty-three pages, Ness gives a largely unvarnished account of himself and his part in the drama. He takes pride in the dangerous work done by the Untouchables, but he also provides a clear-eyed assessment of his role as a supporting player in a larger, multipronged effort to bring down Capone. By the time Fraley recast this raw material into book form, however, Ness had become the central figure of the campaign, a square-jawed hero who all but lassoed Capone from the back of a galloping horse. Ness expressed discomfort over the book's many excesses, but he did little to moderate them. By that stage, he needed the money.

In time, *The Untouchables* provided grist for a wildly popular television series starring Robert Stack and, later, a landmark film directed by Brian De Palma from a script by David Mamet. These portrayals carried Fraley's extravagances to fresh, lofty heights. It may be sufficient here to say that the real Eliot Ness did not throw the gangster Frank Nitti off the roof of the Chicago Federal Building. More than thirty years later, however, everyone remembers that scene from the movie: "He's in the car."

It's easy to see why this version of Ness, a smooth amalgam of Dirty Harry and Atticus Finch, resonates so deeply with people. He's the embodiment of two-fisted justice, so much so that it's even claimed he served as the model for Dick Tracy, the straitlaced supercop of comic strip fame. Few people, myself included, are immune to this appeal. I grew up on the *Untouchables* TV series. Or, more specifically, I spent rainy afternoons watching fuzzy, flickering reruns on Cleveland's Channel 43, with the rabbit ears on our Hotpoint TV carefully set to ten and two. The character on-screen seemed inextricably linked to Chicago, as much a part of the landscape as Wrigley Field. I knew even then that Ness had a Cleveland connection, but the details remained fuzzy.

I was born and raised in Cleveland. I delivered copies of the *Cleveland Press* from the basket of my Schwinn Sting-Ray, and I still have my membership card for the Bernie Kosar Quarterback Fan Club, #1064. That was a tough time to be a Clevelander. Our river caught fire. So did our mayor, the unfortunate Ralph J. Perk, who somehow set his hair alight with an acetylene torch at a metalworkers' convention. Mistakes were made.

Still, when I went looking through Eliot Ness's scrapbooks at the Western Reserve Historical Society, I felt a certain amount of hometown pride. At first glance, his papers make for a strange mishmash, especially as the young Chicago gangbuster slides into a corner office at Cleveland's city hall. Intriguing glimpses of his police-cleanup effort, with headlines such as "Ness is Nemesis of Crooked Cops," are jumbled in with blueprints for a newfangled "coin-in-slot parker," later known as a parking meter. Oddities abound. There's a letter from the "King of Hoboes," thanking Ness for a lunchtime talk, and there's a sheet of lyrics for a children's song on safety awareness: "A Goof Plays on the Roof."

Many familiar faces can be seen peering out from the yellowed clippings and bleached photos. I had expected to see the big-name gangsters. "Scarface Al" Capone covering the unsightly gash on his cheek with a handkerchief. "Machine Gun" Kelly hoisting his trademark tommy gun.

Alvin "Creepy" Karpis with his hands splayed to show the misshapen fingertips with his prints surgically erased. Those men were there, along with several other notorious criminals, but so, too, were many of the era's leaders and shining lights: Franklin D. Roosevelt, John D. Rockefeller, and J. Edgar Hoover, among others. Also, Fred P. Stashower.

There are some for whom this last name will not be familiar. Even for me, his grandson, it came as a surprise to find Fred P. Stashower mentioned several times in Ness's scrapbooks. Many questions sprang to mind. In 1935, the year that Ness became director of public safety, Fred P. Stashower was a rising young ad man. This was well before my time, but I'm fairly sure that he had no criminal record or mob connections, and I know for a fact that he kept his original fingerprints. I knew him, years later, as a genial, pipe-smoking figure in a powder-blue sport coat. A typical day in his company began with an "improving lecture" at the Rowfant Club, a venerable bibliophilic society, and finished on the fifty-yard line of the old Municipal Stadium, commiserating over yet another losing effort from the Browns. He contained multitudes. Wherever he went, some local politician, broadcaster, or sports figure would be sure to cross the room and say hello. Fred greeted all of them the same way. "You're the last of the good guys," he would say. Then, still gripping the guy's hand, he'd tip a wink to anybody who happened to be standing nearby. "But," he would add, "I could tell you stories."

He seemed to know everyone, but even so, it took some digging to figure out how he came to be enshrined in Eliot Ness's scrapbooks. Ness and my grandfather, it seems, crossed paths at least once a year at an event called the Anvil Revue. This was a raucous political roast staged by amateur performers from the City Club, an otherwise sober-minded group of leading businessmen. It was modeled along the lines of the White House Correspondents' Dinner or the Gridiron Club Dinner. A sampling of program titles over the years gives some idea of the tone: "Hoax Populi," "The Pie-eyed Pipers," and "Bombs in Gilead." My grandfather, it appears, was a perennial cast member, and Ness was a frequent target of their japes and gibes—one of the "goats," as they were known. One year, a City Club actor took the stage wearing a child's

Buster Brown uniform, with short pants and a Peter Pan collar, to par-
ody Ness's youth and gee-whiz enthusiasm. "I'm the youngest safety
director in the United States!" he exclaimed. "The G-Man who got Al
Capone single-handed! I'd like to tell you in a few words how to rid the
county of crime and corruption, jaundice, pyorrhea, toothache and body
odor!" Ness took it in stride, apparently. He pasted a caricature of the ac-
tors involved into his scrapbook, including Fred, along with an audience
photo of himself pressing a hand to his forehead, all but doubled over in
appreciation of the joke.

I knew my grandfather for thirty-four years, and he never mentioned any of this. He never mentioned his celebrated turn as FDR,
complete with pince-nez and ivory cigarette holder, or the year that he
had to go on with his arm in a sling, having broken his elbow playing
basketball, or even the year he was branded "an old egg-tossing vandal"
following a prank at City Club headquarters.

In fact, I don't recall that Fred ever mentioned Eliot Ness by name,
but I'm guessing they knew each other well enough to cross the room
and say hello. They were the same age, and—I know for a fact—they
frequented many of the same watering holes. One of these places was a
tavern called Fagan's, said to have been a speakeasy in the Prohibition
era. It catered to the foundry workers and dockhands of "the Flats," a
tangle of shipyards and industrial buildings spread along the banks of
the notoriously twisty Cuyahoga, or "crooked river," that divided the
city into its eastern and western halves.

Fagan's still had a shot-and-a-beer vibe when I went there with my
grandfather in his later years. There was sawdust on the floor and pick-
led eggs on the bar, and Fred's drink would be on the table by the time he
sat down, after exchanging pleasantries with all and sundry. He drank
Canadian whiskey on the rocks. It occurs to me now that for a man born
in 1902, who came of age during Prohibition, this was the good stuff. It
came across Lake Erie straight from Canada, unadulterated, as opposed
to the local brown hooch and needle beer. (My grandmother Hildegarde,
being a woman of more refined tastes, took hers with a splash.)

Fagan's closed a while back, but these days you can get a nice glass of Eliot Ness Amber Lager at the brewpub of the Great Lakes Brewing Co., just across the river. The dark wood behind the bar is pocked with bullet holes where, according to legend, Ness once exchanged gunfire with local hoods. It isn't true, and no one really ever believed it in the first place, but the story persists, as stories about Ness seem to do.

Even now, however, the hunt for the Kingsbury Run killer stands apart from the other stories. "He was that almost unknown creature, a master criminal," one expert would observe. "It can be argued powerfully that he was the greatest murderer of all time." More than eighty years later, the debate over the Mad Butcher and his reign of terror still rages, both in print and over drinks in bullet-pocked saloons. The story also forms a largely undisclosed chapter in the enigmatic saga of Eliot Ness, a grim counterpoint to his camera-ready exploits with the Untouchables, pitting a newly minted American hero against a blood-crazed demon who struck from the shadows.

"One of these days," wrote reporter Bud Silverman in 1961, "before a new generation of Americans becomes indoctrinated with the 'untouchable' version of the life and works of the late Eliot Ness, somebody ought to sit down at his typewriter and describe the man as Cleveland knew him. By almost any measurement, Ness was quite a guy, but he was not the gun-blazing, fist-swinging raider the romantics of the airways are now portraying him."

He was quite a guy; that much is true. You might even say that he was the last of the good guys.

But I could tell you stories.

PART I

AL'S NEMESIS

1

THE LADY IN THE LAKE

"Police business," he said almost gently, "is a hell of a problem.
It's a good deal like politics. It asks for the highest type of men,
and there's nothing in it to attract the highest type of men. So
we have to work with what we get—and we get things like
this."

Raymond Chandler, *The Lady in the Lake*

Before leaving for work each morning, Frank LaGassie, a thirty-four-
year-old photostat operator, often wandered up and down the southern
shore of Lake Erie looking for driftwood. On that particular morning—
September 5, 1934—LaGassie found himself near the familiar stone
archway of the Euclid Beach amusement park. Euclid Beach, patterned
on New York's Coney Island, was a Cleveland institution. It featured
an iconic wooden roller coaster called the Thriller, an elegant carousel
with hand-carved horses and chariots, and a beloved line of concessions
featuring handmade "Humphrey's Kisses" and sugar-coated popcorn
balls. At this stage of its long history, the park operated under an uplift-
ing slogan: "Nothing to depress or demoralize."

For several days, Cleveland's weather had been both depressing
and demoralizing, with heavy banks of low clouds pressing in to trap
the greasy smoke from nearby factories. In the *Cleveland Press*, a local

weatherman explained that there hadn't been enough wind to disperse the city's industrial gloom, creating conditions that all but repelled the sun's rays. Cleveland, according to the *Press*, might soon be known as "The Dark City."

Shortly before eight, Frank LaGassie caught sight of something—a tree trunk, perhaps—half buried in the sand. Moving closer, he saw that the object was in fact a large rotting slab of human flesh. Repulsed, LaGassie took a step back and struggled to make sense of what he was seeing. The blanched, grisly mass appeared to be the lower half of a woman's torso, severed midway through the spine. The legs, still attached, had been hacked off at the knees. From a distance, it might have been a broken mannequin. A closer view brought horrifying angles of bone, viscera, and loose flaps of skin.

Gathering himself, LaGassie turned and ran to a nearby house to call the police. Within hours, the remains had been transported to Cuyahoga County's two-story brick morgue on Lakeside Avenue, where Coroner Arthur J. Pearse took charge. At fifty-one, Pearse had a reputation for a cool head and a sharp eye for detail. Many recalled his decisive courtroom testimony during the sensational 1931 murder trial of "Pittsburgh Hymie" Martin, a rumrunner accused in the vicious slaying of a city councilman named William E. Potter, whose injuries included a skull-crushing blow from the butt of a revolver. Pearse not only offered compelling detail about powder burns and hair samples, but also described the painstaking manner in which he had unscrewed the wooden grips from the suspected murder weapon, finding blood on the interior surfaces. A Republican in heavily Democratic Cuyahoga County, Pearse objected to the necessity of playing politics to hold on to his job, but he was shrewd when the need arose, especially during the Roosevelt landslide of 1932. At one political rally, he drew thunderous applause by insisting that his services were offered without regard to political leaning—or at least, the coroner added slyly, "no one ever complained."

Now, examining the hideously butchered remains on his table, Pearse worked quickly to gather the vital data. He realized at once that the likelihood of establishing the woman's identity—in the absence of a head or hands—was remote at best. Without facial features, dental work, or fingerprints, Pearse had little to go on. He took note of an abdominal scar, indicating a hysterectomy performed "a year or more before death," but admitted that the observation offered only scant hope of identification.

Working methodically through the afternoon, Pearse fixed the time of death within a window of six to eight months prior to the discovery— but, he added, the remains had been in the water "only a short time." He estimated the woman's height at five foot six, and her weight at roughly 125 pounds. Her age, he determined, would have been somewhere from the mid- to late thirties. Curiously, Pearse noted "unmistakable evidence" that the body had been doused in some sort of chemical preservative, giving the skin a hardened, leathery quality described in some accounts as "reddish." He sent a skin sample to local experts, who tentatively identified the chemical as a form of slaked lime. Pearse theorized that the killer might have intended to hasten the decomposition of the body with a caustic quicklime compound, but instead inadvertently applied a preservative. "There are many persons," he told a reporter, "who mistake slaked lime for quick lime and try to do away with bodies in that way."

One thing was clear in Pearse's mind. The woman, whoever she was, had been a victim of foul play. The coroner took pains to rule out the possibility, however remote, that a "prankishly inclined" medical student was pulling a stunt of some kind, using a discarded cadaver to create a stir. Early on, Pearse consulted a local anatomy professor who assured him that such a thing was unlikely, as all "experimental material" was subject to strict cataloging and numbering procedures. When a theory surfaced that the dead woman might instead have been a suicide whose floating corpse was later ground up in the propeller of a passing boat, Pearse batted the idea aside. Close examination of the severed vertebrae, he said, showed the work of a delicate, sharp knife rather than a large, blunt propeller blade. "There is no question," he said, "but this case is a murder."

By the time Pearse finished his initial examination, the story was front-page news: "Hacked Body of Woman Found on E. Side Beach," read the headline in the *Press*, one of the city's afternoon papers. Eager reporters gathered at the morgue, where Pearse provided the facts in unsparing detail. "The torso was severed between the second and third lumbar vertebrae," the coroner said, "apparently with a surgical instrument. The lower limbs were severed at the knee joints." His official report, later reprinted in several newspapers, provided readers with unusually graphic details: "Part of the spinal column had been hacked away," it read. "The head and shoulders were missing."

The following day, as a handyman named Joseph Hejduk read the story in his morning paper, he felt a shock of recognition. Two weeks earlier in North Perry, thirty miles east of the city, he had made a similar discovery. As the *Press* would report, Hejduk had come across "what he believed to be the vertebrae and ribs of a human body." The bones had "a scant amount of flesh remaining," and beside them lay a dead seagull. Hejduk reported the find to a local deputy sheriff, who mistook it for an animal carcass and instructed him to bury it in the sand.

Now, following the reports of LaGassie's discovery, Hejduk realized that he might have inadvertently buried evidence of a crime. He phoned the police and was soon leading a group of detectives on a search of the beach. Coroner Pearse, apprised of the development, acknowledged that Hejduk's description "fitted roughly" with the missing portion of the torso discovered earlier. The coroner's interest was piqued by the dead seagull Hejduk had spotted beside the bones. The specimen in the morgue, he told a reporter, had been treated with a powerful chemical of some kind, and "it was possible for such a chemical to kill a seagull." Since the remains in his possession appeared to have been in the water only a short time, Pearse now speculated that the body parts might have been packed into containers and set adrift in the lake. "It was the coroner's theory," reported the *Plain Dealer*, the city's leading morning paper, "that the trunk, box or other container might have been ripped open by stormy weather and the torso released, to float ashore." At Pearse's urging, Cleveland police announced a plan to drag the lake near the sections of shoreline where the remains had washed ashore.

For the moment, however, it appeared that Joseph Hejduk's promising lead had sputtered out. Heavy rains had battered the shore in recent days, making it difficult to find the spot where he had buried the bones two weeks earlier. Hejduk and a pair of detectives searched for more than two hours but were forced to suspend their efforts as darkness fell.

The following morning, under brighter conditions, Hejduk had better luck. The handyman soon led a group of officials to a set of buried remains that included "three lumbar and 12 dorsal vertebrae of the spine, the ribs, a section of the right shoulder blade and most of the flesh of the upper back." The gruesome find was carefully wrapped and transported to the morgue, where Coroner Pearse declared that it was "indisputably" a match with the earlier remains. "The spinal cut corresponded," the *Press* reported, "and the flesh on both pieces was whitened and hardened by a preservative."

Given that neither set of remains showed much damage from exposure to lake water, Pearse's theory that the body had been packed into one or more containers and set adrift now seemed all the more plausible. Even so, the coroner came no closer to identifying the victim: "Head, arms and lower legs are still being sought," noted the *Press*. Worse, the discovery of the additional body parts appeared to inject a note of uncertainty into Pearse's conclusions. Previously, upon examining the first section, Pearse claimed that it had been "expertly dismembered" by a practiced hand, possibly that of a surgeon. The legs, he explained, had been "unhooked at the knee joints," and the spine had been precisely severed with a delicate knife "between the second and third lumbar vertebrae." Now, as he examined the second section, Pearse seemed to revise his judgment, noting that a cruder instrument—a saw—had been used to sever the right arm, cutting directly through the shoulder blade. "No surgeon would have used a saw," he now insisted. "He would have known how to manipulate a knife around the joint."

Chillingly, Hejduk's discovery appeared to have sparked a trend. "Reports of stray bits of flesh and bone, floating boxes and old trunks— all cast up by Lake Erie—kept detectives busy today," noted the *Press* at the end of the week. At a west-side marina, a ferryboat operator claimed to have seen something that looked like a human head bobbing near a breakwall. Not far away, a pair of fishermen found a clump of what appeared to be blond hair on a snagged line. Another man spotted "two fleshy objects" bouncing in the surf, and even poked at one of them with a stick. "It wasn't a fish," he insisted. "It was flesh of some kind." In each case, police and volunteers carried out a search, but found nothing.

Perhaps the most macabre episode came when a young girl, swimming in the waters of an east-side beach, reported seeing a ghostly hand "waving" at her from below the waves. "Badly frightened, she ran home and told her father," reported the *Press*. "He smiled indulgently and promised to take a look the next day. He kept his promise, and while looking, stepped on the thing his daughter had seen." The police were summoned and dutifully waded out to search below the waterline. Again, they found nothing. The girl's father, badly shaken, was adamant in his statement to a homicide detective: "I'm sure it was a human hand."

These sightings kept the police on high alert for several days. As the *Press* noted, however, "their labors brought no further clew to the identity of the woman or the manner and place in which she met her death." At the morgue on Lakeside Avenue, Coroner Pearse renewed his efforts to identify the body, painstakingly combing through the city's lengthy list of missing women, ranging in age from sixteen to seventy-four. As officers fanned out across the city to question the next of kin, Pearse expressed doubt that the net had been cast wide enough. "Heavy storms this summer could have washed the body from almost any part of the lake," he noted, "or it might have been thrown from a boat or dropped from an airplane." It was reported at one stage that, in the hope of improving the odds, the Boy Scouts might be enlisted, setting aside woodcraft and clove hitches to hunt for missing body parts.

It would have been a big job even with the aid of the Scouts. Because Lake Erie is so vast, stretching to three other states as well as Canada, authorities knew it would be all but impossible to cover the entire shoreline, much less pinpoint the scene of the crime. At the morgue, a frustrated Coroner Pearse was forced to acknowledge that he could not even be certain of the cause of death. Even more puzzling, perhaps, was the motive for the dismemberment. Pearse speculated that the woman might have been killed under conditions that made it difficult to dispose of the corpse without attracting attention—a crowded apartment building, perhaps. By cutting the body into pieces, the killer might have hoped to get rid of the evidence in small, nondescript packages.

Cleveland's "Lady of the Lake," as the newspapers dubbed her, began to fade from the headlines after a week of fruitless effort from the city's police force. Authorities had worked every available lead, questioned hundreds of people, and sloshed through miles of sewers in search of additional body parts. Finally, on September 11, the remains were quietly interred in a potter's field. One detective, asked by a reporter if the murder had been a perfect crime, offered a dispirited response: "No," he said, "but so close to being perfect that we don't know what to do next."

That same day, a team of federal "dry agents" and state officials smashed up an illicit liquor still on Cleveland's east side, the latest chapter in a "vigorous campaign to dry up northern Ohio bootlegging at its source." A few days later, readers of the *Plain Dealer* were introduced to the leader of the federal team: "He is Eliot Ness, 31-year-old University of Chicago graduate, who headed the small band of young men known as the 'Untouchables.'" For several weeks, readers were told, Ness had been in the city working "quietly but effectively" on behalf of the alcohol tax division of the federal government. "Unless Cleveland's bootleg fraternity considers itself bigger and stronger than the Al Capone gang," wrote reporter Charles Lawrence, "it may as well get out of the illegal liquor business now and save itself trouble." On average, he continued, Ness was knocking off at least one still per day, much as he had "wrecked the backbone" of the Capone empire. The article went on to sketch the outlines of Ness's Chicago days, complete with crashing his battering-ram truck through brewery doors, spurning bribes, and calmly brushing aside death threats. "That's just a starter," Lawrence insisted, "to give the Cleveland underworld an idea of what it is in for." The expected result was spelled out in the article's headline: "Gangs Here Face Capone Waterloo."

Ness likely had misgivings over the headline. Capone had been behind bars for more than two years, and in that time Ness had learned to show restraint in his dealings with the press. In Chicago, there had been complaints about his showboating. Now, he made an effort to tamp down the reporter's enthusiasm and present himself as a team player. "I am just finding my way around Cleveland now," he told Lawrence, "and would rather talk about what we can do here after we have accomplished it." As for his work in Chicago, Ness carefully "corrected the general impression" that he and the Untouchables had nailed down the evidence that sent Capone to prison. "We did our part, of course," he said. "But the real work of sending Capone to prison was done by the tax investigators. Our job was more spectacular, that was all."

Spectacular or not, his efforts had already made an impression at the highest levels. Though Ness insisted that he was merely "getting acquainted" with Cleveland, the city had big plans for him.

2

CHICAGO HAS FALLEN

> If, outside of regular working hours, you can get Eliot Ness away from a handball court long enough, you may get him to tell you about his wrecking of Al Capone's breweries.
>
> *The Plain Dealer*, July 14, 1935

"Eliot Ness really was two men," remarked Oscar Fraley, the coauthor of *The Untouchables*. "In public he was the Ness of television: talking little, but with authority and using short, terse phrases. In private, with a few close friends, he was the other Eliot Ness, with a bubbling sense of humor and a ready smile." Once he relaxed, Fraley suggested, the steely mask of the Untouchable dropped away. "Then the words rushed out in a smooth flood which mixed wit, perception and warmth."

Reporters were always after Ness to show his "other" self, but he seldom did. He made himself available to the press without fail, always cordial and polite, but for the most part he held himself at arm's length. "His speech sounds candid," a friend recalled, "but it rarely ever is." To some, his clipped, guarded manner suggested hidden depths, a trained observer who was never off the clock. To others, he appeared wary and insecure, a man who wore a smirk to hide his failings. At least one newsman sensed a note of artifice behind the laconic manner: "He immediately strikes one as 'all business,' then smiles and winks, as if the fact that he is merely acting a role is just between you and him. He is, in short, an enigma—but an enigma with lots of promise."

He had always been an enigma. Friends noticed it even when he was a teenager at Fenger High School, on the South Side of Chicago. "Some people considered him arrogant," a classmate recalled, "like he thought he was better than everybody else, but I think he was just uneasy in social settings. Once you started talking to him, he loosened right up and was fine. He just didn't ever take the first step." This social awkwardness, which made a sharp contrast with his well-groomed appearance and crisp attire, landed him with a nickname that neatly captured his contradictory nature. Schoolmates called him "Elegant Mess."

Even the earliest details of his life are mired in contradiction. He was born in Chicago on April 19, probably in 1902, but there remains a lingering confusion over the year of his birth, arising from a mistake in his college records. He was named for the British novelist George Eliot, but it is not clear if his parents, for whom English was a second language, understood this to be the pen name of a female author. Peter and Emma Ness had emigrated from Norway some twenty years earlier, arriving at Ellis Island in 1881 just as the nation was struggling to come to grips with the assassination of President James A. Garfield. "I knew that something big was going on," Peter Ness would recall. "But I didn't speak English and nobody around me spoke Norwegian, so I didn't know what."

Peter Ness settled his family in a close-knit Scandinavian enclave in Chicago's South Side neighborhood of Kensington, where he opened a family bakery that would eventually grow to four locations. The business absorbed most of his time and energy, setting an industrious example for his young son, to whom he became a remote, if admired, figure. Eliot was the last of five children, with a ten-year gap separating him from his youngest sister. As the older siblings left home, Emma Ness doted on her youngest child. "I never saw a baby like him," she would say. "He was so terribly good that he never got a spanking."

By the time Eliot was nine, his father had set him to work mopping floors at the bakery. "He made sure I recognized the importance of hard work, honesty and compassion," Ness would recall. Years later, he would credit his parents with instilling a powerful sense of morality. "I'm so proud," he would say, "to be the son of two people who built a successful business and raised a large family while never cheating anyone out of a nickel." But there was always a wistful note of regret about his father. "He never had a lot to say, but when he did speak, I knew it was something worth listening to," Ness said. "I always took it to heart because I didn't see him all that much."

A quiet, self-contained child, Ness spent much of his time reading detective stories, especially Sherlock Holmes. When he sought out company, he tended to avoid the neighborhood gang of boys. "We used to tease him for playing with girls," a classmate recalled. "We'd play army, or baseball, or other games that were just for boys. We'd invite him to play, and he would just look away and say, 'Naw, no thanks.' He seemed uncomfortable—nervous, I guess. After a while, we quit asking him."

During his teenage years, Ness began to come out of his shell under the influence of his brother-in-law Alexander Jamie, an investigator with the US Justice Department. Jamie, who was twenty years older, saw potential in Ness, teaching him in turn to use his fists, drive a car, and handle a gun. Local newspapers described Jamie in much the same terms they would later apply to Ness. Jamie, they wrote, was a "courageous federal operative" who was known to have "refused huge bribes" in the course of his duties. Ness idolized him, carefully cutting out newspaper clippings that detailed his activities.

In October of 1919, following the passage of the National Prohibition Act, known informally as the Volstead Act, Jamie's career path took a sharp turn. The Volstead Act provided for the enforcement of the Eighteenth Amendment, ratified nine months earlier to establish the prohibition of "intoxicating liquors" in the United States. Jamie soon found himself assigned to the Chicago office of the Prohibition Bureau. Enforcing the new laws, as one official noted, looked to be all but impossible, "like trying to dry up the Atlantic Ocean with a blotter." Even so, Jamie put his back into it. An article headlined "Wield Mop on Chicago Rum" hailed him as the leader of a raid that seized 12,000 gallons of liquor and five hundred cases of beer. Another had him breaking up a drunken high school party and confiscating "twenty-six assorted bottles of poison bearing the label of 'gin.'" Ness, watching from the sidelines, cataloged these exploits as if collecting baseball cards.

Ness graduated near the top of his high school class in 1921, but rather than enroll in college, he bounced around doing manual labor at a munitions factory and dipping radiators at an auto plant. After a time, his father took him aside for a bracing piece of advice: "He said he hadn't worked day and night so that his youngest child would be a failure." Ness promptly went out, bought a suit and a briefcase, and enrolled at the University of Chicago. Only then did he inform his parents of his plans. "The enrollment first and announcement later was typical of Eliot," his mother said.

By all accounts, Ness cut a dashing figure as a college man. Slim and athletic, he began to take an interest in women and was gratified to find his attentions returned. In particular, he focused his energies on Edna Ståhle, a striking dark-haired young woman from the neighborhood who now worked as a stenographer in Alexander Jamie's office. Ness began to find excuses to drop by and linger beside her desk, tossing his hat from hand to hand as he made awkward conversation about the weather and college football.

Ness proved to be an indifferent student at the University of Chicago, drifting through various majors. He still worked part-time at his father's bakery, but he also managed to immerse himself in campus life, pledging a fraternity, working doggedly on his tennis game, and carving out three nights a week to study the martial arts. During his college years, he also discovered a taste for alcohol. His admiration for his brother-in-law's Prohibition work had limits. "The trouble with the Prohibition Law," he later wrote, "was that such a large section of the public did not believe in it; they either were against it in its entirety or figured it was for the other fellow." More often than not, Ness himself figured that it was for "the other fellow."

Ness graduated in 1925 with a degree in business administration and political science. He spent more than a year working for the Re-tail Credit Company, checking credit ratings and verifying insurance claims. It was mind-numbing work for meager pay. "I don't think I could stand the monotony of an office," he later told an interviewer.

After work, he occasionally tagged along with his brother-in-law on the hunt for illicit stills and speakeasies. These ride-alongs offered a glimpse of a more exciting life, and also showed him a city undergoing a transformation at the hands of Al Capone. Alcohol had been the fifth largest business in the country when Prohibition went into effect in 1920, and the new laws did nothing to curb the public's enthusiasm for spirits. Capone rose to power on "a tidal wave of beer," as the *Chicago Tribune* noted, "ministering to a $20,000,000 a year thirst." He built his empire like a Gilded Age robber baron, with interlocking networks of bootlegging, extortion, gambling, and prostitution designed to eliminate competition and maximize profits. As one North Side gangster remarked, "We're big business without high hats." Capone himself, who rode around town in an armor-plated Cadillac, understood what set him apart from other tycoons. "You can get a lot farther with a smile and a gun," he was quoted as saying, "than you can with just a smile."

Ness, the recent business graduate, developed a grudging appreciation. "Together with his ruthlessness, he has the qualities of a great businessman," he later wrote. He added, taking a swipe at the gangster's carefully coiffed appearance: "Under that patent leather hair he has sound judgment, diplomatic shrewdness, and the diamond-hard nerves of a gambler, all balanced by cold common sense."

Even allowing for Ness's hero worship of Alexander Jamie, the decision to follow in his brother-in-law's footsteps would not have been an obvious one. The Prohibition Bureau was riddled with corruption at the time, and held in contempt by honest lawmen and members of the public alike. As Capone set to the work of "giving the public what the public wants," he found that the average Prohibition agent was happy to look the other way for a price. In fact, said an assistant attorney general, the majority of them "were as devoid of honesty and integrity as the bootlegging fraternity." Each month, by some estimates, the Chicago bootlegging empire set aside a staggering $1 million to grease the palms of crooked officials. At times, even Capone himself seemed exasperated. "They talk to me about not being on the legitimate," he snapped at one female reporter. "Why, lady, *nobody's* on the legit. You know that and so do they."

"The skies were black with smoke from 'alky' cooking plants," recalled Treasury Department official Elmer Irey, "beer was as easy to get as water, and it was a foolhardy policeman who dared molest a citizen peddling whiskey that would eat a hole in a battleship." Over time, Capone's enforcers tightened their grip on the city, cutting down rival gangsters with tommy guns, sometimes while leaning from the window of a speeding Cadillac V-63. One reporter summed up the situation in a phrase: "Chicago, the world's Fourth City, has fallen."

Years later, Ness would be notably vague about how he came to join the Prohibition Bureau. "Corruption was apparently a continuous problem," he wrote. "I came in presently to work on personnel." No doubt his brother-in-law exerted some influence, but Ness, who had been sitting behind a desk running credit checks for more than a year, would not have been a hot prospect. For a year or so, he appears to have been little more than a warm body at the bureau. He struggled to make a good impression, and even took to carrying around a copy of the office rule book at all times. His only real distinction, it appears, was that he had managed to pass the civil service exam, unlike most of the other local hires.

Even so, Ness felt confident. "I looked around me after a little while," he would tell a friend, "and decided there really wouldn't be much competition in that field." He set his sights on the bureau's Special Agency Division, a cluster of "small, highly trained mobile forces of investigators," led by an uncompromising veteran named George Golding, a former New York City policeman. "Hardboiled Golding," as he was known, liked to work in the spotlight, and "led his men through miles of popping photographers' flash guns as he rounded up dozens of illicit backroom gin mills and bathroom alcohol stills." Under Golding's command, the tight-knit, well-trained squad "swooped down on unsuspecting Chicago, their eyes blazing and their guns in hand." Ness wanted in. He filled out a transfer request and interviewed with Golding, but he doubted that the boss would give him a second look.

Soon, the landscape shifted. In March of 1928, one of Golding's special agents shot a civilian in the back while raiding a South Side saloon. In a flash, public opinion turned against Golding's raiders, who were now derided in the press as lawless thugs. In the midst of the chaos, while Golding scrambled to repair the damage, Ness received word that his transfer request had been approved. The special squad could no longer afford to be picky. Having made it onto the elite team, Ness resolved to make his mark.

Much confusion hangs over the accounts of Ness's early work as a special agent, with crucial details lost in a fog of conflicting sources. One well-traveled tale has Ness resorting to ugly violence in the neighborhood of Chicago Heights, a notorious hotbed of bootlegging thirty miles south of the city. He and his colleagues, the story goes, had gone there pretending to be in the market for a payoff, hoping to gather evidence of police corruption while sniffing out illicit breweries. "One time two truckloads of merchandise were coming in," longtime resident Sam Pontarelli claimed. "Ness and his men stopped the trucks, grabbed the drivers, squeezed their balls, and beat the shit out of them. Hit them with clubs. It looked as though the shipment would not be delivered, but then money changed hands, and the trucks got through." The account must be treated with caution, as Pontarelli was an intimate of Al Capone's, but in his view Ness was no paragon of virtue: "He was on the take." Even Ness's fellow Prohibition agents noted occasional lapses. "He bent a few rules," said a colleague named Al Wolff, "and even broke a few." Ness would have waved the accusations aside, insisting that he was simply playing a role to get information. Whenever money changed hands, he claimed, it was turned over to his superiors.

On February 15, 1929, Chicagoans awoke to an unusually grim headline, "Firing Squad Kills Seven in Big Gangland Massacre," accompanied by a gruesome photo of the fallen thugs in a spreading pool of blood. Seven members of the powerful North Side gang headed by George "Bugs" Moran had been gunned down in a "murderous fusillade" at their headquarters on North Clark Street. Within hours the press had fastened an enduring label on the murders—the St. Valentine's Day

massacre—describing the crime as "the most sensational wholesale killing in the long and bloody history of Chicago gangland warfare." Police
were said to be "struggling manfully through a maze of theories," but
the anonymous assassins remained at large. In the absence of evidence
to the contrary, it was widely assumed that Al Capone had ordered the
killings to consolidate his power.

Up to this point, Capone had been an object of benign fascination
for many Chicagoans, and his frequent acts of public largesse, including the biggest soup kitchen in the city, had won him a reputation as
"Good-Hearted Al." Now, in the wake of the massacre, public opinion
went sour. "About this time," Ness would recall, "the law-abiding people
of Chicago had had just about their fill of gangs, gangsters and killings.
The Federal government also had had about enough. President Hoover
sent for George E. Q. Johnson and together they planned the downfall
of the Capone mob. The government was out to give him the works."

In truth, George E. Q. Johnson, the US attorney for the Northern
District of Illinois, had been out to give Capone the works for some time.
Johnson was spearheading a bold strategy against the gangster on two
fronts—income tax evasion and conspiracy charges centered on violations of the Volstead Act. President Hoover's directive gave fresh impetus
to Johnson's efforts, and encouraged the escalation of a campaign to rattle
Capone's empire by disrupting his cash flow. A plan now took shape
for a new and improved "Capone squad," created from the ruins of the
Special Agency Division, whose leader, George Golding, had now been
recalled to Washington. In the shuffling of chairs that followed Golding's
departure, the twenty-eight-year-old Ness emerged as "the oldest Special
Agent in this office in point of service." Alexander Jamie, now assigned
elsewhere, recommended Ness take charge of the Chicago office, citing
his "reputation for honesty" as well as "coolness, aggressiveness and fearlessness in raids." In truth, Ness was just about the last man standing
after the Golding debacle. District Attorney Johnson had other ideas,
handing Ness a job more in line with his abilities: leader of the new
Capone squad.

For all of Jamie's praise, Ness had given his supervisors little reason to hope that he would succeed. Ted Kuhn, a veteran agent, recalled Ness's naïve excitement, during his first weeks on the job, over a forth-coming liquor bust: "He thought it would have some kind of domino effect and scare away all of the other moonshiners." Kuhn asked if Ness had kept the details to himself or spread the word around the office. "Just a couple of guys in the department," Ness replied.

"I knew right then that we'd never be arresting anyone in that case," Kuhn recalled, "but I figured it would be a good lesson." Sure enough, by the time the agents arrived on the scene, the brewing apparatus was nowhere to be found. "You've got a lot to learn, kid," Kuhn told his de-jected colleague. "I'll say this for him, he was a fast learner."

District Attorney Johnson was banking on it. Ness would get his marching orders from a determined group of Treasury agents, or "T-men," who had made it their business to learn as much as they could about Ca-pone's sources of income. These men, Ness wrote, could plainly see that Capone and his men "were not paying enough income tax on the huge sums they were making from the illicit beer and alcohol racket." As *The New York Times* would explain, Ness and his men had a clear set of in-structions: "Go out and actually prove that Al Capone is at the head of this liquor conspiracy." At the same time, Ness's raids on Capone's brew-eries would dry up the mobster's revenue, disrupting his web of bribes and payouts and thereby removing "the aura of immunity that had been placed upon the dark brow of 'Scarface Al' by his gangland followers."

Ness intended to pick up where Hardboiled Golding had left off, but with an even greater focus on incorruptibility. To make a serious dent in Capone's bottom line, he would need men who couldn't be bought. "I was allowed to pick a number of agents from any government service that I wished," he wrote. "I was to have a squad of about 12 men who would work with me directly under the authority of the U.S. Attorney." Later Ness would claim that he had "very definite ideas on the type of men" suited to this work. "I ticked off the general qualities I desired: single, no older than thirty, both the mental and physical stamina to work long hours and the courage and ability to use fist or gun."

The reality fell well short of this ideal. For all the talk of a rigorous vetting process, at least a few of the men assigned to the Capone squad were already in place when Ness took charge. And while he might have preferred a team of young single men, what he got was a group of agents who were all older than he was—one of them, Bill Gardner, was forty-six. Most had wives and children, and some of these older veterans had reservations about the fresh-faced "Boy Scout," as Ness soon came to be known. Worse yet, at least one recruit wasn't quite as immune to bribes as the later folklore would suggest, and there were also accusations of "consuming liquor not in the line of duty." It was not a promising start, but Ness found ways to navigate this rocky terrain as he grew into the job. He quietly transferred some men into other divisions, and isolated others from sensitive information.

In time, he winnowed the group down to a select core, beginning with Sam Seager, a former guard at "the death house at Sing Sing," and Marty Lahart, a "tall, happy Irishman" whom Ness had known since his first days on the job. Ness also tapped Joe Leeson, a soft-spoken agent from Detroit who had a reputation as the best "tail car" man in the country, along with the "barrel-chested giant" Barney Cloonan, known to be rough and ready in a fight. Paul Robsky, a former marine, brought a useful array of technical skills, including the know-how to tap phone lines. Not all of the men were happy with their new assignment. "I remember my knees shook like jelly when I got the orders telling me what was up," recalled Lyle Chapman, who was brought aboard as a detail-oriented "pencil detective." For several days, he admitted, "I pondered how to get out of it."

Ness believed he had found the best men available. "They fitted my every qualification," he claimed. Actually, this could no longer be said even of Ness himself, who was certainly young and eager, but no longer single. Ness had married Edna Stahle on August 9, 1929, and the couple moved into a modest apartment on the South Side. For Ness, who had been living at home with his parents up to this point, marriage brought a welcome sense of independence. Edna might well have felt the opposite. She was keenly aware of the demands of the Prohibition job, having worked in Alexander Jamie's office, and knew that these pressures took a toll. During this period, as Ness would tell a reporter, he would put in "hours and hours of intensive work to insure Alphonse Capone's ultimate sojourn behind bars." Edna, meanwhile, found herself sitting alone in their empty apartment.

For the moment, Ness's most intensive work involved drawing up a plan of action for the new team. "Our first move," he said, "was to make an analysis of how we could hurt the Capone mob and its income the most." Everything rested on whether the team could actually locate any of the gangster's breweries. Capone had built several layers of deception into his network of alcohol production, designed to shield the workings and throw off any law enforcement officials who weren't on the payroll. The breweries and supply chain featured a cunning series of blinds and decoys, including duplicate trucks and fake storefronts, along with an ever-changing system of delivery routes and schedules. To Ness, it resembled a street corner shell-and-pea game.

The breakthrough came when the team began to focus on the shell rather than the pea. Instead of putting their attention on the beer itself, Ness and his new squad attempted to track the barrels used to deliver it. "The first observation we made was that the barrels had to be used over and over again," Ness recalled, "and that if we could successfully follow a beer barrel from a speakeasy, we would wind up locating a Capone brewery." This was easier said than done. Capone's operatives were well aware of this weak link in the supply chain and took appropriate precautions. Often the barrels would only be moved in stages, traveling short distances over a period of several days, even when empty. Similar safeguards were applied to the delivery trucks, with lookouts and escort cars keeping watch for any sign of pursuit.

The first opening came when a cluster of empty barrels was tracked to an old factory building near Comiskey Park, the baseball field on the south side of the city. "We, of course, thought at last we had located a Capone brewery," Ness recalled. "But the Capone gang, in its typically efficient manner, had specialized operations. This plant was used for cleaning barrels." Even so, Ness and his men had caught a big break, and they knew what to do with it. "I had on my squad two of the greatest automobile drivers I have ever known," Ness explained. "They could tail a car or a truck so that most times they were undetected."

With the help of his "wheel men," Ness resolved to track the barrels from the cleaning plant to their final destination, which was certain to be a brewery. This was done by slow and cautious degrees because a convoy of "white-hatted gangsters in souped-up Ford coupes" invariably accompanied the barrel trucks. To avoid being spotted, the Capone squad did the tailing in short relays, covering just a few blocks at a time on consecutive days, always keeping a discreet distance or running along a parallel street so as not to tip their hand. "Finally, they tailed it to a large garage in Cicero," Ness recalled, and after several more days of observation, their suspicions were confirmed. "At last we felt we had a Capone brewery," he reported. "We were now ready to make a Federal raid."

Many others, including Hardboiled George Golding, had launched brewery raids before. Capone had always shrugged off these efforts. If one operation got scuttled, two more popped up elsewhere. More important, the men who ran the operations always escaped, each and every time. "No prisoners had ever been taken during a Capone brewery raid," Ness acknowledged. "To us, that meant that the influence of graft had successfully protected these breweries through the years."

Bitter experience had taught Ness to keep his mouth shut as his plans took shape so that no advance word would leak out. Even so, with so many dry agents on the take, Capone would be tipped off soon enough. "If this group of 12 were to make a dent where 250 Prohibition Agents and quite a few thousand police had not," Ness declared, "a different kind of game would have to be played." Ness realized that the team would have to strike hard and fast since they might not get another chance.

"We designed our raid," Ness would recall, "as we would design a football play." For several days, he and his men pored over charts, maps, and timetables in a rented room near the targeted brewery. Earlier raids had bogged down as agents tried to force their way through brewery doors reinforced with steel. These delays allowed the workers inside to slip away through escape hatches, often taking their valuable brewing equipment with them. To overcome a costly bottleneck of this type, Ness intended to deploy his secret weapon: a ten-ton truck rigged up with a heavy steel prow. Again and again, he laid emphasis on the crucial fact that no prisoners had ever been taken during a Capone brewery raid. "It was our plan not to give them a chance to escape," he said, which meant getting through the reinforced entryway as quickly as possible. That being the case, he explained, "it was decided that we would drive the truck through the doors of the brewery."

By the morning of March 11, 1931, Ness reported, everything was ready. Shortly after dawn, his men took up their positions. At the last minute, Ness brought in reinforcements to cover all the exits, including the skylight. Five men would ride in the truck, and ten more in a pair of sedans. The sedans would move in just ahead of the truck, rolling out ladders so the men could scramble onto the roof. "Each man was given an assignment," Ness said. "Each man was instructed to stay at his post until he got word from me."

A short distance away, the raiders could see faint trails of steam blowing through the building's vents, a sign that the brewing vats were churning. Ness, sitting in the cab of the truck, poked his arm through the window and gave a signal. The sedans rolled forward. Ness counted off sixty seconds, then gave a nod to Joe Leeson, who sat behind the wheel. Leeson eased the truck into low gear and started off down the cobbled street, lining up for a direct hit on the heavy entry doors. The engine bucked and whined as the truck gathered speed. Ness braced for impact.

In years to come, this moment would be showcased again and again in books, television programs, and movies: the determined squad of Prohibition agents battering through the doors of an illicit brewery, arriving like the hammer of justice. At the time, as Ness related, the bold maneuver appeared to have misfired. "The doors fell with a great loud clap," he recalled, "and at that moment my heart sank. There was no brewery!"

This had been his great fear—either that his information was faulty or, worse, that someone on his team had tipped off the "alky cookers" that raiders were on the way. As he glumly pondered the empty warehouse, however, Ness caught sight of something peculiar. "What I was looking at was a wooden wall," he said, "painted black, about two truck lengths away from the front door of the building, thus giving the illusion of a vacant garage." The raiders realized at once that the interior of the warehouse had been cunningly dressed like a stage set, concealing a large space at the rear that hid the brewery operation from prying eyes. Gathering themselves, Ness and his men found a set of swinging doors hidden in the painted wall and "were on the necks of five operators in less time than it takes to tell it."

At last, a raid on a Capone brewery had netted prisoners. The raiders had seized not only Capone's men but three trucks, a vast supply of beer in barrels, and more than a dozen massive brewing vats, each with a capacity of several hundred gallons. Ness and Lyle Chapman, the pencil detective, took careful notes on everything they found, including the registration numbers of the trucks, hoping for evidence of the type that could tie Capone to the operation in a courtroom. Once the data had been recorded, the destruction began. Ness and his men brought out axes and gleefully smashed up the barrels and brewing vats, sending glossy waves of beer and foam swirling through a drain in the floor. Ness stood and watched as the last of it gurgled away, while several of his agents came forward to pat him on the back. The Boy Scout had pulled it off.

More raids followed in the early months of 1931. "We seized some 45 trucks and 25 breweries as the days of the investigation went on," Ness recalled. "Each raid was made exactly in the same way, and each brewery was found to be erected on the scale of 100 barrels of beer a day." Ness and his team also scooped up brewmasters such as Steve Svoboda, whose expertise was essential to the operation. Svoboda would be arrested again and again in the weeks to come. He and his colleagues were always released on bail soon enough, but the process caused further delays and disruptions, putting additional strain on Capone's fine-tuned supply chain.

Over time, Ness and his team refined their strategy to enhance their stealth and speed. The ladders were rigged with padding to mask the sound of the raiders clambering onto rooftops. A set of handles fitted into the cab of the battering-ram truck kept the agents from knocking their heads on impact. Even so, Ness would sometimes slip on a leather football helmet as the lumbering vehicle gathered speed.

Before long, the raids took a heavy toll on Capone's bottom line. Ness told reporters that his team was bleeding Capone of $10,000 a day. More than once, however, they found themselves chasing down a false lead. "We'd go in blazing, like real gangbusters, and come up with dry holes," Al Wolff would recall. "This went on for several weeks. Finally, we learned to distinguish between the real leads and the phony ones."

Sometimes it came down to a coin toss. One hot night in July, Ness and his men swarmed into a garage on North Clark Street only to find a large, empty warehouse instead of the expected brewery setup. This time, there were no fake walls or hidden doors. "Well, boys," said Ness dejectedly, "it looks like we're dished again." Behind him, one of the men pulled out a handkerchief to mop his brow, sending a half-dollar coin clattering to the floor. The coin rolled away and slipped through a floor drain at the center of the room. Instead of the expected clink or splash as it dropped away, however, the agents heard a strange, oddly wooden thunk. Ness exchanged a glance with his men as he bent down to pull up the grate. At their feet, they found a hoard of more than a hundred crates of the "finest imported liquors." The loss of a fifty-cent piece had brought in a haul estimated at $15,000.

Over time, Ness expanded his operations with the help of a network of informants. One of them, known only as "the Kid," appeared determined to place himself in harm's way because he wanted "to look good for his wife, who was a burlesk [sic] queen." Ness also sought to gather information through telephone wiretaps, including a daring plan to bug the phones at the Capone gang's sales office in a downtown hotel, "where the telephones rang without let-up with orders from speakeasies for beer and liquor." In order to gain access to an awkwardly placed junction box, Ness hit on an audacious scheme to draw the hotel's guards away from their posts, taunting them with a fancy Cadillac he'd impounded in an earlier raid. "I got the Cadillac touring car out, took down the top, and put my four biggest special agents in the car," he recalled. "In ten minutes a great deal of interest had been aroused, and the guards got into cars and followed my four agents from a distance." With the guards pulled away from their posts, Ness managed to send Paul Robsky, his electronics expert, clambering up the telephone pole at the back of the building to rig a wiretap. "This tap was kept alive for many, many months," Ness reported, "and we learned a great deal about the operations and personnel of the gang through it."

"It was dangerous," Ness would say of these exploits. "We always travelled with sawed-off shot guns in our pockets, and when we went into a restaurant, we always took a corner table as the danger of our undertaking was becoming more imminent." For a time, Capone's henchmen tried to buy off Ness and his men, becoming more and more insistent as the raids took their toll. At one stage, Ness was offered "two crisp $1000.00 bills on my desk every Monday morning." It must have been tempting, given that his government salary came to less than $3,000 per year, but he waved it away. "As my investigation of the Capone mob went on," he said, "and they were being so squeezed that they could barely operate, they became more desperate and more bold. One day as two of my agents followed a barrel truck a car pulled up beside them and the driver threw a huge roll of bills in the window, which landed in the lap of one of my men." Ness added, with evident pride: "He immediately threw it back."

When bribery failed, Capone's men tried other tactics. At first, these efforts were fairly benign. One morning, as Ness emerged from his apartment, he found his sedan propped up on blocks with the front wheels missing. As time wore on, however, Ness and his agents began to receive threatening phone calls, and "hoods in pearl grey hats" could be seen lounging around near their homes. Ness arranged for police protection, but his safeguards failed to prevent a break-in at the squad's headquarters, where the team's files were rifled. Later he learned that the mob had taken a page from his own playbook and tapped the phone lines leading into their headquarters.

On occasion, the strong-arm methods took a more sinister turn. "Just keep in mind," Ness was told at one stage, "that sometime soon you're going to be found layin' in a ditch with a hole in your head and your wang slashed off." More than once, Ness had reason to believe the gruesome threat would be carried out. One night, as he and a partner were scouting the Chicago Heights neighborhood, they noticed a "flashy new car" tailing them. "I suggested that we go to an area in Chicago Heights where the street was very narrow," Ness recalled. They quickly turned off the main thoroughfare and blocked the narrower road with their sedan, forcing the tail car to a halt. Ness frisked the driver while his partner covered him with a shotgun. "I found a gun on him which had all the numbers filed off," Ness said. He knew what this meant. "This was a killer's gun," he reported, "because the mob's method of killing was to shoot the victim and throw the gun next to the body."

Later that night, his fears were confirmed by a phone call from an informant who, Ness said, had overheard a pair of gang members "talking about killing me." The clinching detail came when the caller mentioned that the assassin had been told to use "dum dum" bullets. "This obviously was the man whom we had caught following us," Ness explained, "as the bullets in his gun were of that variety, having a cross cut across the nose of the bullets so that they would make a large hole in the body." Ness and his fellow agent spent the night lying low in a boardinghouse. "This gun," he said, "was obviously meant for us."

On June 5, 1931, the United States indicted Al Capone on twenty-two counts of income tax evasion, alleging more than $1 million of undeclared income between 1924 and 1929. One week later, Capone was indicted a second time for Prohibition violations, in "one gigantic conspiracy case" that alleged some $13 million of annual beer sales over roughly the same period of time. "Capone was brought to the bar of justice on two indictments," Ness would recall, "one with 5,000 violations of the liquor law in collusion with 68 others."

This terse statement glossed over a great many frustrations. Even now, having amassed so much evidence, District Attorney Johnson and his aggressive team of Treasury agents could not be sure if either of the

twin pillars of their case—income tax evasion and liquor conspiracy—
would hold up in court. At the same time, they had to contend with
swirling rumors of murder plots personally arranged by Capone so as
to "forestall the indictment" and derail any further attempts at prosecution. For a time, Johnson came under the protection of a Secret Service
detail, while Ness requested police surveillance for his wife and parents.

As national attention focused on the forthcoming trial, Johnson
found himself swarmed by reporters. In one of his first official statements to the press, the district attorney took special pains to highlight
the work of Ness and his elite squad. Johnson modestly insisted that "all
the praise heaped on him for the dogged pursuit of the gangsters should
be shared," because Ness and his men had "perfected the conspiracy
case" against Capone. These efforts, according to the *Times*, proved to be
"the opening wedge" of the district attorney's campaign.

Johnson's remarks, landing squarely in the midst of a dry thicket
of facts about income tax law, lit a fire under the press. The exploits of
Ness and his "rugged young drys" were now described in terms usually
reserved for the heroes of cowboy movies: "Faced Many Perils in Capone
Round-up," declared a headline in *The New York Times*; "Dared Death to
Get Liquor Evidence," said the *Chicago Tribune*. "No soldier on the battlefield ever performed more heroic work than has Eliot Ness performed,"
read one particularly breathless account. "The country needs more of the
heroism displayed by Eliot Ness." Over the next few weeks, the praise
was picked up and amplified in newspapers across the country, gaining
luster with each repetition.

The district attorney had laid particular emphasis on the "zeal and
incorruptibility" of Ness and his team. "They were the men on the firing
line," Johnson said. "They worked at the risk of death and resisted the
temptation of bribes several times as high as their salaries." At a time
when graft had been elevated to a fine art, this aspect of the story stood
out. Soon, Ness and his team had a colorful new nickname: the Untouchables. It caught on immediately. "The 'Untouchables' have accomplished
their mission," declared the *Times*, and "are waiting for further orders."

In fact, Ness and the newly minted Untouchables were about to find themselves on the sidelines. "Did you ever think you wanted something more than anything else in the world," he reportedly said, "and then, after you got it, it wasn't half as good as you expected? Has that ever happened to you?"

3

JACKASS HILL

Outside a red fuse flickers fitfully by the rails where an engine
is switching, and in the distance the sky glows dully with the
lights around Public Square. A Rapid Transit train rattles and
rolls, leaning on the curve, its windows a streak against the
black cliffs; and for an instant its headlight sweeps the foot of
Jackass Hill. But only for an instant: the blackness closes in, the
night on Jackass Hill is impenetrable as ever.

John Bartlow Martin, *Butcher's Dozen*

In years to come, as the words "Kingsbury Run" became infused with
darkness, the name would be spoken in hushed tones, as if the slightest
whisper might call the demons forth. This was especially true for children, who saw that the subject made their elders uneasy. Conversations
broke off in mid-sentence at their approach, leaving sinister outlines
hanging in the air. At campfires along the Ohio Valley, and at slumber
parties in the safe, tidy suburbs of Cleveland, Kingsbury Run was a tale
told by flashlight, a place where monsters walked and innocents lost
their lives.

It was not always so. The ancient riverbed had always presented
a forbidding terrain, cutting through the city's southeast side like the
track of an angry serpent, but its plunging valleys and craggy cliffs were

spelled off by pockets of uncommon beauty. Generations of Clevelanders, many of them Central European immigrants, came to enjoy picnics
on lush, winding glades and to wade in ice-clear brooks.

Soon enough, the garden spots gave way to industry. Railroad tracks
threaded across the dry bed of the ravine by the end of the nineteenth
century, running alongside John D. Rockefeller's oil refinery, William
Halsey Doan's naphtha works, and many others. Columns of gray smoke
and tall jets of burning gas veiled the skyline, above the clanking and
thudding of heavy machinery behind tall wire fences. Kingsbury Run
became a valley of ashes, but it seemed a small price for the thunderclap
of prosperity that followed.

A pair of ambitious homegrown railroad tycoons, the Van Swerin-
gen brothers, parlayed a modest real estate speculation into a $3 billion
empire during these boom years, much of it resting on the right-of-
way grants along a six-mile stretch of Kingsbury Run. At one end, on a
lush, sparsely populated plateau at the eastern edge of the city, the Van
Sweringens developed a showplace suburb known as Shaker Village,
later Shaker Heights, that became the envy of the nation. At the other
end, at the center of Public Square, the brothers broke ground for an
ambitious downtown rail terminal, a "city within a city" that would
anchor their holdings and reshape the skyline, capped off by a majestic
skyscraper called the Terminal Tower. Each day, the city's businessmen
would be ferried back and forth between Shaker Heights and the Terminal Tower, passing along the natural ravine formed by Kingsbury Run,
on a commuter railroad called the Shaker Rapid Transit, also owned by
the Van Sweringens. This was financial swagger on a global scale, as
one editorial noted, sparking the city's transition "from an overgrown
country town to a real metropolis." At the time of completion, on
June 28, 1930, the Terminal Tower would be the world's tallest building
outside of New York.

The timing had seemed fortuitous when the Van Sweringens
launched the project in their glory years, but the doors of their gilded
terminal complex now opened onto the vacuum of the Great Depression.
In the words of journalist George Condon, the effects of the stock market

crash "swept in with a silent roar like the sound that fills the ears of a drowning man." One factory after another went dark and upended the lives of thousands of workers, many of whom had lived in "rookeries and dives" pulled down to make way for the terminal complex. Makeshift shantytowns with names like Cinder Park and Whiskey Island bracketed the lakefront's Tin Can Plaza and extended into the depths of Kingsbury Run. Workingmen and their families found shelter in shacks of scavenged cardboard and corrugated metal, and slept beneath "Hoover blankets" of discarded newspaper. Each night, as the city's disheartened businessmen made their way home to Shaker Heights, many of them wondering how much longer they would have jobs, the headlamps of the Rapid Transit would send a brief flicker of light across the cooking fires and tar paper shacks of Kingsbury Run. Most of the commuters preferred to look away, as if whistling past a graveyard.

By this time, Kingsbury Run had become a place of violence and sudden death. "If you enjoy feeling your flesh creep," one journalist wrote, "just take a midnight tour through Kingsbury Run." People came there to settle grudges and, occasionally, to dump corpses. As far back as January of 1874, the body of a day laborer named Charles Hartman was found floating in a shallow pool of water following "some trouble in a saloon." Other reports would surface in the years to come—an infant found dead beside railroad tracks, a boy's skull fractured by a passing stranger, and finally, in November of 1905, the discovery of a "headless and limbless form" on a garbage dump. The gruesome nature of this last horror left reporters straining for acceptable language. One writer fastened on a phrase that would recur again and again in the days to come: "torso murder."

Immigrant workers, some of whom had quite literally pulled themselves up from the depths of Kingsbury Run, occasionally chose to build homes along the jagged cliffs overlooking the valley. Often their houses were perched along streets that sheared off like broken twigs as the terrain plunged downward. One of these neighborhoods stood at the southern edge of the Run near East 49th and Praha Avenue, at the top of a steep, sixty-foot slope known as Jackass Hill.

Toward the end of the afternoon of September 23, 1935, two boys were seen walking near the top of Jackass Hill. Sixteen-year-old James Wagner and twelve-year-old Peter Kostura were tossing a ball back and forth as they headed home. When the ball sailed wide and rolled down the sharp incline, Wagner challenged his friend to a race to the bottom. The footing was treacherous, and both boys were off balance as their momentum carried them downward. At the bottom, a clump of brush stood beside the path. Wagner got there first, and as he waited for Kostura to catch up, he caught sight of something white and strange among the branches. He took a step closer and then shrank back, eyes wide. Turning away, he scrambled back up the hill, shouting at the younger boy. Turn around, he called, there's "a dead man with no head down there."

First on the scene were Sergeant Arthur Marsh and Patrolman Arthur Stitt, a pair of railway "bulls" hired by the Erie Railroad to police their yard. In the brush at the foot of Jackass Hill, they found what James Wagner had glimpsed: the body of a headless man. The man was pale white and lying on his side, nude but for a pair of black cotton socks. One early report would insist that the corpse had been "neatly positioned as though by an undertaker" with the heels together and the hands stiff at the sides, but a photo taken at the scene shows the remains in an oddly restful pose, with the arms gently crossed as if clutching a pillow.

The railroad men could see no blood on the body or on the ground nearby, a fact that struck them as highly irregular. The jugular vein, as one investigator would point out, "is a snaky thing, it splatters blood everywhere when you cut it." Marsh and Stitt surmised that the victim had been killed elsewhere, drained of blood, and cleaned up. Only then had the body been dumped at Kingsbury Run. As they examined the body more closely, they noticed a horrifying slash mark between the legs— along with the beheading, the victim had been castrated.

Marsh put in a call to the Cleveland police while Stitt backed away and made a search of the surrounding area. According to one account, only a few moments passed before Stitt began shouting for his partner.

"You find the head?" Marsh called back.

"No," Stitt replied. "It's another body."

Stitt had uncovered a second male corpse some thirty feet away, also missing its head and genitals. This victim appeared older than the first, and the body was in a more advanced state of decomposition, with a peculiar, darkened tinge to the skin. Close by, Stitt noticed a thatch of dark hairs poking out of the ground. Kneeling down, he began brushing away a mound of loose sand. He drew back at once, startled. As the sand broke up, he found himself staring down at a severed human head.

By now, detectives and patrolmen from the Cleveland Police Department had arrived to begin a systematic search. Orley May and Emil Musil of the detective bureau arrived in the first wave, having responded to a radio call. Within moments, a second severed head was uncovered a short distance from the first. One account holds that it rolled out like a wilted cabbage as detectives tunneled into the bank of a sandy ravine, coming to a stop at their feet.

Officers also found an assortment of clothing nearby, some of it bloodstained. The items included a white shirt and pants, a blue suit coat, some underwear, and a checked cap. In addition, police found scattered lengths of rope and a rusty metal pail filled with oily liquid, later identified as motor oil. Detectives speculated that the oil, subsequently found to contain traces of blood and hair, might have been brought to the scene as a means of burning the bodies. No sooner had this theory been raised than a final, horrific discovery drew the attention of the investigators. A clump of tangled flesh found near one of the bodies proved to be the severed genitals of both men.

This last detail presented an awkward problem for the horde of reporters now converging on the scene. Already, they knew, the discovery of headless corpses would push the limits of propriety in a family newspaper. Any discussion of this brutal emasculation risked a total breach, especially for the somewhat staid and businesslike *Plain Dealer*, a fixture of breakfast tables throughout the city. In the days to come, journalists would strain for acceptable euphemisms. Some made oblique reference to a "murder of passion" or "love vengeance," but most adhered to the example of the following morning's *Plain Dealer*. There, in a model of economy and restraint, the victims were described as "headless and otherwise mutilated."

Coroner Arthur J. Pearse reached Jackass Hill at about six, roughly one hour after the initial discovery. Glancing down at the headless corpses, he briskly fulfilled the first of his official obligations and pronounced that the two men were, in fact, dead. This done, he set to work. Studying the remains more closely, Pearse estimated that the first victim had been killed four days prior to discovery and the second perhaps three weeks earlier. The condition of the second body, he told reporters, would make identification a challenge, but he was hopeful where the first victim was concerned. Missing persons reports would be carefully checked. As Pearse continued his examination, a police photographer pressed forward with his camera to document the scene.

As evening fell, curious residents of the surrounding neighborhoods began to gather along the rim of Jackass Hill, peering down at the unfolding drama. They watched silently as investigators combed through the brush and peered into tangles of branches and debris. They stayed long after the remains had been loaded onto stretchers for transport to the morgue. The children of the neighborhood would speak of it for decades afterward. "I saw the head," one would recall. "That was a terrible thing for a child to see."

By 7:30, the remains had arrived at the Lakeside morgue, where it was quickly confirmed that the two decapitated heads were a match to the bodies found at the scene. Deputy Coroner Wilson Chamberlain began the autopsies early the following morning, recording that the first body was that of a "handsome" man, five feet eleven inches tall and weighing about 150 pounds, with a light complexion and brown hair. Rope burns on the wrists indicated that the victim had been tied up and struggling at some point before death occurred. A heavy, sharp knife had been used to sever the head, leaving clean edges to the skin, indicating a strong, practiced hand. A telltale retraction of the neck muscles, together with an almost total absence of blood in the heart, brought Chamberlain to a chilling verdict: "This man's death resulted from decapitation with a sharp instrument."

Coroner Pearse's official report echoed this uncompromising conclusion: "Murder and mutilation," he recorded. "Death due to decapitation
and shock—Homicide." In a statement to a *Cleveland News* reporter, the
coroner would go even further, expressing his belief that "either a butcher
knife or an axe was used to hack off the heads of the two men after their
hands had been tied behind their backs."

It could not be said for certain whether either man had been con-
scious at the time of death, but, as one homicide detective remarked
during the autopsy, decapitation seemed an extremely odd method of
murder. "Usually," the detective observed, "a murderer kills by other
means—stabbing, shooting, strangulation, poison. Sometimes, not often, the heads are removed to prevent identification, but almost never to
kill." He added: "It's a hell of a job to remove a human head, anyway."

The second body, despite its more advanced state of decomposition, offered intriguing contrasts to the first. This victim appeared
older and stockier, roughly forty-five years of age and perhaps
165 pounds. He measured five feet six inches tall, with "brown eyes,
very dark hair and perfect teeth." Again, the decapitation had been
clean and precise. Stranger still, as a lab technician noted, the body
appeared to have been doused in "some unknown chemical," turning
the skin a dark oak color.

This last detail—the apparent application of a preservative of some
type—would eventually suggest a link to the Lady of the Lake, whose
remains had been discovered on the shore of Lake Erie one year earlier. For the moment, Chamberlain and Pearse drew no connection, perhaps owing to the large number of corpses that had passed through
the morgue in the intervening months, nor does the parallel seem to
have occurred to any of the investigators at the scene. As in the earlier
case, however, samples of skin were submitted for lab analysis, in the
hope of identifying the chemical used. The results only served to raise
more questions. While Chamberlain had estimated that the second victim had been dead anywhere from seven to ten days, revising Pearse's
findings at the scene, the lab report indicated that it might have been as

long as four weeks. And where Chamberlain had suggested that an acid might have been used, the lab report drew attention to the bucket of oil and hair found at the scene, suggesting the possibility that the body had been "saturated with oil and fire applied," accounting for "the peculiar condition of the skin."

By this time, a far more promising lead had surfaced to draw the focus away from the many contradictions. The decomposition of the second victim had been too advanced to allow for fingerprints, but investigators were able to lift a clear set from the corpse of the younger man. These provided an immediate match to a well-thumbed file in the police records room. The younger victim was now positively identified as twenty-nine-year-old Edward Andrassy, a figure familiar to neighborhood police. Andrassy had a reputation as a "snotty punk," according to one officer, and had often been found boozing and brawling along an east-side cluster of saloons and gambling parlors known as Rowdy Row. Police had picked him up more than once for public drunkenness, and occasionally he could be found sleeping off his latest bender in a graveyard near some train tracks. "Andrassy was the type of fellow gives a cop a lot of lip when he's questioned," a railroad bull would say of him. "Once I had to knock him down."

Andrassy's livelihood was a mystery, even to his family. His police file included reports of marijuana trafficking and panhandling, and he had once served thirty days in a workhouse on a concealed weapons charge. More recently, he had boasted to a friend about "a very risky business" involving some form of mail fraud. There were even rumors concerning a voodoo cult.

"Young Andrassy was a worry to his hard-working parents," the *Press* would report. "He had long been idle, and refused to look for work." This was not entirely true. Andrassy had worked various jobs over the years, pulling stints as a hotel bellhop, a magazine salesman, and a laborer on a government relief project. His only steady employment, relatively so, had been as an orderly in the psychiatric ward of Cleveland City Hospital, a job he found in his late teens. Apparently his work habits left something to be desired; over an eight-year stretch, he would be fired and rehired eleven times.

During one stretch of employment at the hospital, Andrassy stepped in to intervene when an agitated patient lashed out at a nurse named Lillian Kardotska. The nurse's gratitude soon led to romance, and she and Andrassy would be married a short time later. Within three weeks, it became clear that Andrassy wasn't cut out for domesticity. His bride, who was now pregnant, grew so enraged with his bad behavior that she bashed him across the forehead with a high-heeled shoe. The blow left a pockmark that could be plainly seen on Andrassy's severed head six years later.

Cleveland police interviewed dozens of people who had worked with Andrassy at City Hospital, as well as the staff at the Warrensville workhouse where he'd been incarcerated four years earlier. Officers also carried out an extensive canvass of the neighborhoods surrounding Jackass Hill. No potential lead went unchecked, no matter how slim. Upon learning that Andrassy's older brother had been killed in a brawl some thirteen years earlier, police tracked down the man responsible and questioned him closely, to no avail. When officers discovered a pile of old newspapers among the dead man's effects, with a handful of names and addresses jotted in the margins, they doggedly followed up each notation. Again, their efforts went nowhere.

Many of the people interviewed gave bizarre and contradictory statements. One man reported finding a bloody typewritten note at the base of Jackass Hill, containing instructions for cremating a body. Another pair claimed to have spotted an elderly man crouching over the spot that had concealed Andrassy's remains; he hurried away, they said, when approached. At one stage, a watchman with the New York Central Railroad came forward with an especially tantalizing lead. In the weeks prior to the discovery of the bodies, he said, there had been sightings of a green coupe at the top of Jackass Hill. Inside was a man with a pair of binoculars who could be seen scanning the horizon through his windshield. In time, Detectives May and Musil traced the owner of the car, but the seemingly hot lead ended in disappointment. The man with the binoculars had selected the spot because it commanded a view of a particular window on the other side of the Run, belonging to a married woman with whom he was having an affair. Whenever the woman's husband was safely out of the house, she would signal the all-clear by hanging out a white tablecloth.

Police also made the rounds of a vast number of cheap hotels, rooming houses, pool halls, and bars, hoping to construct a timeline of Andrassy's final days. Here again the specifics proved difficult to pin down, even in the accounts given by members of Andrassy's immediate family. The victim's father, Joseph, was an industrious Hungarian immigrant who had been in Cleveland for more than thirty years, variously working as a painter, shoemaker, and metalworker. He told a detective that he had last seen his son four days earlier, adding that Edward often "associated with persons of questionable character" in the city's notorious third police precinct, known as the "Roaring Third," in a seedy neighborhood near the town center at Public Square. In those days, one journalist would write, the Roaring Third was "a region of Italian and Greek vendettas, of speakeasies and secret distilleries, of narcotics dens and houses of prostitution; and more than one man went to the electric chair."

Andrassy's mother, meanwhile, reported that her son had been afraid to leave home for several days, but she recalled seeing him earlier with an unknown companion riding around in a fancy dark car—the type of car, she said, that a gangster might own. One night he had come home bleeding from a gash to the head, but claimed that he could not remember how he came to be injured. On another occasion, Andrassy told his sister Edna that he had "stabbed an Italian" during a fight, and now feared reprisals from "the gang." He refused to supply any further details, saying only that he would have to lie low for a while. "Edward lived in continual fear of his life," his parents told the police. "He always told us to mind our own business when we told him to straighten out." It would not have been easy for them to mind their own business since the evidence of their son's shady behavior always seemed to wash up on their doorstep. Mrs. Andrassy would recall that a middle-aged man had turned up a couple of months earlier, claiming that "he was going to kill Edward for paying attention to his wife."

Threats like this one led some investigators to speculate that the murderer might have been a cuckolded husband. The days leading up to Andrassy's death seemed to feature a parade of young women, at least some of whom were married. He frequently had been spotted at a particular downtown nightclub, always with someone new on his arm, and there were whispers that he traded in "Spanish fly," an illicit aphrodisiac. Many other vaporous, unsubstantiated rumors would surface in the days to come, and each new claim brought another round of prurient speculation. "His associates were questionable characters, suspected perverts," the *Press* insisted. "Andrassy's known background included incidents of strange behavior." At times, it was claimed, he had dabbled in pornography and prostitution.

Among Andrassy's effects, police discovered a pair of medical books, one of which involved the treatment of female disorders. The find appeared to support a particularly distasteful story told to police by a man named Peter Feltes, who had known the victim since childhood. Andrassy, Feltes said, occasionally attempted to pass himself off as some sort of "female doctor." On one occasion, Andrassy told his friend that his wife was looking unwell and proposed to examine her. He offered to go home and get his instruments in order to do a thorough job, claiming that he "could fix her within a month, so that she could have children." Some accounts suggest that Feltes offered no objection, while others claim that Andrassy threatened him with an ice pick. In any case, police were told, Andrassy proceeded to force his attentions on his friend's wife and, according to one account, "committed sodomy" under the pretense of carrying out an examination. It is difficult to know what to make of this ugly tale, as Andrassy's saga is filled with lurid accusations made by unreliable witnesses. The ill-treated woman does not appear to have brought charges of any kind, but perhaps it would have been more remarkable if she had, given the unwelcome notoriety that it would have brought and the largely unsympathetic attitudes of the time.

By the same token, the discovery of a stack of "physical culture" and "muscle" magazines in Andrassy's room sparked a great deal of hazy speculation. "Our journey will take us into the lower depths of American life, indeed, into the very lowest depths," wrote John Bartlow Martin, an early chronicler of the case, "inhabited by prostitutes, pimps, hobos, dwellers of caves and shanties, homosexuals, and the kind of twisted persons that interested Krafft-Ebing." Views of this type, though typical of the era, would throw a long shadow over the investigation in the coming months. The terms "pervert" and "deviant" would be used with unsettling frequency, often with the suggestion that such unsavory characters deserved whatever life handed them. Given that both of the bodies at Jackass Hill had been brutally castrated, it was natural that investigators should focus on the role that sex had played in the crime. "Because of the nature of the mutilation practiced on the bodies," reported a Chicago paper, "police are inclined to characterize the crime as one of passion." For some investigators, however, the violence done to the corpses only served to narrow their focus. "The police believed this indicated that the murderer was a sexual pervert," wrote Martin, "and they wondered if Andrassy was one himself." It was a question that would occupy a great many hours, perhaps at the expense of other lines of inquiry. It bears mentioning that Andrassy's former wife, Lillian, airily dismissed the notion of homosexuality. "He was anything but," she said.

Other investigators, taking note of the victim's Hungarian descent, believed the crime might have had its roots in a blood feud among immigrant factions, at a time when Cleveland boasted one of the largest Hungarian populations outside of Budapest. "At first we thought it was a 'nationality case,'" one detective would say. "It's not unusual for a Hungarian or Bohemian to cut up people, they learn to butcher in the old country. So we figured what the hell, we'll send a couple of detectives up on Jackass Hill that can speak the language, ask a few questions, and that's it."

Meanwhile, authorities continued their efforts to uncover the identity of the second victim. Detectives grew hopeful when reports surfaced that Andrassy had been seen in the company of a friend he introduced as "Eddie," a chauffeur for a wealthy woman said to be receiving Andrassy's dubious services as a "female doctor." The two men had been spotted in an expensive sedan, perhaps a Lincoln or a Buick, which might well have been the same "gangster" car Andrassy's mother had mentioned. "Eddie seemed very nervous," one witness would say, adding an unexpectedly detailed description of him as "good looking, very good set of teeth, appeared to have a broken nose and wore dark trousers, blue shirt, checkered gray cap, and dark brown hair." At least some of these details, notably the "very good set of teeth," tallied with the description of the older man found at Jackass Hill. Frustratingly, when witnesses were taken to the morgue to view the remains, the results were inconclusive.

Even so, as the investigation gathered steam, the *Press* offered its readers a tidy recap of the "gruesome double-murder mystery." A now-familiar image of Andrassy ran at the top of the account, flanked by photos of James Wagner and Peter Kostura, the two boys who had discovered his body. Police were said to be pursuing "several clews" and working from a detailed list of theories:

THAT the bodies of the two victims were taken to the foot of the hill, known as 'Jackass Hill,' after the murders had been committed elsewhere.

THAT the victims knew each other and were killed by the same person.

THAT the unidentified victim was killed first, and his body immersed in some sort of fluid until the murderer could trap Andrassy, who, according to Coroner A. J. Pearse, was killed a week later.

THAT both men first were beheaded, then stripped of their clothing, after which they were further mutilated.

THAT each victim, after his hands were tied, was 'executed' with some sharp instrument, probably an ax or a butcher knife.

Many readers would have found themselves bewildered by this list, and most especially by the head-scratching notion that the killer had preserved the body of the older victim in a bid to "trap" Andrassy. The summary exposed a mass of gaps and contradictions, and one crucial point, in particular, appeared to have slipped through the cracks. The *Press* noted that the two victims had been killed elsewhere and taken to the foot of Jackass Hill, but this deceptively straightforward statement brushed past the problem of how the bodies had been transported to this remote and inaccessible spot. One assumes the killer fastened on Jackass Hill as an isolated dumping ground where the remains could be easily hidden, and where they might lie undisturbed at least for a few days. He might well have driven a car to the top of the hill, but he then would have faced the daunting problem of getting the bodies down the steep, sixty-foot incline. A car could not have handled the sharp angle, and there is no record of drag marks or tracks from a cart or wheelbarrow. This suggests that the killer might have carried the remains from the top to the bottom, perhaps in darkness, making at least two trips, and somehow completing the grim task without being seen. If so, the killer was likely a figure of considerable size and strength, possessing either a steely nerve or a reckless disregard for the possibility of being caught in the act.

If, as some investigators assumed, the process had been carried out in the dark, it might help to explain why the remains were not particularly well hidden. Though the heads were at least partially buried, the bodies had been poorly concealed in the underbrush. Stranger still, the genitalia and bloodied clothing appeared to have been tossed carelessly aside. Perhaps the killer had been interrupted in the midst of the concealment. Possibly he intended to burn the remains and clothing, using the pail of oil found at the scene, only to be forced to improvise when someone approached. If so, given all of the attention focused on the crime afterward, it seems remarkable that no one came forward and no supporting evidence was uncovered in the canvass of the surrounding neighborhoods. One theory of the case posited that Edward Andrassy might have interrupted the killer at his work. Perhaps, the reasoning went, Andrassy came upon the killer as he attempted to dispose of the earlier victim, and was subsequently killed himself. Or, as others have suggested, Andrassy might have been complicit in the earlier murder, even helping the killer carry the body down the steep incline, only to fall victim once the heavy lifting was done. This scenario has several points against it, not least being the absence of signs of struggle or traces of blood at the dumping ground.

Through the final days of September, the drama at Jackass Hill dominated the front pages of the city's three major papers, but a number of other stories vied for the public's attention that week. A dramatic photo sequence from Yankee Stadium captured the climax of the historic boxing match between Joe Louis and "lone white hope" Max Baer, in which the "Brown Bomber" pummeled his opponent in the fourth round. From Hollywood came rumors of the potential breakup of the dance team of Fred Astaire and Ginger Rogers, a calamity "akin to homicide on Santa Claus." And from Chicago came a report that bank robber Alvin Karpis, who now supplanted Al Capone as Public Enemy No. 1, had been thwarted at the scene of his latest heist by a "flood of tear gas and bullets."

In this parade of headlines, many readers would have skimmed past "U.S. Sentences Five Dover Men," a wire service report detailing the "stiff and consequential" penalties handed down to a group of renegade bootleggers in Cleveland. "The gang was rounded up by Eliot Ness, official of the federal alcohol tax unit," the article related, "who was one of the agents instrumental in wiping out the Chicago Capone gang." No mention was made of how Ness happened to find himself in Cleveland, and few readers would have paused to wonder. The city's attention remained focused on Jackass Hill, where the mysterious killer appeared to have escaped capture, at least for the moment. One by one, each of the promising leads went cold and had to be tossed aside in frustration. As the hope of a quick arrest faded, many of the officers working the case realized that they were at the start of a long and difficult path.

Detective Orley May, who had been first on the scene with his partner, Emil Musil, spoke for many as he summed up the mood on Jackass Hill:

"I've got a bad feeling about this one."

4

SNORKY'S LAST RIDE

Eliot Ness was totally unlike the picture the public now sees. He had a baby face, a soft voice, a disarming youthful ingenuousness, but a brilliant mind. He knew how to perform honest, devoted public service in the name of the law, and he had a natural yen for that.

Philip W. Porter, journalist and friend, 1976

In the days following the raft of indictments against Al Capone, Eliot Ness became suddenly, dizzyingly famous. "I was now receiving a great deal of newspaper publicity," he would recall, "and gradually becoming known as a 'gangbuster.'" This was a considerable understatement. Over the space of a frantic two weeks in the summer of 1931, Ness got about as much press as Al Capone, Lou Gehrig, and the president of the United States. "The way to become famous fast," as the legendary journalist Walter Winchell declared, "is to throw a brick at someone who is famous." Ness had thrown a brick at one of the most famous men of his time, creating an irresistible story in the process—the blue-eyed, all-American college boy going toe-to-toe with the sinister Italian mobster. The press couldn't get enough of it, though Capone himself would have objected to the characterization. "I'm no Italian," he would often say. "I was born in Brooklyn."

Ness, for his part, often seemed to be trying too hard. He presented himself as Prohibition's answer to Jack Armstrong, the All-American Boy, and sprinkled his speech with exclamations of "Gosh!" and "Gee!" Occasionally he embroidered details in ways that gave rise to confusion, as when he attempted to clarify the origin of the newly famous Untouchables label, now widely used to describe his team of raiders. Ness claimed that the name arose as a response to the "extremely undignified and unprintable names" being hurled at his men by Capone's henchmen. "He remembered that the appellations employed to describe his group had been used in the caste history of India to describe the 'untouchables,'" reported the *Times*. "So 'Untouchables' it was." The *Times* reporter would attribute this odd piece of window dressing to Ness's irrepressible sense of humor, but like so much of what he told the press in those early years, the explanation somehow raised more questions than it answered.

Often, he tripped over his own feet, as when he sat down with Priscilla Higinbotham, a striking twenty-three-year-old "girl reporter" from the *Chicago Herald and Examiner*. Higinbotham took a special interest in Ness's doings, having recently graduated in the inaugural class of students at Northwestern University's Scientific Crime Detection Laboratory, the only woman in a class of thirty-five men. A photograph taken at the time showed her cradling a Thompson submachine gun.

This interview should have brought out the best in Ness, who spent much of his spare time at the Northwestern crime lab, boning up on the latest advancements in ballistics, fiber analysis, and fingerprinting. At a time when few law enforcement officers had college degrees, Higinbotham appeared eager to present Ness as the face of the future, an earnest young man who had prepared diligently for the task at hand. For a few minutes, at least, Ness seemed to fill the bill. He offered compelling thoughts on "the business of modern crime fighting," along with his "very definite views" about Prohibition and its unintended consequences. "It is not only his desire to run Capone and his henchmen out of town," Higinbotham reported, "but he particularly wishes to destroy the corruptive influences in politics that have resulted from the Capone reign." These corruptive influences formed a theme that would dominate

Ness's career well beyond the era of speakeasies and bathtub gin. So long as the police were on the take, he would say over and over again, it naturally followed that crime would flourish.

As Higinbotham pressed for details about the doings of the Untouchables, however, Ness made a sudden, jarring pivot. He now adopted a breezy, insouciant manner, as if going head-to-head with Al Capone had simply been a pleasant diversion to fill the time between croquet tournaments. It had been "merely by chance" that he joined the Prohibition Bureau, he now insisted. "It offered a lot of excitement, too," he added, "for there certainly is a thrill in pitting your wits against others." His most notable exploit, smashing through the doors of Capone's breweries in a battering-ram truck, was now rendered as something of a jolly lark. "It's funny, I think, when you back up a truck to a brewery door and smash it in," he said. "And then find some individuals inside that you hadn't expected." He even made light of a death threat from a hired assassin, brushing the matter aside with a quip: "We had thought everything was going so well, too." Higinbotham seemed nonplussed at this air of merriment. "Ness has a sense of humor of rather an unusual variety," she observed dryly, "for it would seem rather difficult to laugh in the face of death with any degree of amusement." Mercifully, Ness soon stopped laughing and cut the interview short, recalling suddenly that he was late for a tennis match. He hurried away, leaving his interviewer to sum up his contrary nature in a headline: "Al's Nemesis Boasts Ph.B.; Finds Humor in Dry Work."

Interviews of this type did little to endear Ness to his colleagues, especially those who had shared in the burden of building the case against Capone. To some of his fellow agents, Ness appeared to be hogging a disproportionate share of the credit. Even worse, when speaking with Higinbotham and others, he could come off as a clueless young man who didn't quite understand the stakes—Bertie Wooster with a badge and a .38.

Though he had much to learn about dealing with the press, Ness could justify his openness as a lesson handed down by August Vollmer, "the father of modern law enforcement." Two years earlier, Ness had taken an advanced course on criminology at the University of Chicago taught by Vollmer, who advised close cooperation with journalists as a means of forging better community relations. Ness embraced the message but was ill-prepared for the consequences. Already, as the building blocks of his renown dropped into place, he had sparked resentments that would shadow his career.

The press found a splashy hook in the Untouchables and their battering-ram truck, but the reality of these long months of effort had more to do with a laborious accumulation of facts and figures. Victor Hackler, an Associated Press reporter, aptly described the coordinated efforts of the T-men and dry agents as "colorless work" with "tedious attention to detail" that had flushed Capone out into open court. "Little groups of men," he wrote, "working methodically, quietly, poring over bank records, following beer trucks and clutching at straws, have accomplished what all the gangs in Chicago couldn't do—overthrow the Capone dynasty."

The celebrations appeared premature to District Attorney Johnson, who worried that his evidence might not hold up in court. Behind the scenes, his team held meetings with Capone's attorneys to discuss a plea bargain. Soon, they were reported to have hammered out a deal that carried a two-and-a-half-year sentence. In Johnson's view, this was the only safe bet: a plea bargain would put Capone behind bars. In spite of the vast accumulation of evidence, Capone had been scrupulous about keeping his name off any potentially incriminating records or documents. He kept no bank accounts, owned no property in his own name, and signed no checks. For Treasury Agent Frank Wilson, Capone's slippery accounting became a source of enduring frustration. "He had bought himself a Florida Palace on Palm Island, imported a chef from Chicago, and was spending $1,000 a week on banquets," Wilson groused, "and I couldn't show that this satrap of Chicago earned more than $5,000 a year!"

As the date of the sentencing hearing approached, Capone himself seemed resigned to serving time, which one interviewer characterized as "an easy way out of his hazardous calling, with a peaceful life as his reward after he has served his term." Capone appeared smug and confident as he arrived at his sentencing hearing on the morning of July 30, having told reporters that he was going to face the music and "hoped everybody was satisfied."

Everybody was not satisfied. As the proceedings came to order, Judge James H. Wilkerson, who had handed down a contempt of court ruling against Capone earlier that year, abruptly tossed out the laboriously crafted agreement, declaring that the court would not be bound by any pretrial arrangements. "It is time," the judge announced to a stunned courtroom, "for somebody to impress upon this defendant that it is utterly impossible to bargain with a Federal court." The message was clear: Wilkerson intended to put Capone on trial, come what may.

For Ness, the judge's bombshell proved especially galling. Capone's plea bargain had included a six-month prison term on Prohibition charges, a small but gratifying victory for the Untouchables. Now that the evidence was to be tested in the courtroom, Johnson laid plans to lead with the tax evasion case, holding the Prohibition charges in reserve. This put the Untouchables on the sidelines, at least for the moment. In setting the plea bargain aside, however, Judge Wilkerson also had issued pointed instructions to reindict Capone on the Prohibition offenses so that a federal grand jury might bring more serious charges under the so-called Jones Law, an amendment to the Volstead Act that carried heavier penalties. Ness had every reason to believe that he would get his day in court. "Judge Wilkerson has set the income tax case for trial on Oct. 6," one report noted. "The prohibition case will be tried later."

The press, meanwhile, continued to shower attention on Ness, "the especial thorn in the side of the Capone mob," as the *Chicago Daily News* described him. In the days to come, much attention would be paid to the role that the Untouchables had played in lancing the bull, weakening Capone's empire and setting the stage for his prosecution. "College Drys Cost Capone Half Million," ran a typical headline; "Sleuths Draining Capone Coffers," declared another.

On the first day of the trial—October 6, 1931—thousands of Chicagoans lined the streets, straining for a glimpse of the famous defendant.

Outside the beaux arts Chicago Federal Building, at the corner of Dearborn and Adams, photographers set up tripods on the tops of their cars to snap photos as Capone ducked inside.

"Are you worried?" a reporter shouted at him.

Capone turned, smiling. "Worried?" he answered with a shrug. "Well, who wouldn't be?"

In fact, Capone had seemed conspicuously relaxed in the days leading up to the trial, giving rise to suspicions that he had found a way to game the system. "Capone's boys have a complete list of the prospective jurors," an informant claimed. "They're fixing them one by one. They're passing out $1,000 bills." District Attorney Johnson and Treasury Agent Frank Wilson brought their suspicions to the courthouse, but Judge Wilkerson seemed curiously unperturbed. "Bring your case into court as planned, gentlemen," he said. "Leave the rest to me."

Two months earlier, the judge had blindsided both legal teams by tossing out the elaborately crafted plea bargain agreement. Now, at the opening gavel of the trial both sides had sought to avoid, Wilkerson hurled another thunderbolt. "Judge Edwards has another trial commencing today," Wilkerson announced as he took his seat. "Go to his courtroom and bring me his entire panel of jurors. Take my entire panel to Judge Edwards." With a sweep of his hand Wilkerson had replaced the potentially compromised jury pool with a fresh and untainted one, a maneuver that drew audible gasps from the spectators' gallery. Capone sat rigid beside his lawyers, apparently crestfallen.

In the front row of seats behind the prosecutors' table, Ness sat clutching a battered leather document case, hoping that his liquor conspiracy evidence might yet come into play. At various stages, it was reported that "records of intercepted telephone conversations" would be entered into evidence, and that "Eliot Ness, in charge of the 'Capone detail' of the prohibition unit, may take the stand."

It is unlikely that Ness had ever seen Capone at such close quarters. The pool of replacement jurors, comprised mostly of farmers and other out-of-towners, also stared at the famous defendant with frank interest. The celebrated newsman Damon Runyon, covering the trial for the

Hearst newspaper chain, observed that these "tillers of the fruitful soil" appeared greatly disappointed. The "moon-faced fellow" behind the defense table, Runyon said, did not live up to their expectations of a ruthless gang chieftain. Something was missing: "Perhaps a cartridge belt."

A cartridge belt would have been just about the only thing missing. As the proceedings got under way, the prosecution sought to illustrate the scale of Capone's wealth with a showy display of confiscated treasures, including diamond jewelry, silver champagne buckets, and a $50,000 pinkie ring. Over the next few days, some fifty prosecution witnesses would take the stand to testify to the defendant's lavish spending. "The butcher, the baker, and the landscape maker from Miami were among the witnesses," said Runyon, "not to mention the real estate man, the dock builder, the telephone agent, and the chap who supplied the drapes." A salesman from Marshall Field's, Chicago's best-known department store, spoke at impressive length about Capone's preference for one-piece long underwear crafted from "the finest Italian glove silk." Capone paid twelve dollars a set, he said. The gangster's wardrobe also included dozens of artfully tailored suits, running the gamut from "sulpher-colored" to "dusky purple," at a cost of $135 each. In happier times, Capone's gangland cronies called him "Snorky," a term meaning elegant or spiffy. At one stage, jurors were even invited to handle a diamond-studded belt buckle that belonged to the defendant. At a time when a quart of milk cost twenty-five cents, Capone's belt buckle carried a $275 price tag—and he ordered them by the dozen to pass out to friends. "Is it conceivable," asked the prosecutors, "that he had no taxable income?"

The point seemed obvious, but the prosecution team had difficulty translating the catalog of extravagance into proof of income. In the absence of financial records, this all-but-literal airing of Capone's dirty laundry became the foundation of Johnson's strategy. Much of Capone's defense rested on the contention that he had no income to speak of, and that any money he might have made in the years under consideration had been offset by heavy gambling losses. "I never had much of an income, a large income," Capone had insisted in an interview with

Treasury agents the previous year. The government intended to show that Capone drew huge profits from speakeasies, gambling houses, and brothels, and that he not only failed to pay income tax but also conspired to evade payment. The distinction was important; failure to pay was a misdemeanor, but conspiracy to evade payment was a felony. Much of the evidence was "circumstantial in character," as Treasury Agent Frank Wilson candidly admitted, but over the course of the ten-day trial, the accumulation gathered a potent force, much like fermenting beer.

Ness, whose suits cost less than Capone's underwear, followed the proceedings closely as the days wore on, hoping to catch sight of some of the evidence that the Untouchables had brought to the table. For him, the crucial moment came as the prosecution attempted to link Capone to a fleet of trucks used to make beer deliveries. Ness and the Untouchables had made a specialty of delivery trucks, having seized dozens of them during their campaign of brewery raids. For a time, Capone's fleet had been so depleted that his men resorted to making deliveries in ordinary Ford automobiles, after pulling out the seats to make room for the bulky barrels.

Later, the impounded beer trucks would feature prominently in the pages of *The Untouchables*. Readers were told that Ness, under orders to transfer some forty-five confiscated vehicles to a garage across town, drew up plans for "an impressive motorcade" to spite Capone. Leaving nothing to chance, Ness primed the pump with a taunting phone call to Capone himself: "Well, Snorky, I just wanted to tell you that if you look out your front windows down onto Michigan Avenue at exactly eleven o'clock, you'll see something that should interest you." At the appointed hour, a heavily guarded convoy of captured vehicles, cleaned and polished to a high gloss, rolled slowly past the gangster's Lexington Hotel headquarters. Capone was said to be livid: "I'll kill 'im! I'll kill 'im with my own bare hands!"

Like so many of the tales told in *The Untouchables*, this account is fragrant with artifice. Ness's personal writings make no mention of a parade of captured trucks, and there is little evidence to confirm that the episode ever occurred, though at least one policeman of the era insisted that it did.

Ness himself, as he sat in Wilkerson's courtroom, would have been more concerned with proving ownership of the trucks. When he came to write his account of his first brewery raid, he would stress that he and his men took careful note of the registration numbers of the vehicles they seized in an effort to get "some tie-up" to Capone. "Later," he explained, "it was found that a truck seized on this occasion had been bought several years previously, and as part of the purchase price, another truck turned in. Circumstances connected Al Capone with this purchase, with the activities of the racket, and also with income from the fruit of the racket." It was a small point, but it mattered to Ness. He did not take the stand in October of 1931, but he wanted it known that he had landed a punch.

In any case, the prosecution team soon moved on to more damaging evidence, including an incriminating memo produced by a Capone attorney during settlement talks the previous year, and the testimony of a cashier from a local gambling den who helped to unravel the workings of Capone's web of bookkeepers and middlemen. "There was more of it—lots more—but the curious in the audience seemed to be tiring," noted the reporter from *The New York Times*. After ten days of proceedings, it fell to Damon Runyon to summarize the "gale of oratory" heard in the courtroom: "What the defense said, when you boiled it down to a nubbin, was that your Uncle Sam hasn't proved all those things said about Al Capone in the indictments, and that he is entitled to his liberty forthwith." The argument of the prosecutors, "reduced to a mere hatful," stated that the defendant "had a lot of income and didn't pay tax on said income, and therefore ought to be put in the cooler."

In the end, it took the jury only eight hours to return a verdict. They found Capone guilty on five of the twenty-three counts contained in the indictments against him: three felonies and two misdemeanors. If the maximum penalties were enforced, Capone would face seventeen years in prison, but it was widely expected that he would serve the terms concurrently, rather than consecutively, resulting in a much lighter penalty. At the sentencing hearing one week later, however, Judge Wilkerson once again confounded expectations. Two of the three felony counts, he announced, would be consecutive. "The result," Wilkerson said, "is that the aggregate sentence of the defendant is eleven years in the penitentiary." Capone's eyes seemed to harden as the enormity of it settled over him. "He tried to smile," noted the *Times*, "but the smile was bitter."

On the surface, this appeared to be a decisive victory for the prosecution, but Capone's team saw an opening. "I'm not through fighting yet," the gangster told the press. "I'm not going to admit defeat until the higher court rules against me." This was the scenario that District Attorney Johnson had labored to avoid. The plea bargain that Wilkerson dismissed two months earlier would have sent Capone away without any detours. Now, as the gangster made his way to Chicago's Cook County jail, his lawyers retrenched for a series of appeals.

The prospect of further legal battles meant a fresh set of marching orders for the Untouchables. District Attorney Johnson told the press that they were now building an "airtight" liquor conspiracy case so that new charges could be filed if Capone's lawyers mounted a serious challenge to the tax conviction. Even if Capone served his time, Ness was told, the Prohibition case would be kept current for use in the event that he came up for parole. Ness, spoiling for a fight, rallied the Untouchables for a sweep of Chicago's remaining breweries.

Weeks stretched into months as Capone's attorneys played out their legal options. Soon, Ness would be promoted to chief investigator of the Chicago office of the Prohibition Bureau, but each day brought unmistakable signs that his work was winding down. The years of Prohibition, wrote H. L. Mencken, the legendary "sage of Baltimore," had been an abject failure. "None of the great boons and usufructs that were to follow the passage of the Eighteenth Amendment has come to pass," Mencken declared. "There is not less drunkenness in the Republic, but more. There is not less crime, but more. There is not less insanity, but more." Privately, Ness would have agreed. He continued to put in long hours, but already, in spite of the call for a "new booze conspiracy indictment," his agents were being pulled away and reassigned to other divisions. As calls for the repeal of Prohibition gathered force, Ness could see that his days as leader of the Untouchables were numbered.

As the year drew to a close, Ness found himself further preoccupied with thoughts of his father, who had suffered a debilitating stroke. On December 23, 1931, Peter Ness passed away at the age of eighty-one. "I just wish," Ness would say, "I had gotten to know him better." In his personal scrapbooks, he preserved a clipping that appeared in Chicago's *South End News* long after he had left the city. It identified him as "Eliot Ness, Son of Local Baker."

By the spring of 1932, it became clear that Capone's lawyers were running out of options. In early May, Capone received word that his petition to the Supreme Court for review of his case had been rejected. This, said lawyer Michael Ahern, marked "the end of three bitter years for us and the end of Al Capone." After months in the relative comfort of the Cook County jail, serving whiskey and cigars to a parade of gangland visitors, Capone would do hard time at the federal penitentiary in Atlanta, said to be the "meanest" facility in the entire US prison system.

Just after nine in the evening of May 3, Capone was handcuffed to a "petty auto thief" named Vito Morici, who was also scheduled for transfer. Knowing that photographers would be waiting outside, Capone took steps to conceal his restraints, telling Morici to drape his overcoat over their manacled wrists.

The prison warden arrived at 9:30 to lead Capone and Morici out of the facility. Fellow inmates called out words of encouragement as Capone passed. "You got a bum break, Al!" said one. "You'll own the joint before you're there very long!" shouted another. Flashbulbs popped as Capone reached the prison's inner courtyard. "Jeez," he muttered, "you'd think Mussolini was passin' through."

Ness stepped forward. The job of escorting Capone out of the prison had fallen to the Untouchables, and Ness had arranged for a five-car caravan to transfer him from the prison to the Dearborn railway station, where Capone would board a Dixie Flyer passenger train bound for Atlanta. Later, the scene would be painted as the tense climax to a long and dangerous pursuit, with Ness and his men alert to potential threats on all sides, armed with sawed-off shotguns, revolvers, and automatics.

"Keep your eyes open," Ness was quoted as saying. "You can never be certain what these monkeys will try."

The reality, as the motorcade rolled through the prison gates, proved to be a free-for-all. "The jail gates opened quickly and the Capone car dashed through the crowd, which gave way in V fashion to avoid being run down," reported the *Times*. "After that it was every driver for himself. Fenders and bumpers clashed and pedestrians were trampled in the stampede to avoid being hit." Officers along the way described the ride as the wildest and noisiest ever seen on the streets of Chicago. For both Ness and Capone, the two-and-a-half-mile drive presented a lurching, blurred triptych of the gangland era, hurtling by the site of the St. Valentine's Day massacre on Clark Street, racing past a chain of speakeasies and betting parlors, and finally barreling around the corner at Dearborn and Adams beside the darkened Federal Building, the scene of Capone's conviction in Judge Wilkerson's courtroom.

Sirens blaring, the five cars reached the Dearborn station just after ten. Reporters and photographers pushed forward as Capone, still chained to Vito Morici, climbed awkwardly from the second car. Ness and his men battered through the unyielding ranks of journalists in an "urgent flying wedge," sending a photographer's camera clattering to the sidewalk. Capone tugged at Morici's wrist. "Damn it, come on," he said. "Let's get the hell out of this."

Finally, climbing aboard a Pullman car, Capone settled in for the long ride. Still handcuffed, he managed to light a cigar before offering a smile to photographers. "I don't know much about Atlanta," he told an eager group of reporters. "For one thing, it'll be hot." He joked that he might shed a few pounds by joining the prison baseball team, having once been a "pretty good pitcher and first baseman, if I do say so myself."

Ness, meanwhile, busied himself with a last-minute check of the eight-car train. This done, he made his way back to the compartment where Capone sat chatting with reporters. Here, as recounted in the pages of *The Untouchables*, he and Capone faced each other for the first and only time. "Well, I'm on my way to do eleven years," Capone told his adversary. "I've got to do it, that's all. I'm not sore at anybody. Some people are lucky. I wasn't. There was too much overhead in my business anyhow, paying off all the time and replacing trucks and breweries. They ought to make it legitimate."

Ness shook his head slowly. "That's a strange idea coming from you," he answered. "If it was legitimate, you certainly wouldn't want anything to do with it."

Capone's eyes stayed on him, Ness would report, as he backed out of the train compartment. He jumped down onto the platform and stood watching as the Dixie Flyer pulled away from the station and gathered speed. "There goes two and a half years of my life," Ness recalled thinking. "Only then did it come to me that the work of 'The Untouchables' was finished."

Of all the many inventions and exaggerations of *The Untouchables*, this elegiac face-off with Capone is the most transparent. Though much of the dialogue attributed to Capone appears in the newspapers of the day, there is no mention of a snappy retort from Ness, and no account of it appears in his personal memoir. It is, in all probability, one of many fabrications by his collaborator, Oscar Fraley. And though Ness might well have wanted to believe that he recognized the passing of an era as the lights of the Dixie Flyer faded away, he would, in fact, be at his desk the following morning, and for many days to come, still convinced that he needed to keep his shoulder to the wheel if Capone were to remain in prison.

There were many things that Ness simply could not have known at the time. One fact, in particular, would loom large in the days to come. On arrival in Atlanta, Capone would undergo a routine examination by prison doctors, testing positive for tertiary syphilis. Soon, he would exhibit signs of progressive dementia, and he would never again be a force in the underworld. Received wisdom tells us that the Capone era ended with the tax conviction, but he was only thirty-three years old at the time, and full of plans to keep hold of his power. "I guess," he had told a visitor at the Cook County jail, "if it ain't too stiff a rap, why the

organization would sort of hold together until I got back." Ness hoped
to have a hand in thwarting those plans, buttressing the tax conviction
with Prohibition charges, but it was not to be. In his scrapbooks, Ness
would preserve a pair of headlines from February of 1938, by which time
a badly deteriorating Capone had been transferred to the brand-new
Alcatraz Federal Penitentiary: "Al Capone has Mental Break" and "Put
Capone in Strait-Jacket." The following year Capone would be released
on parole, a broken man, and he would die in January of 1947, within a
few days of his forty-eighth birthday. Ness and the Untouchables would
never have their day in court. They became redundant almost at the
moment Capone arrived in Atlanta.

This became a lifelong disappointment for Ness. Though he took
great pride in the role he had played in putting Capone behind bars, he
remained frustrated that the full weight of the liquor conspiracy evidence was never brought to bear. At the same time, he faced a daunting
challenge of living up to his own press as "the college boy who took
on Capone." Ness was not yet thirty years old when Capone went to
prison, and already the Untouchables saga was becoming a double-
edged sword. Soon, he would tell friends that "he was pretty well fed
up" with the subject.

"All I know about Capone," he said, "everybody knows—now."

PART II

THE MAD BUTCHER STRIKES AGAIN

5

CAPONE NEMESIS GETS BIG JOB

This is the kind of merciless war on crime Cleveland has long awaited. The community pins its faith on Ness, the man who knows what it's all about!

The Plain Dealer, December 12, 1935

The arrival of Eliot Ness, the celebrated gangbuster, drew scant notice in Cleveland in the summer of 1934—"little more than a municipal side glance," as reporter George Condon would recall. "The city was too much caught up in the toils of the deepening Depression and the many serious problems that plagued the community to get excited over the arrival of a young man to take up a government post that seemed remote and unimportant."

Even so, Ness felt ready for a change of scene and eager to make his mark. His last days in Chicago had been dispiriting as one by one the members of the Untouchables peeled off and went their separate ways, a process hastened by the consolidation of government agencies under the new administration of Franklin D. Roosevelt. For a time, Ness had joined the Justice Department's transitional Alcohol Beverage Unit, but soon he began angling for a job with the United States Bureau of Investigation, which would shortly be reconstituted as the Federal Bureau of Investigation under its thirty-eight-year-old director, J. Edgar Hoover.

Ness considered himself a shoo-in at the FBI. Technically, he had already worked for the bureau earlier that year, when the shuffling of government agencies briefly placed the Prohibition Bureau under Hoover's jurisdiction. With his college degree and his glittering record of service, he appeared to conform perfectly to Hoover's ideal of an all-American G-Man—smart, clean-cut, and morally upright. Ness submitted his application in the fall of 1933, bolstered by a letter to Hoover from District Attorney George E. Q. Johnson, who praised the "splendid piece of work" Ness had done in the pursuit of Capone. "Boss is using his influence," Ness told a friend. "Everything appears to be OK."

Everything was not OK. The famously thin-skinned Hoover had no tolerance for agents who got more press than he did. Worse yet, Hoover harbored a seething resentment against Johnson, having become incensed at the praise heaped on the district attorney during the Capone drama. Hoover dismissed the press accounts as "bunk" and claimed that he himself deserved much of the credit, having pressed an otherwise reluctant Johnson to take action.

Nevertheless, Hoover went through the motions with Ness's application. He wrote to inform Ness that federal agents started off at a salary of $2,465 a year, well below the $3,800 Ness was earning at the time. "Kindly advise this Division whether you would be willing to accept the regular entrance salary," Hoover wrote, "in the event it is possible to utilize your services."

There is no record of Ness's response, but it soon became apparent that Hoover would not utilize his services at any price. Ness had imprudently told a friend that he expected to be put in charge of Hoover's Chicago office, and would accept nothing less. Word of this boast made its way to Washington, and Hoover was not amused. The director now began amassing a file of reports and press clippings on Chicago's golden boy. On December 4, 1933, Hoover made a terse notation: "I do not think we want this applicant."

The following day, the Prohibition era officially came to a close with the passage of the Twenty-First Amendment. The "ghastly farce," as Congressman James Montgomery Beck phrased it, was finally over. It marked a rare moment of high spirits amid the lingering gloom of the Depression, with a quarter of the work force still unemployed and the Dow more than two-thirds below its 1929 peak. One of the most vocal celebrants was journalist H. L. Mencken. To illustrate his belief that Prohibition had increased rather than reduced the country's consumption of alcohol, Mencken marked the repeal by downing a large glass of water—"my first," he said, "in thirteen years."

The repeal found Ness "passing through a rather unsettled period," as he later admitted. He had been as much a figure of Prohibition as Carrie Nation, the hatchet-wielding "avenging angel" of the temperance movement, and he seemed certain to fade into irrelevance now that the battle was over. The FBI had offered a chance to move forward with the times. Now, with his application stalled, Ness feared he would be cast aside with the other relics of the failed experiment.

For the moment, there was still plenty of mopping up to do, and a great deal of money at stake. Now that alcohol was legal again, the Treasury Department was already making plans for the massive windfall of liquor taxes that had abruptly come to life. At a stroke, the job of former "drys" like Ness shifted to protecting the government's interests. Much of this work was the same as it had been before: stamping out bootleg operations wherever they could be found. A robust network of illicit stills had sprung up in the "Moonshine Mountains" of Ohio, Kentucky, and Tennessee, and the difficult work of imposing federal law on these backwoods "alky kitchens" fell to Ness. In early 1934, he landed in Cincinnati as assistant investigator-in-charge for the region. At the age of thirty-one, Ness was done with Chicago for good.

Life as a "revenoor" proved difficult. "Those mountain men and their squirrel rifles gave me almost as many chills as the Capone mob," Ness would recall. Even so, he turned down other, more comfortable job offers, certain that his current post would pay dividends in the long run. Finally, in August of 1934, he won an appointment as investigator-in-charge for northern Ohio. Ness and a four-member staff established their headquarters in the stolid twenty-one-story Standard Building in downtown Cleveland, amid the marble fixtures and bronze metalwork of the recently defunct Standard Trust Bank. This felt luxurious after the rough-and-tumble of the Moonshine Mountains, and both Ness and his wife expressed pleasure at regaining their domestic comforts. Edna had remained behind in Chicago while her husband chased through the backwoods, but now, with the promise of stability in the new job, she settled into a small lakefront cottage in Bay Village, an hour's drive from downtown. For the moment, she appeared content. As before, however, her husband's work kept him out until all hours. Edna spent a great deal of time at home with only her six cats for company.

For Ness, Cleveland presented a familiar landscape, even in its darkest aspects. Like Chicago, the city had become a stronghold of organized crime during Prohibition, with a rail hub and shipping network that proved ideal for the distribution of bootleg liquor. Even after repeal, bootleggers continued to produce and sell alcohol in staggering quantities. Powerful crime syndicates such as the Mayfield Road Mob controlled all aspects of the pipeline, beginning with the corn sugar that fed the stills and ending with rake-offs from the city's innumerable saloons and gambling parlors. In Chicago, Ness and the Untouchables had tracked empty beer barrels. In Cleveland, his team sprang into action whenever a large shipment of raw sugar rolled through town, as the cargo almost always made its way to an underground distillery. Some of his most significant busts, Ness reported, began when he caught a whiff of pungent sour mash or spotted a faint thread of molasses in the Cuyahoga River.

After work, when another man might have headed home to his wife, Ness could be found having drinks and swapping stories with the city's press corps, looking to get his name back in the papers after the relative obscurity of his stint in the boondocks. Ness had come to enjoy seeing his name in the headlines, above the fold if possible. He understood that there were advantages to be wrought, especially now that he hoped to leverage his Chicago experience into a better job. "He is ambitious for Eliot Ness, admits it and is no hypocrite," one reporter would say of him. "The publicity spotlight and the crowds' adulation appeal to him."

In time, he would cultivate close relationships with reporters at each of the city's three largest newspapers—the *Plain Dealer*, the *Press*, and the *News*. At a time when Ness was still learning his way around, both figuratively and literally, the press could be counted on to point him in the right direction, and many of his biggest liquor busts began with a tip from a reporter. Ness had learned from his missteps, and now took pains to share credit, often mentioning his colleagues by name. It is too much to say, as the *Plain Dealer* would claim, that Ness "was not one to blow his own horn," but at least he was no longer off-key, as he had so often been in Chicago. "Ness is a public official dear to the hearts of reporters," wrote Philip Porter, the city editor of the *Plain Dealer*. "They admire his courage and his skill, and they like him personally. Few government officials have won them in such a short time as he has. It's a pretty safe rule that when reporters respect and admire an official, he's the goods. They see so many phonies that they can smell them out like bird dogs."

Phony or not, Ness could be counted on to supply a clinching detail or snappy quote that made each of his stories irresistible. One anecdote involved a face-off with a former wrestler known as "Big Louie," who mercifully put up no resistance as Ness and his agents moved in: "Had he done so," Ness admitted, "I seriously doubt that we would be having this conversation." He also regaled the newsmen with a story about a 150-gallon still that he and his men had discovered on East 114th Street. Beside the still, he said, was a notice intended for the workers: "Don't forget the drops!" This referred to the flavorings used to add taste to otherwise unpalatable mixtures so that customers "could tell the different brands apart." Ness finished the story by raising a suspicious eyebrow at the cocktail glass in his own hand.

Soon, the sheer number of stories about Ness took on a life of its own, with newspaper columnists tracking the "miraculous streak" as if he and his men were a baseball team on a playoff run. Each day brought fresh accounts of the raiders kicking down doors, lowering themselves through skylights on dangling fire hoses, or battering through concrete to rescue trapped colleagues. A typical photo showed Ness and his grinning raiders hoisting their sledgehammers, ready to punch holes in yet another boiler. "Cleveland is learning that liquor laws can be enforced," wrote Charles Lawrence in the *Plain Dealer*, "if a government sets its mind to it and those charged with the enforcement are honest men."

This was a swipe at Mayor Harry Davis, a Republican stalwart whose administration was widely seen as "a classic example of boodling and incompetence." Mayor Davis gave lip service to the government's call for a clampdown on bootleggers, but Safety Director Martin Lavelle, in charge of both the police and fire departments, doubted that it could succeed as long as criminals continued to undercut the alcohol tax. No one could stop bootlegging and eliminate speakeasies, said Cleveland's top lawman, "until the city has five-cent beer and ten-cent whisky." In general, Lavelle preferred to look the other way. "You can have as good a time as you can imagine," he once told New Year's Eve revelers, "so long as you don't interfere with the safety of anybody else."

Soon enough, this philosophy would be sorely tested. On a hot Friday afternoon, June 28, 1935, a boisterous "drinking party" aboard a speedboat on Lake Erie ended with the drowning death of thirty-four-year-old Mildred Brockman, an employee of the city's public works department. Early reports of the tragedy were sketchy, and Safety Director Lavelle seemed unwilling to investigate. "I don't know what we can do about it," he told a reporter. The press smelled a rat. Twenty-four hours later, Lavelle admitted under growing pressure that he had been aboard the speedboat at the time of Mildred Brockman's death. Worse yet, he'd been a guest of Martin O'Boyle, a well-known bootlegger of Prohibition days and "still a potent figure in Cleveland racketeering."

The press opened fire, lambasting Lavelle for attempting to cover up his involvement in the tragedy and for "consorting on terms of social intimacy" with a known racketeer. The latter offense touched an especially raw nerve. "Rumors have been current for months that an alliance existed between local rackets and local politics—an alliance profitable to both sides but destructive of decent government in Cleveland," one reporter noted. As calls for the safety director's resignation gathered force, Lavelle appeared baffled. "I've done nothing wrong," he insisted. "The thing could have happened to anyone." Mayor Davis stood by him, expressing confidence that the Lavelle scandal "won't hurt us a bit" in the fall reelection campaign.

He was wrong. Harold H. Burton, an independent Republican candidate, took to the hustings to batter Davis for having "surrendered without a fight to lawlessness." Burton, a Harvard Law graduate, brought impressive credentials to his campaign, having served as the city's law director. He also saw action in World War I, rising to the rank of captain and returning home with a Purple Heart. Supporters were quick to point out that "a man who had the courage to face bullets in France and Belgium will have the courage to face racketeers in Cleveland." In a pointed reminder of the Lavelle scandal, the *Plain Dealer* hailed Burton as a politician who would "resist evil political influences, exerted by so-called 'friends.'"

In the end, a record voter turnout pushed Burton past Davis in the primary, and he went on to win easily in the November election. The victory "came like a breath of spring after a long hard winter," Philip Porter would recall, but many believed that the new mayor faced an impossible task. Burton had promised to clean up the city, and as he settled into his new office at city hall, the streets were literally heaped with trash. The outgoing Mayor Davis, citing budgetary restrictions, had ordered a halt to the city's rubbish collections following his defeat in the primary, a transparent act of spite.

Burton dug in. His most urgent priority, given his law-and-order platform, would be to clamp down on the police department and wrest control of the city away from the criminal element. That being the case, Burton knew that his success or failure would rest on the choice of Lavelle's replacement as safety director. Burton had an ideal candidate in mind: Joseph Keenan, the assistant US attorney general, who had earned a national reputation directing the prosecution of Machine Gun Kelly and the Ma Barker gang. Burton flew to Washington, DC, and courted Keenan aggressively at a national conference of mayors, even taking President Roosevelt aside at a White House reception to warn that he intended to lure Keenan away. "He's a good man," FDR responded. "I'd hate to lose him."

In the end, the president need not have worried; Keenan turned down the offer after two days of intense lobbying. As the reports of this setback made the rounds, the city's newsmen speculated openly on a possible replacement. Instead of a slick, high-flying lawyer like Keenan, they suggested, why not take a blunt instrument to the problem? At the city desk of the *Plain Dealer*, reporter Wes Lawrence threw out a seemingly outlandish suggestion. What about this new kid, the booze cop? It seemed wildly impractical at first, but soon the reporters began warming to the idea. The guy who took on Machine Gun Kelly had turned them down, so why not the guy who went up against Al Capone? "He'd be just the kind of guy Burton needs," Lawrence insisted. "So what about it? What about Eliot Ness?"

Though the newly elected mayor was only dimly aware of Ness's existence, the idea quickly took root. Soon, all three newspapers were touting the qualifications of the "boyish-looking, scientifically-trained" liquor agent, and suggesting that the "bright young G-man" had the inside track. "In case you didn't know," readers of the *Plain Dealer* were informed, "Ness was the boy who put the Al Capone breweries out of business in Chicago. After that, the local mobs don't alarm him too much."

Privately, Ness's supporters doubted that Burton could afford to gamble on a political unknown. For that matter, no one seemed entirely clear as to whether Ness was a Republican or a Democrat. "How elections are won," said one observer, "is a matter which does not interest him." Nevertheless, Burton was said to have concluded that "he really ought to look into the qualifications of this marvel."

The mayor could not have been reassured by what he found. Ness was younger by far than any previous safety director, and unlike Martin Lavelle and most of his predecessors, Ness had never been a police officer. Worse, Ness had spent barely a year in Cleveland at this stage, hardly long enough to find a decent laundry service, much less to grasp and untangle the political intricacies of the police department. Ever hopeful, the press attempted to spin his lack of experience into a selling point, insisting that Ness was "removed from the muddy main currents of politics." Ness himself, when cornered by a *Press* reporter, responded with "his blue eyes twinkling good-naturedly" at the prospect. "I would like to get the job," he said. "I would like to see what I could do. But whoever does get that job will have his hands full."

Burton and Ness met for the first time on Saturday, December 7, 1935. Both men had cause to be wary. By this time, Burton felt cornered by the press, who had turned Ness's candidacy into a referendum on the mayor's reform agenda. Ness, for his part, had been warned that the new safety director was doomed to fail, but he knew a lifeline when he saw one. His application to the FBI remained in limbo, and his work as a liquor agent offered no future. The post of safety director, if he could land it, would revive his career. "I will accept the position if it is offered," he told reporters. "The same tactics we used against Capone and others could be used in combatting crime in Cleveland. All crime is alike."

This was naïve, and Burton knew it. In Chicago, Ness had been in charge of a squad of eight men, more or less. Cleveland's safety director would control not only the entire police department, but also the fire and building departments, with more than 2,500 city employees under his command. There was nothing in Ness's background to suggest that he could meet an administrative challenge at this level. By the same token, the problems facing Cleveland could not be ascribed to a towering crime boss like Capone. Instead, the city's next safety director would have to deal with the more ingrained consequences of a long-standing culture of corruption. Instead of knocking down brewery doors, the new "top cop" would have to fight a rot from within.

Burton knew the stakes all too well. "We were beginning to be tagged as a city unable to enforce the law," he would say, which threatened to scuttle any chance of economic recovery. This was an equation Ness understood after his work in Chicago, and he spoke persuasively about the ripple effects of corruption. "Racketeering here is rampant," Ness would write in a letter to his mentor, August Vollmer, a few days later, "much more so than is apparent on the surface. Almost every business association in the city is paying some sort of tribute to a well-organized Sicilian gang."

So long as these "Sicilian gangs" held power, Burton feared, the city would never shake off the lingering effects of the Depression. Here, Ness saw an opening. He had heard much the same concern expressed by powerful, disgruntled businessmen in Chicago as they came together to form an elite group called the "Secret Six," putting up private funds to back the anti-Capone effort. If Cleveland's business leaders would support a similar effort, he told Burton, he could launch a frontline assault on crime. He would begin by assembling a small force of trusted men who would serve as his eyes and ears—a Cleveland version of the Untouchables. These investigators would appear on the city payroll as laborers and garage attendants, but their operating budget would be off the books. Like the Untouchables, this group of "Unknowns" would be shielded from citywide corruption, and would answer only to Ness.

It was an audacious proposal, but Burton seems to have liked the sound of it. More important, he was uniquely qualified to put the plan into action. As a former acting city manager, Burton knew that his colleagues at the Chamber of Commerce were "tired of being shaken down" by a corrupt system. He felt sure that they would cheerfully shell out for Ness's secret squad if it helped to break the stranglehold of mobsters and racketeers. Even as the two men spoke, Cleveland was bidding furiously to host the following year's Republican National Convention, with a decision expected at the end of the week. If successful, the city would have a once-in-a-generation opportunity to showcase Cleveland, in Burton's words, as "a place to do business." If Ness's Unknowns helped to clear the decks, his sub-rosa budget would be money well spent.

On the morning of Wednesday, December 11, Burton called Ness at the Standard Building and formally offered him the job. Ness threw on his camel hair coat and hurried over to city hall, two blocks away, for his swearing-in ceremony. Arriving at the mayor's office, Ness found the reception area packed with reporters and job-seekers, none of whom took any notice as he politely found a place at the back of the line. For some time, he stood quietly with his hands in his pockets, not certain if he should push his way forward and announce himself, oblivious to the fact that he was no longer a man who had to take a number. At last, someone recognized him and bundled him into the mayor's chambers, where a city official waited to administer the oath of office. The following day, newspapers across the country carried photos of the "mild-mannered, collegiate-looking" Ness being sworn in as the city's youngest-ever safety director. In all the rush, he hadn't bothered to take off his coat.

"Of course I am greatly honored by the appointment," Ness told reporters afterward, and he brandished a thick copy of the city charter as an example of the "homework" that lay ahead. "After that I don't know what I'll do," he told reporters, "but I hope to take necessary action first and talk about it later." The *Plain Dealer*, more than a little giddy over the appointment, made a virtue of his reluctance to say more: "Facts First, Then Talk, Says Ness."

Mayor Burton had "surprised everybody, including himself," with the bold move, said one insider. "It just didn't seem possible," Philip Porter would recall. Not everyone was so besotted. Many on the police force were reported to be in a state of "mingled anxiety and high expectations," fearing that the era of lax discipline and under-the-table payoffs would come to an end. Officers knew better than to criticize the new boss openly, but many took a dismissive tone. "Policemen have seen safety directors come and safety directors go," said one, "and things don't usually change much under the surface." The *Press* echoed this skepticism: "Mr. Ness's first discovery about the Cleveland Police Department probably will be that there aren't any G-men in it," one columnist observed. "He'll find some clever maneuverers, however."

For two days, Ness busied himself learning the ropes, trailing along with Burton on a monotonous round of meetings with city officials. Finally, on the evening of Friday, December 13, Ness found an opportunity to make good on his promise to lead from the front lines. He and Edna had joined friends for a quiet, celebratory dinner at a restaurant near Public Square. For Edna, it was a chance to step out and bask in the glow of her husband's sudden rise in status. She had seen precious little of him since the move to Cleveland, and she could not have been pleased at some of the errors and exaggerations that had crept into the announcements of his appointment. Two days earlier, a front-page story in the *Press* had described the new safety director as "32 and single," as if an eligible young bachelor had stepped into the spotlight. For one evening, at least, Edna could relax over dinner and drinks at her husband's side.

Suddenly a shadow fell across the table as Ness's driver appeared at his elbow. A bulletin had come over the two-way radio in Ness's official car. A cleaning woman, it seemed, had spotted a pair of safecrackers at work in a City Savings & Loan at the Williamson Building, nearby on Euclid Avenue. Ness stood up, dropped a pile of cash on the table, and muttered a few words of apology before sprinting toward the door, leaving his unhappy wife staring after him.

Ness arrived at the Savings & Loan just as police entered the marbled lobby with their weapons drawn. Some of the officers, he noted, were carrying machine guns. No one recognized the tall, unassuming figure in the camel hair coat until he identified himself to the officer in charge, drawing surprised looks from nearby patrolmen. None of them had ever seen Martin Lavelle or any of his predecessors at the scene of a bank heist. Stepping forward, Ness borrowed a gun from a detective and fell in step. This was the part of the job he knew how to do.

As the officers pushed their way into the building's interior, they discovered that the safecrackers had managed to peel open one of the bank's vaults, but instead of cash, they found it stuffed with useless papers. Another safe stood nearby, but the burglars had been interrupted before they could get to work on it, and no one had seen them leave the building. Ness joined in as police searched the premises, a process that carried them up seventeen floors to the building's roof. There they discovered that the crooks had escaped by means of a makeshift drawbridge—a heavy oak door laid across a window ledge to the fire escape of the building next door.

The bad guys had slipped through his fingers, but Ness wasn't done for the night. Shrugging off the disappointment, he joined a group of officers for an impromptu tour of the city's police precincts, each one known for a specific set of vices. The Fifth Precinct, for instance, was a hotbed of "policy games," also known as the numbers racket, an illegal type of three-digit lottery that thrived in downtrodden neighborhoods.

The Fourth Precinct, Ness learned, was a center of prostitution, while much of the city's bootleg liquor flowed through the Eleventh, in Little Italy, the stronghold of the notorious Mayfield Road Mob. And the infamous Roaring Third, northeast of Public Square, was the city's answer to New York's Tenderloin district, offering sin of every description, including "plain and fancy gambling, speakeasies and prostitution."

Over the next few hours, the new safety director appeared to be everywhere, overseeing the fire department's response to a five-alarm warehouse fire and scoping out more than a dozen gambling parlors. At two in the morning, he joined a raid on a "suspected disorderly house," the type of establishment where women stood at the windows in hope of "attracting the attention of male passersby." After calling for a paddy wagon, Ness crept along an alley at the side of the house, as he had so often done as a liquor cop, in order to surprise the occupants. As he stepped through a rear door, however, he found the place deserted. It seemed that the "working girls" had slipped away through the front while Ness made his way to the back. "They're jittery anyway," he said, putting a gloss on the episode for reporters. "That was a quick getaway."

Actually, as Ness knew perfectly well, the "quick getaway" meant that some of his officers had looked the other way at the crucial moment. He had a long way to go if he hoped to make good on his promise to clean up the police department. Even so, Ness had sent a powerful message to the rank and file. "I've served under five safety directors," one sergeant would say when Ness dropped by the station house unexpectedly, "and this is the first time I ever saw the face of one of them." Ness would keep hold of the gun he had borrowed at the beginning of the night, a .38 Smith & Wesson, for years to come.

The timing of this "Friday night surprise" was excellent. Mayor Burton planned to unveil his crisis plan for the city budget, which included emergency funds for the police and fire departments, on Monday. Glowing accounts of the doings of the "Safety Director turned raider" dominated the weekend papers, suggesting that Burton's plan could work with proper support. But the coverage also made it clear how much difficult work lay ahead. "A quarter century of political favoritism, phenagling and chiseling has left the honest cops disheartened and cynical," wrote Philip Porter in the *Plain Dealer*. "If Eliot Ness can do anything about it, his task will be as tough as Hercules' in cleaning out the Augean stables."

In other words, if Ness hoped to make any headway in his new job, he would have to wade through a great deal of shit.

6

WOMAN SLAIN, HEAD SOUGHT IN COAL BINS

Dismembered parts of approximately half of the body of a
woman who had been dead from two to four days were found
yesterday morning in two burlap sacks and a half-bushel basket left in the rear of the Hart Manufacturing Co. plant at 2315
E. 20th Street.

The Plain Dealer, January 27, 1936

Charles Page, owner of the White Front Meat Market on Central Avenue,
couldn't understand why anyone would leave a ham outside in the snow.
A woman had burst in moments earlier, highly agitated, complaining
about the frantic barking of a dog. At the back of the shop, she said,
she'd found the dog tied to a fence, howling furiously and straining to
get at a couple of small bushel baskets. The baskets sat at the back wall
of a neighboring building, the Hart Manufacturing Company, and they
appeared to be filled with parcels of meat. Hams, maybe. Page jumped
to his feet. "That sounds like something meat shop burglars might have
left behind," he cried. Grabbing his coat, he hurried outside.

Page could not have been eager to venture outside on that frigid
Sunday morning. A bitter cold snap, the worst in recent memory, had
gripped the region and would eventually claim dozens of lives. Page's
neighborhood would have felt especially bleak and forbidding. On one

side it was hemmed in by a clattering spur of the Nickel Plate Railroad, with tracks extending through the basin of Kingsbury Run. On the other was the massive Lorain-Carnegie Bridge, completed four years earlier, a series of cantilever truss spans stretching for nearly a mile across the nearby Cuyahoga River. The bridge was anchored at both ends by massive sandstone pylons, forty-three feet tall and carved with grim classical figures that glowered over the horizon. Known as the *Guardians of Traffic*, they each clutched a different vehicle to illustrate "progress in transportation," from the stagecoach to the modern automobile.

Very little of that progress could be felt in Page's neighborhood, where the streets had been disrupted and realigned to make way for the bridge. What remained was a strange hodgepodge of crumbling factories and sagging houses, with a handful of brothels and betting parlors mixed in. Even under a hard crust of recent snow, the dirt lot behind the meat market looked dingy and forlorn, with a stiff wind rattling the chain-link fence that ran along the far edge.

In spite of the snow, Page had no trouble spotting a pair of small woven baskets sitting by the back wall of the Hart Manufacturing Company. The baskets were covered with burlap gunnysacks that had been tugged loose in the wind, revealing neatly packed bundles wrapped in newspaper. Stepping forward, Page reached into one of the baskets and began to unwrap a parcel. Inside was a human arm, severed at the shoulder, alongside a second clump of flesh that appeared to be a section of a thigh.

Horrified, Page dropped the parcel and took a step back. Then, unable to stop himself, he bent down and tugged at the corner of one of the burlap gunnysacks. "From the gunnysack," the *Press* would report, "Mr. Page withdrew the torso, which had been hacked away from the upper body at the region of the stomach, and from which the legs had been clumsily hacked at the beginning of the thighs."

At last, Page had seen enough. Dropping the second parcel, he hurried back to his shop to call the police. They arrived within minutes, swarming across the lot that separated Page's shop from the Hart Manufacturing Company. The first wave included Joseph Sweeney and James Hogan. Both men were in their fifties, and both had seen their fortunes rise in the shuffle that accompanied the appointment of Eliot Ness the previous month. The balding, bespectacled Sweeney had been on the force for nearly forty years by this time, and two weeks earlier, he had scored top marks on a civil service examination, leading to his appointment as acting chief of the detective bureau. Sergeant Hogan, a lanky, thirty-year veteran, was serving as head of the city's homicide squad. Hogan had a reputation for doggedness, never letting go of a case until the last detail had been nailed down, even if the details literally ate away at him. He suffered from ulcers that regularly sent him to the hospital.

Under Sweeney and Hogan's direction, police carefully unwrapped the remaining bundles in the two baskets, revealing a ghastly assortment of body parts that included a second thigh, described as "obese." Detectives took note of the fact that the body parts were wrapped in local newspapers of widely varying dates, some several months old and others as recent as the previous day. In addition, the remains were marked with black dust and appeared to bear the imprint of lumps of coal, suggesting that the body might have been stored in a coal bin. Sergeant Hogan was said to be giving close attention to this detail, and gave orders for a search of the coal bins in the neighborhood.

Soon, a "suit of cheap cotton underwear" turned up nearby, wrapped in the pages of a two-month-old newspaper, along with a tag marked with the name of William Danches, the owner of an east-side poultry market. The poultry market clue appeared to gain significance as the police widened the search area, turning up another burlap gunnysack. The sack bore traces of blood and chicken feathers. "This sack was found near a factory that makes pillows from poultry feathers," the *Press* would note. "A driver for this firm failed to report to work today and detectives were attempting to find him."

As investigators scrambled to chase down the leads, Inspector Sweeney pieced together a possible timeline, drawing heavily on various reports of dogs howling in the night. He told reporters that the remains had likely been dumped sometime around 2:30 the previous morning, when a woman named Josephine Marco had been awakened by the barking of her dog, who had been left on the back porch of her home. Mrs. Marco told police that she thought she'd heard someone moving around outside but did not get up to investigate. Meanwhile, a pair of neighborhood watchmen making their regular rounds near the Hart building had seen nothing unusual, and had evidently not noticed the baskets. If the baskets had in fact been left at 2:30, as signaled by Mrs. Marco's dog, they had sat undisturbed for roughly eight hours. They might have gone unnoticed even longer if not for the second dog tied up in the alley, whose insistent barking had drawn the attention of Charles Page.

From the first moments, it was clear that the body parts were those of a female victim. For this reason, perhaps, investigators did not immediately draw a connection to the pair of decapitated bodies discovered four months earlier at Jackass Hill. Though dismembered corpses were by no means a regular feature of a Cleveland police officer's experience, the two crime scenes appeared to have little in common. There had been no tidy bundles of newspaper at Jackass Hill, and the salient feature of the earlier investigation—the discovery of the severed heads—had so far not been repeated. The *Cleveland News*, however, would remark in passing on the connection between this latest horror and the "still unsolved torso murder" of the so-called Lady of the Lake, which had occurred sixteen months earlier. The "dismembered pieces" in that case had also been those of a woman, the reporter noted, but investigators "never were able to identify her."

Having learned all they could at the Hart Manufacturing building, police moved quickly to process evidence that might identify this fresh set of remains. Detective Emil Musil, who had been one of the first on the scene at Jackass Hill, joined Detective George Zicarelli to comb through missing persons reports in search of a possible match. Another pair of detectives canvassed the neighborhood, knocking on the doors of local brothels. To their way of thinking, the degree of violence and the questionable neighborhood suggested that the victim had been a prostitute. Their efforts brought no results—none of the "white girls," they were told, had gone missing.

Shortly after one in the afternoon, Coroner Arthur Pearse began his examination of the remains at the county morgue. A preliminary report in the *Plain Dealer* placed Pearse's estimate of her age between thirty and thirty-five, and her weight somewhere in the range of 150 pounds. Her death, Pearse concluded, had occurred somewhere between two and four days earlier. The coroner took note of an old vaccination mark, as well as the scar of what he described as "an abdominal operation performed years ago," or perhaps two of them, since the notes made reference to both a hysterectomy and a partial appendectomy. Death was attributed to murder and "criminal violence."

Significantly, Pearse told reporters that the dismemberment had been carried out with "an exceptionally sharp knife," and that the person doing it had been "apparently inexperienced." His official verdict would underscore the point, describing the work as "crude." In this, Pearse appeared to disagree with the findings of County Pathologist Reuben Straus, who performed the official autopsy. Straus's report noted clean edges at all of the incision points, indicating a practiced hand. This apparent discrepancy would loom large in days to come. Earlier, when examining the remains of the Lady of the Lake, Pearse claimed the body had been "expertly dismembered," perhaps by a surgeon. A short time later, finding that the second set of remains bore the traces of a saw blade, Pearse had revised his opinion. "No surgeon would have used a saw," he insisted at the time. "He would have known how to manipulate a knife around the joint."

Now, a similar fog of uncertainty settled over the current investigation. According to Pearse, the dismemberment had been crude. According to Straus, it had been precise and assured. If, as Straus reported, the incisions were clean at the edges, it suggested that the murderer possessed both experience and anatomical knowledge, and might belong to a profession that equipped him to perform the gruesome procedure efficiently—perhaps a butcher, if not a surgeon. If Pearse was correct, no such assumptions could be made. Much would hinge on this point as investigators attempted to draw up a profile of their quarry.

For the moment, Pearse and the rest of the investigators continued to focus their energies on identifying the victim, a task greatly complicated by their failure to locate her missing head. Unexpectedly, a quick breakthrough came at the hands of a seventy-year-old police veteran named George Koestle.

Koestle, superintendent of the city's Bureau of Criminal Identification, knew that his career was winding down. Eliot Ness had arrived promising to update and modernize the department's resources, but Koestle stood firmly rooted in the techniques of the previous century. He began his service with the Cleveland police in 1897, five years before Ness's birth. Koestle had been "twirling his night stick on a lonely beat" when his chief tapped him to set up a revolutionary new system of criminal identification, supplanting a large but inefficient "rogue's gallery" of criminal mug shots. Up to this point, the city had been slow to adopt innovation in police work, as one newspaper noted at the time, but "had now at last embraced the value of a world famous method."

This method was Bertillonage, a system of classifying and identifying criminals pioneered in France by Alphonse Bertillon in 1879, and introduced to the United States a short time later. The Bertillon method was rooted in the science of anthropometry, the study of the measurements and proportions of the human body. Under Bertillon's guidelines, criminals would be photographed and carefully measured with special calipers, gauges, and rulers, so as to develop a unique profile that could be shared throughout the world. The system placed a particular emphasis on some eight hundred possible shapes and aspects of the human ear, which carried an "immutable legacy," as Bertillon himself explained, because it was "unchangeable in form from birth."

Koestle, who had been a professional photographer earlier in his career, was thought to have the training and sensibility needed to make a success of the Bertillon method in Cleveland. In a dusty third-floor corner of police headquarters, he set up a darkroom and a measuring station and set to work. Over the course of nearly forty years of continuous service, he amassed a catalog of more than 125,000 "Bertillon cards" and some seventy thousand photographs.

By 1936, however, the once-celebrated system had become passé, and Koestle himself would soon face a compulsory retirement as Eliot Ness phased in his reforms. Nevertheless, when Coroner Pearse managed to pull a usable thumbprint from the severed arm found behind Charles Page's shop, he had reason to hope that Koestle would find a match. Alongside his work with the Bertillon system, Koestle had also been an early proponent of fingerprint identification, adopting the system in 1906, well before fingerprints had been accepted as evidence in an American courtroom. In one year alone, he matched the prints of nearly two thousand suspects to fingerprint cards already on file, and identified seven John Does in the county morgue. On a wall of his office, he proudly displayed a photograph showing the handprint of a burglar convicted in 1917, the first conviction in a Cleveland court that had rested solely on print evidence. A visitor to the archive reported that Koestle needed "only about two minutes" to find a particular fingerprint record, in spite of the "bewildering mass of data" he'd collected.

Even so, Koestle knew that he faced long odds in the current case. Even after ruling out a large number of potential fingerprint cards, he noted with despair that Pearse's print still appeared "similar to 12,000 others in police files." Worse yet, as a reporter noted, "there was a big chance that the woman had never been arrested and fingerprinted" on a prior offense, in which case her prints would not be on file at all. Undaunted, Koestle bent to his task, hoping that his cherished archive, the labor of a lifetime, could unlock one last puzzle. Sitting alone in his records room, he flipped through hundreds of cards, one after another, doggedly comparing each one to the print taken from the victim, and trying not to grow discouraged as the pile of discards grew larger.

Amazingly, by 1:30 that afternoon, Koestle emerged from his cluttered archive brandishing a single manila card. Not only had he made a positive identification, he had done it while the victim's remains were still on Pearse's table at the morgue. Koestle, his colleagues believed, had broken the case wide open.

The victim was Mrs. Florence Polillo, described as "a police character" and "relief client." Her prints and photograph came to be recorded in Koestle's files five years earlier, owing to a charge of "occupying a room for immoral purposes." Her name at birth, it appeared, had been Florence Genevieve Sawdey, and she was a native of nearby Ashtabula, but she had acquired a dizzying number of aliases over the years, including Florence Martin, Clara Dunn, and Florence Gallagher. She was thought to be in her early forties, and her police photograph—the only image of her known to exist—shows that hard living and heavy drinking had taken their toll. She was "a big woman, fat, squat, with dark stringy hair, tiny eyes, and almost no neck," according to one early account. Her hair had been dyed a reddish color at the time of her death, her skin was sallow and discolored, and she had a mouthful of false teeth. Although she was a familiar figure on the streets of the Roaring Third, especially among saloonkeepers and bootleggers, police had trouble reconciling the contradictory details of her background. She was said to have spent time in Buffalo, New York, and Erie, Pennsylvania, scraping out a living as a barmaid and a waitress, and augmenting her meager earnings by cashing welfare checks and turning tricks. "For years she had been a prostitute, sinking lower and lower in the levels of that oldest profession," one reporter noted. "She was available to any man of any sex desires." In addition to her brush with the law in Cleveland, there had been at least one earlier arrest for solicitation in Washington, DC.

The quick identification "cleared up half of the mystery of the grisly contents of the basket and gunny-sack," as the *Press* observed. "Why the victim was hacked to death, and by whom, remained unsolved." Police hoped to find further clues at Mrs. Polillo's rooming house on Carnegie Avenue, not far from the White Front Meat Market, where residents remembered her as "a pleasant sort" who got along well with her fellow lodgers. According to Mary Ford, her landlady, Mrs. Polillo never had company during her nine months there, and paid her rent on time with government relief checks. "She never gave us any trouble," Mrs. Ford insisted. "The only bad habit I noticed was that she would go out occasionally and get a quart of liquor—bad liquor, too—and drink it all by her lonesome in her room. When she was drinking she was pecky—quarrelsome, you know." The landlady claimed to have no knowledge of criminal activity of any kind, much less prostitution. "She never spoke of men," she insisted, "and didn't go out very much." When told where the body had been discovered, Mrs. Ford could think of only one reason why Mrs. Polillo might have been there. "I bet that's where she went to get her liquor," she said. "It was mean stuff."

In the victim's small bedroom, investigators found a sad, oddly chilling collection of dolls, more than a dozen of them, carefully arranged on the bed, chairs, and davenport as if keeping a vigil for their owner. "She had a name for every one of those dolls," Mrs. Ford told the police. In fact, she continued, Mrs. Polillo would dress the dolls up in a variety of outfits, and often invited the landlady's daughters to join her in playing with them. Reporters were quick to link this detail to Coroner Pearse's assertion that the victim had been "physically incapable" of bearing children. A bold subhead in the *Press* announced: "Maternity Denied Her."

Mrs. Polillo's room also contained a trunk of personal effects that the detectives hoped would shed light on her murder. From a notebook, police gathered names of the dead woman's acquaintances, all of whom would eventually be located and questioned. Investigators also learned that she had been married at least twice, first to a man named Ghent, about whom little could be discovered, and next to Andrew Polillo of Buffalo, a union that had lasted roughly six years. When notified of his former wife's death, Polillo sent word that he would board a bus and make his way to Cleveland.

As police pored over a collection of letters and other papers in the trunk, a portrait of the victim as an itinerant hard-luck case slowly took shape. A letter from a man in the Allegheny County jail begged for a loan of ten dollars to pay off a vice fine; another informed her that her radio had been taken to a pawn shop: "If you'll send me the $2, I'll get it out." Why the dead woman had preserved these letters was impossible to say. Police also puzzled over a record of payments involving an unknown "Dr. Manzella," but a rigorous search failed to locate him or even to discover what sort of services he provided. An acquaintance recalled that Mrs. Polillo had once undergone "some kind of treatment" at Cleveland's Lakeside Hospital, but no further details could be uncovered.

Mrs. Ford had last seen her lodger at 8:30 on the evening of Friday, January 24, two days before the body was discovered. "She usually ironed on Saturday," the landlady said, "and when I found she wasn't here I was worried." Mrs. Ford's statement, together with the county pathologist's estimate of the time of death, led police to conclude that the murder had occurred late Friday night or early Saturday morning.

As the timeline came into focus, police worked to shed light on the victim's whereabouts prior to her death, quickly accumulating a great many striking, if often contradictory, details. Mrs. Polillo's path had crossed with a number of gamblers, bootleggers, and other seedy characters in the previous days and weeks. More than once, she had been seen with both eyes blackened, suggesting that she'd been beaten up, perhaps repeatedly. Three months earlier, police had arrested her for selling "intoxicating beverages," and at one stage, she had done a stint in a workhouse. At least one report placed her in the company of "a very dirty looking" man, possibly a pimp, while others mentioned an addict by the name of Al, who was said to have furnished her with liquor and drugs. Police also turned up a long line of former "paramours," one of whom went by the name of One-Armed Willie, who might have fought with her just hours before her death. Another shadowy figure told police that Mrs. Polillo had tried to sell him a gun, and still another was overheard to say that he "was looking for Florence" and would "cut her all up" when he found her.

Detectives also uncovered reports of yet another marriage, roughly two years earlier, to a tall, blond truck driver whom the victim had introduced as Harry Martin. The couple lived for a time in a run-down hotel on the east side, where the manager remembered Martin as "nice looking" but prone to violence. Police could find no trace of him in the city, but shortly before Mrs. Polillo's death, they learned, she had returned to the hotel and asked about some jigsaw puzzles that had been kept around for the guests. She left after being told that the puzzles had been given away.

One incident in particular gives a measure of the difficulties facing detectives as they attempted to shed light on Mrs. Polillo's checkered past.

A *Press* reporter recounted the peculiar saga of a suspect known as "Captain Swing," who came to the attention of police after jumping out of a third-floor window while "on a prolonged drunk." Somehow he emerged with no worse injury than a pair of broken feet, and told police that he had not jumped at all but instead had been "blown out" of the room. Afterward, however, he was reported to have "mumbled things that tended to implicate him in the killing" of Mrs. Polillo. Sergeant Hogan was said to be waiting—"on the advice of doctors"—for Captain Swing to sober up before questioning could begin. This colorful suspect apparently became less promising as his blood alcohol level dropped. Within a few days, his name disappeared from the inquiry.

In the meantime, investigators pursed the slender clue afforded by the tag found at the scene bearing the name of the William Danches poultry store. Detectives Musil and Zicarelli traced the lead to the Cleveland Feather Company, purveyor of feathers for furniture and bedding, located on Central Avenue near the spot where the remains were found. Police made a thorough search of the premises, giving special attention to the coal bins in the boiler room. They also carried out a search at the home of truck driver John Willis, who had transported feathers from the poultry store to the feather company, but could find no link to the crime. Once again, a promising lead had sputtered out.

Andrew Polillo, whose marriage to the victim had ended roughly eight years earlier, arrived in Cleveland on January 28, two days after the discovery of the remains. Some accounts suggest that he made the trip in hope of collecting on an insurance policy. Whatever his motivation, he agreed to speak with Sergeant Hogan soon after stepping off his bus. Polillo's recollections proved hazy and incomplete, so much so that he could not even be sure of the dates of the marriage. If some details had faded, however, he retained a sharp and bitter memory of how his wife had left him in Buffalo. "She said that she was going to visit her mother for two weeks," he told Hogan, "as she wanted to get straightened out." His wife had been "drinking quite hard" at the time, Polillo recalled, and he hoped that a change of scene would do her good. Roughly two weeks later, while coming home from a restaurant late one night, Polillo was

surprised to see his wife walking toward him from the opposite direction. "She was with a man and she had a hold of him by the arm," Polillo
recalled. "I looked at her and she looked at me, and after she passed I
turned and looked at her and she turned and looked at me." Apparently
they arrived at a tacit understanding in this moment, with both parties
recognizing that the marriage had reached its end. "The next night," Polillo said, "while I was out she went to the flat and took all of her clothes
and went away." Their paths would cross again only once, in the office
of a lawyer. Polillo told Hogan that he had no idea where she had gone
or what she had been doing in the years that followed.

By the end of the month the investigation appeared to be stalling.
As the story faded from the headlines, the public's attention shifted to
the funeral of King George V, the uproar over a thirty-day stay of execution for Bruno Hauptmann—who had been convicted of the Lind-
bergh kidnapping the previous year—and a near-fatal prison attack on
"thrill slayer" Richard Loeb. On the heels of the discovery of the so-
called "Doubleday baseball" in Cooperstown, New York, a spirited debate erupted over the announcement of the first-ever class of inductees
into the Baseball Hall of Fame, which included Ty Cobb, Babe Ruth, and
Honus Wagner. "You can tie Wagner," one sports columnist quipped,
"but you can't Ty Cobb."

On the morning of Friday, February 7, Clevelanders woke to the
news that the "murky, partly frozen waters" of the Cuyahoga River had
caught fire, owing to a slick of industrial oil on the surface. The blaze
caused $20,000 worth of damage to the Erie Railroad "jackknife," one of
several bridges that stitched the two halves of the city together across the
coils of the river like the seams of a well-worn baseball. Though the *Plain
Dealer* described the inferno as "the thing that fire officials and business
men of the Flats fear most," the *News* adopted a more cavalier point of
view, referring the episode to the attention of Robert Ripley's famous
Believe It or Not franchise: "Oh, Mr. Ripley!" their headline announced,
"Our River's on Fire!"

The day's other significant piece of news, an important break in
the Polillo murder, was given a surprisingly muted treatment on page

five of the following day's *Plain Dealer*. Under the headline "Find More Pieces of Woman's Body," readers learned that a second set of remains had been discovered "in a hole partly filled with rubbish" at the rear of a vacant building on Orange Avenue, not far from the White Front Meat Market. A young man taking a shortcut behind the building had made the find at about five in the evening, and police were on the scene within minutes. The additional body parts included the upper half of a female torso, along with the left arm and both lower legs. The grisly remnants had been "unwrapped and exposed to view," readers were told, and "appeared to have been deposited in haste."

Soon enough, County Pathologist Reuben Straus would confirm what the responding officers had already guessed: the second set of remains matched up with those of Florence Polillo already at the morgue. Straus's report, according to some sources, would add a notably ghastly detail. As in the case of Edward Andrassy at Jackass Hill, Mrs. Polillo's remains were said to show a retraction of the muscles at the neck, together with an almost total absence of blood in the heart, suggesting that the head had been removed just before death or immediately afterward. In other words, Florence Polillo's cause of death, like Edward Andrassy's, might well have been decapitation.

More unsettling details would emerge as Dr. Straus studied the incision marks on the upper torso. Sergeant Hogan, who was present for the examination, took special note of Straus's observation that the killer had made neat incisions around the arms and legs but had subsequently "wrenched" the limbs from their sockets, signaling a surge of brute force rather than surgical precision. More than one commentator would suggest that the killer had been worked up into a state of rage at the time of the dismemberment.

In spite of these new details, Sergeant Hogan told reporters that the discovery "shed little light on where the murder was committed." Hogan believed that Mrs. Polillo's murderer had sought to avoid detection by disposing of the body parts in scattered locations, and that he had apparently "driven up to the edge of the spot and thrown the pieces out." For all anyone knew, the second set of remains might have been discarded at the same time as the first, only to lie unnoticed beneath a blanket of snow. Possibly this second set had originally been wrapped in tidy bundles of newspaper or burlap coverings, which had either deteriorated or blown away in the damp, bitter weather.

The police had now recovered nearly all of Mrs. Polillo's remains, with the notable exception of her head. Spurred on by the latest find, Sergeant Hogan renewed the search effort and directed a team of officers as they spread across the neighborhood, lifting trash can lids and peering into coal bins. The head, he told them, must be found.

Across town at that very moment, Eliot Ness stepped forward to address a group of Boy Scouts at the May Company, a local department store, where he shared the podium with a bluegrass fiddle group. This type of appearance was fast becoming a signature piece of his new administration. A few days earlier, Ness had told stories of his Capone days to an auditorium filled with "howling, yelling, whistling youngsters," the local chapter of the Dick Tracy Detective Club. "You have a badge just like mine," he told them, flashing his gold shield. "When you grow up to be a man with long pants perhaps your badge will grow with you, and when that time comes I'd like to have you all working for me."

It looked as if there were going to be plenty of vacancies. Three days after his all-night ride-along with the Cleveland police, Ness launched a massive cleanup campaign: "Ness Fires 2 Policemen Drunk On Job," announced a headline in the *Plain Dealer*. "I will not stand for this sort of thing in my department," Ness insisted. "These men have a past record of prior offenses. They don't fit." Both officers were called in for a formal hearing, but neither could mount a defense: "I didn't sleep," one of them insisted. "I dozed."

Drinking on duty seemed like a fairly minor offense in the grand scheme of things, but Ness wanted to send a message: it was time to straighten up. The department had become so lax that even this modest show of discipline made page one of the next day's papers. "In a decently operated police department," one reporter groused, the action "wouldn't have been worth mentioning."

For the moment, every move Ness made seemed worth mentioning. As Mayor Burton mounted a full-court press to pass his new budget, Ness was trotted out at every opportunity as the public face of the new administration, a symbol of action and change. For several weeks, Ness appeared to be everywhere—addressing the Rotary Club, judging horse shows, and flashing his "winning smile" at garden club meetings. Though Burton himself was "a personable gentleman," as George Condon would note, he had no particular knack for public speaking and needed a standard-bearer to get his message out. Ness, by virtue of his youth and high profile, gave the new administration "a glamor and a glow that it sorely needed." More than once, the newspapers found occasion to run photos of Ness in tight-fitting gym shorts, showing off his trim physique as he demonstrated his skill in the martial arts.

On December 23, after less than two weeks in office, Ness announced an unprecedented shake-up of the Cleveland Police Department. He understood that he couldn't fire every officer with a stain on his record, so instead he arranged transfers for 122 men in a sweeping effort to flush out the most egregious offenders. It would be the first of several personnel shuffles intended to sever political alliances and break up entrenched patterns of bribes and payoffs. "My order should not be construed as a reflection on the men transferred," Ness declared, attempting to smooth ruffled feathers. "I have not gone into their individual integrity. I have faith in most of them, but, as matters stand now, they are working in a shadow of suspicion that is detrimental to both themselves and the community."

In particular, the shake-up focused on the department's detective bureau, a division where advancement and political favoritism went hand in hand. "A great deal of worriment has settled on that ancient nest of intrigue," wrote Philip Porter in the *Plain Dealer*, noting that one detective had carefully placed a manual of scientific police work on his desk, "in case Ness should happen around and see it." The veterans had cause for concern. Twenty-six new patrolmen would come onto the detective force under the Ness reforms, and many of them had barely a year of service under their belts. Their inexperience was seen as an advantage, the press reported, because they had not yet "fallen into the rut of routine police procedure," but it remained to be seen whether they were up to a challenge on the scale of the Florence Polillo investigation.

Ness also made a dramatic change at the top, replacing the detective bureau's Captain Emmet Potts, "the fair-haired boy" of the previous administration. Ness handled this departmental coup with notable delicacy, letting it be known that Potts's rank would not change despite a reassignment that involved determining the location of improperly placed stoplights. In other words, the former superintendent of the detective bureau had been placed on traffic duty. The message was clear: Ness was playing hardball. In the meantime, Potts had been replaced with the "strictly non-political" Joseph Sweeney, who was now directing the Florence Polillo investigation.

Given the scale of these maneuvers, political insiders expected that Ness would move to replace George Matowitz, the chief of police. Matowitz had served as interim safety director during Burton's transition and clearly had been angling for the job himself, "exuding the additional prestige most exceedingly." Though he promised full cooperation, Matowitz resented being passed over for the upstart Ness, and responded in "sulphurous language" when reporters asked if he expected to be fired. Even so, Ness decided to keep the thirty-one-year veteran at his post. The chief had a reputation for honesty, and though he had turned a blind eye to a great many shady dealings over the years, a colleague noted that Matowitz "deserved and held the liking of every man on the force." Ness saw that leaving him at the helm would quiet some of the grumbling and project a sense of stability to the rank and file.

In speech after speech to the city's business community, Ness insisted that his police department cleanup was the key to economic recovery. The city would stagnate, he maintained, if the mob continued to flourish, and the mob could only flourish if the police were complicit. "In any city where corruption continues, it follows that some officials are playing ball with the underworld," he said. "The dishonest public servant hiding behind a badge or political office is more detestable than any street criminal or mob boss." Even the honest cops were certain to grow discouraged, he said, and they would "see as little crime as possible." Others, like the pair he had already suspended, simply wouldn't bother to do their jobs properly, and would think nothing of drowning their sorrows on duty. "And the worst part," he concluded, "is that we have officers who match all three descriptions—crooked, lazy, and drunk!"

Ness's approach to crime, as George Condon would note, "was about as emotional as an accountant's approach to double-entry booking." Even so, his ambitious agenda thrust him back into the national spotlight alongside a wave of highly visible "gangbusters" led by New York's special prosecutor Thomas Dewey, who was in the midst of a major anti-vice campaign in New York City. Dewey, a future governor and presidential candidate, would soon capture the nation's attention with his dogged pursuit of Dutch Schultz and Lucky Luciano, but an editorial in the February 8 edition of the *Plain Dealer* offered a decidedly parochial take on his efforts: "New York, it appears, has its Eliot Ness."

That same day, the *Press* ran a photo gallery of local luminaries at a banquet for the Cleveland Safety Council. Edna Ness was seen chatting amiably with the council president while her husband sat nearby, looking polished and elegant in his dinner jacket. Jarringly, the adjacent column of the newspaper featured a grim update on the Florence Polillo investigation. Ness was inadvertently positioned so that his head seemed to turn away from the stark headline: "Find More of Torso Victim: Police Push for Head of Woman in Lot on Orange Avenue."

In time, the Safety Council photos would be clipped out and pasted into the Ness family scrapbook, carefully trimmed with scissors so that no trace of the Polillo story impinged on the festive mood. In a matter of days, however, Ness would be forced to turn and face the story directly.

7

"LET'S GO"

Then, an easy target in his tan trench coat, Ness raised one foot
and gave the door a violent kick. The force of the blow tore off
the lock, springing the door, but it still was held by the safety
chain inside. One more expert kick snapped the chain and the
door flew open. As it did, a man stepped in the breach and
leveled a pistol at the taut-faced Safety Director. . . .

Oscar Fraley, *4 Against the Mob*

"I lost my shirt," said one visitor after a bruising tour of the city's gambling parlors in the early days of 1936. "Also, my shoes, trousers and
dignity."

The comment highlighted an ongoing challenge for Eliot Ness. Even
as the illicit alcohol business dried up, a robust and pervasive network of
illegal betting houses continued to pump money into the mob's coffers.
At a time when a five-bedroom home in Shaker Heights could be had
for $15,000, Cleveland's gamblers laid down nearly a quarter of a million
dollars each week, much of it at glitzy casinos like the Thomas Club and
the Harvard Club on the outskirts of the city. It wasn't just the locals who
became ensnared in these "sucker traps," George Condon would recall.
"Long before there was a Las Vegas, there was Cleveland, and its place
on the gambling map was most prominent." Every night, a fleet of town

cars, buses, and lake cruisers brought in high rollers from all points of the compass. There were few winners in this equation. One man, despondent after a ruinous night at the tables, drew up a mock suicide note. "Have my body cremated and give my ashes to the Thomas Club," he wrote. "They have everything else."

From his first days in office, Ness had been carrying out raids on gambling parlors and "horse rooms." Personally, Ness had no particular beef with gamblers. "It's debatable whether gambling is morally wrong," he admitted. "I am inclined to be liberal in my views of amusements." He believed, however, that gambling served as a magnet for every other form of lawlessness, including prostitution, racketeering, and graft. "He doesn't relish being labeled a 'bookie raider,'" a reporter noted, "but he firmly believes a direct connection exists between gambling and more serious forms of crime. He tells you this over and over again." One headline writer summed it up in a phrase: "Choke Crime By its Purse, Ness Urges."

Ness could do little about the Thomas and Harvard Clubs, both of which had set up shop just outside the city limits, beyond the reach of Cleveland police. The Harvard Club had a particularly storied history under the ownership of Frank Joiner, a so-called "slot machine baron," whose nude body had turned up a few months earlier with three bullets in the head. Under the new owners, Arthur Hebebrand and James "Shimmy" Patton, the Harvard Club operated out of a converted warehouse in Newburgh Heights, south of the city, and enjoyed a reputation as one of the best and largest gambling joints to be found between New York and Chicago. As many as a thousand people per night passed through the club's gaudy plywood facade, which was painted to suggest the pillars and tall windows of a southern plantation. Inside, patrons sipped on gin rickeys and old-fashioneds, and tried their luck at craps, roulette, and all-night poker. The club even provided a special window at which gamblers could cash their government relief checks.

Hebebrand and Patton enjoyed a cozy relationship with local law enforcement. "Honest John" Sulzmann, the sheriff of Cuyahoga County, had the authority to shut their operations down at any time, but for years he had resolutely declined to do so. Whenever the Harvard and Thomas

Clubs were brought to his attention, Sulzmann shook his head sadly and cited a vague "home rule" policy to the effect that he would "not cross municipal lines on official business unless asked to do so by municipal authorities." When pressed, the sheriff denied all knowledge of gambling in his jurisdiction, insisting at one stage that the Harvard Club—with its dozens of gaming tables, betting windows, and cashier's cages—was nothing more than a popular restaurant. By January of 1936, reporters had spent nearly five years trying to goad the sheriff into action. On one occasion, a detailed account of the Harvard Club's "multifarious activities" appeared in the papers alongside a helpful road map—"telling Sheriff Sulzmann how to get there."

Frank Cullitan, the Cuyahoga County prosecutor, had made it his mission to close down both clubs, peppering the operators with misdemeanor warrants. A bookish man with a face "as Irish as the keeper of the Blarney Stone," Cullitan had come to his government post only four years earlier in 1932, after twenty-five years as a trial lawyer. "He hits hard," a colleague would say of him, "but never low blows." His efforts to shut down the gambling clubs had been largely brushed aside, but his doggedness made an impression. "Anyone who knows Frank Cullitan," a colleague would remark, "knows he will act when the time is right."

On January 10, 1936, Cullitan decided the time was right. Determined to strike "suddenly and hard," the prosecutor rolled out a bold plan to launch coordinated raids on both the Thomas and Harvard Clubs. He secured two sets of search and seizure warrants, hired moving vans to cart away impounded gambling equipment, and took out arrest warrants for Shimmy Patton and Arthur Hebebrand.

Cullitan knew that if any advance word of his plan leaked out to local law enforcement officers, both clubs would be stripped to the walls before he arrived. "It was impossible to conduct a successful raid if the sheriff's office or suburban police were alerted," one source admitted. "It was a public joke." To avoid any chance of a tip-off, Cullitan sidestepped the police altogether. Instead, he hired a group of twenty-five men from a local private detective agency and had them sworn in as special constables. He also recruited a trio of young, ambitious assistant prosecutors to help lead the charge: Charles McNamee, Frank Celebrezze, and Thomas Burke.

Cullitan mustered his forces in a suburban parking lot at four that afternoon, dividing his recruits into two groups. McNamee and Celebrezze took their places at the head of the convoy headed south to the Harvard Club, while Cullitan and Burke would lead the other group east to the Thomas Club. At a signal from Cullitan, the raiders climbed into their cars and started their engines. Moments later, two convoys peeled away in opposite directions, each with a moving truck bringing up the rear.

The Thomas Club was "boldly lit and busy as a bus terminal" when Cullitan's team arrived a short time later. Brandishing his warrants, the prosecutor forced his way inside and scooped up a bonanza of gambling equipment, including craps tables, roulette wheels, slot machines, and a special telegraph hookup for up-to-the-minute race results. The club's operators, Patton and Hebebrand, were nowhere to be found, and many of their employees managed to slip away in the confusion, some of them carrying sacks full of cash beneath their coats. Still, Cullitan's men seized an impressive arsenal of Thompson submachine guns and tear gas canisters, along with a small fortune in silver coins that had been abandoned as too unwieldy to carry. In all, it would take two trips in a one-and-a-half-ton moving van before all the equipment could be cleared away. Cullitan also grabbed up a large haul of incriminating ledgers and receipts. These would shed light on the club's dirty finances, the prosecutor hoped, and "give the public an idea of how large a sucker it really had been." Feeling satisfied with their efforts, Cullitan and his men climbed back into their cars and headed across town to the Harvard Club.

Charles McNamee and Frank Celebrezze had reached the heavily fortified entrance of the Harvard Club at 5:20 that afternoon. Backed by their team of special constables, the two prosecutors pounded on the door and demanded entry. A voice from inside called back: "You can't get in here without getting your head bashed in."

McNamee and Celebrezze drew back, startled. They had expected only token resistance. Instead, the assistant prosecutors watched in amazement as dark-suited henchmen took up positions in the club's windows and along a high balcony, brandishing machine guns. Incredibly, Patton and Hebebrand's men appeared ready to defend the building as if it were a military fortress. "The huge club," the *Press* would report, "was then in a state of siege," with several hundred well-heeled gamblers still milling about inside.

Moments later, a large, gleaming sedan pulled up in front. Shimmy Patton, a short, stubby man in a green hat and billowing white scarf, scrambled out with a stone-faced bodyguard at his side. After conferring with his employees, Patton hurried over to confront the assistant prosecutors. "If one of you tries to stick his goddamned neck in that door we'll mow him down with machine guns," he announced. "We've got them and we'll use them." He jabbed a thumb toward the balcony at the side of the building, now bristling with heavily armed men.

"We don't want any bloodshed," McNamee insisted. Hoping to defuse the situation, he offered to let the club's patrons exit safely before the raiders swept through.

"The hell with that," Patton snapped. "You aren't coming in here. If you do, you'll get killed."

This uncompromising resistance was hard to explain. If anything, the raiders had imagined that Hebebrand and Patton would cooperate in a spirit of amused contempt, knowing that their friends in law enforcement would straighten out the "misunderstanding" soon enough. Now, seeing the anger and fixed determination in the gangster's face, McNamee and his men drew back in confusion. Meanwhile, according to the *Press*, "a steady line of men with bulging overcoats, presumably removing money and gambling equipment, filed out of the club door, in full view." Adding to the confusion, hundreds of Newburgh Heights residents had now massed outside, eager to see how the standoff would play out.

Frank Cullitan and his team arrived half an hour later. Climbing out of his car, the prosecutor caught sight of gun barrels glinting in the windows of the club. "This is the most brazen defiance of law and order I ever have heard of anywhere," he said, shaking his head. As Cullitan weighed his options, Shimmy Patton hurried toward him. "Mr. Patton," Cullitan said, "I've tried to go about this as decently as I could, and we're going to see it through."

"No," Patton snapped, "you ain't gonna make a pinch here! No pinches! Understand?" As a reporter edged toward them, Patton turned and vented his fury. "Don't try to get your ear in here!" he shouted. "Lightning is liable to strike you, buddy!" He continued in this vein for some time, one observer would recall, "cursing more profusely than most of the quiet group of waiters expected." While Patton ranted, his partner, Arthur Hebebrand, sidled up to Cullitan and drove the point home with chilling finality. "If an arrest is made," he told the prosecutor, "you won't get out of here alive."

Cullitan had heard enough. He had two dozen men and the full force of the law on his side, but he saw now that he needed reinforcements. Turning away, the prosecutor hurried to a pay phone. First, Cullitan put in a call to the county sheriff's office, only to be told that Sheriff Sulzmann was "ill in bed at his home." Next, he tried without success to reach the mayor of Newburgh Heights and Police Chief George Matowitz. Finally, at the end of his rope, Cullitan fished another coin out of his pocket and called Eliot Ness.

It is impossible to know what was going through Cullitan's mind as he called Cleveland's new safety director, who had been on the job for less than a month. Ness was younger than Cullitan by more than twenty years, and likely seemed raw and untested to the more seasoned prosecutor. But if the stories of facing down Capone and his mob were true, or even half true, Ness would know how to handle Patton and Hebebrand. If ever a situation cried out for an Untouchable, this was it.

An aide answered the phone in Ness's office and went down the hall to pull him out of a city council meeting. Cullitan sounded tense and out of breath as he gave Ness the broad strokes. "They're threatening to open fire if we come inside," the prosecutor said. "We need help!"

Ness told Cullitan to hold tight and clicked over to another phone line, hoping to cut through some of the red tape that came with his new job. Ness knew perfectly well that he had no authority outside the city limits, so his first thought was to call the sheriff's office and pile on the pressure, in hope of rousing Sulzmann to action. William Murphy, the chief jailer, answered the sheriff's phone. "Prosecutor Cullitan is at the Harvard Club with several of his staff and their lives are endangered," Ness told him. "As a citizen, I am calling on you to send deputies out there." This was an exceptional circumstance, Ness insisted, and it demanded a direct response from Sulzmann: "Will you go out or won't you?" He waited for several tense moments until the jailer returned, having phoned the sheriff at home. "No," Ness was told. "We won't go out there."

The sheriff's refusal put Ness in a tight spot. Charging into Cullitan's operation at the Harvard Club, which appeared to have gone entirely off the rails, carried huge risks. Ness would be overstepping his own authority and exposing himself to a potentially humiliating misstep. It was one thing to plan and carry out a raid of his own, but in this case he would be trying to clean up Cullitan's mess. If things went badly, it could hobble his own cleanup campaign before it really began, demonstrating that the city's entrenched gambling network was too much for the young, inexperienced safety director. On the other hand, Cullitan had presented Ness with a problem he understood. Here was a chance to prove himself in the field, and to show how they'd done things in Chicago.

Ness could not have spent much time wrestling with the dilemma since Cullitan was still waiting on the open phone line when he clicked back over. "I'll be there," Ness told the prosecutor. "I'll come as a private citizen and I'll ask some policemen to go with me as volunteers. Hold everything!"

After a brief consultation with Mayor Burton, who left him in no doubt of his dubious legal standing, Ness drove over to the Central Police Station, arriving just as a large group of officers came in for a ten o'clock change of shift. Few of the men had ever laid eyes on Ness before, and all had reason to be wary of the upstart who had already rattled the department to its core. Ness stood at the center of the room with his hat in hand, explaining in quiet, urgent tones that Cullitan and his men were in a serious fix. "I found the boys just coming off duty and preparing to take off their uniforms and go home," he recalled. "I told them the circumstances and informed them I was going out there, even if I had to go alone." The room fell silent as Ness outlined the risks. "I told the men the city's responsibility for them ended when they crossed the boundary line," he said. "If they were killed out there their families might be cut off the pension rolls. I told them I wouldn't hold it against them if they didn't go. It was voluntary service."

For a long moment the room remained silent as the men weighed their young commander's words. Then, with a shrug, a man stepped forward, followed by two or three more, until at last every officer in the room signaled his intention to follow Ness to the Harvard Club. "Without an exception," Ness recalled proudly, "they all agreed to go." Moments later, a convoy of squad cars rolled out of the station garage with sirens blaring. For all his haste, Ness had not omitted to notify the press of the brewing drama. The police cars were trailed by three sedans filled with newsmen.

Ness and his reinforcements arrived at the Harvard Club at 10:30. As his car drew closer, Ness could see that a group of "tough-looking birds" had Cullitan hemmed in. "I would be unable to exaggerate the gravity of the situation," he recalled. "I told our driver to open up his siren and split a way through the crowd."

Ness made his way to Cullitan's side while his officers got the crowd under control. The two men quickly hammered out a plan, but first Ness had to dispense with a troublesome legal formality. "I told Mr. Cullitan we could not participate in a raid because the Harvard Club was outside the city," Ness explained. "I added, however: 'We are here to protect you, and to do that we must go where you go.'" In other words, if Cullitan pressed ahead with his raid, Ness would be at his side. Moreover, he added, certain circumstances might arise that would justify a more active role. "You know," Ness said, "an old law gives any citizen the right to make an arrest if a felony is committed in his presence." In fact, he went on to say, he and his men had brought along tear gas rifles—"in case a felony should start."

Ness was on dangerous ground, and Cullitan knew it. Worse yet, the prosecutor saw that tear gas rifles were the least of the safety director's "precautions." Sawed-off shotguns, rifles, pistols, and heavy truncheons were also in evidence. Cullitan, who had armed himself with nothing more than a handful of arrest warrants, blanched at the sight of so much firepower. Turning to Ness, he echoed what Charles McNamee had said earlier: "I don't want any bloodshed."

Ness gave no response, or if he did, it was not recorded by the eager group of reporters who stood watching his every move, with blue Eagle pencils hovering over open notepads. Some of them, huddled together behind makeshift barricades, believed that Ness had taken on "the most hazardous task of his career," with nothing less than the city's future hanging in the balance. "It was an issue no less important than that," the *Plain Dealer* would declare. "If this most populous of Ohio counties were to be bluffed to a standstill by a gang of suburban gamblers, it might as well run up the white flag in token of its surrender to outlawry. It might as well admit itself buffaloed by a do-nothing sheriff." Ness, for his part, just wanted to get on with it. After five hours, the standoff had reached its crisis.

By this time, all of the lights inside the club had been extinguished and only the glint of gun barrels could be seen in the darkened outline. "They strutted and preened themselves," a *Press* reporter said of the club's gunmen, "promising to 'mow down' anyone who tried to enter." Though the police were also heavily armed, Ness himself had not thought to bring the .38 Smith & Wesson he had appropriated a few weeks earlier. In fact, he seldom carried a gun in any circumstances. "I don't need it," he once told a friend, "the holster's enough." Now, standing at the center of a large, restless group of city officials and lawmen, Ness took a moment to pin his gold safety director's badge to his lapel. Glancing at a row of squad cars behind him, he pointed into the shadows. "Let's have a light here," he said quietly. The drivers turned the beams of their swing-lamps toward the club's entrance. Ness squared his shoulders. "All right?" he said. "Let's go."

With that, he started forward. The off-duty officers fell in step behind him, their ranks swelled by Cullitan's special constables. "Four-score armed men, led by the unarmed Ness, came marching forward in a solid phalanx," the *News* would report. Ahead stood a line of machine-gun-toting thugs, just beyond the splash of illumination from the police beacons. One witness recalled a sharp intake of breath from the bystanders as Ness advanced, taking no heed of the gun barrels that now swung in his direction, convinced that none of the club's lookouts would have the brass to shoot him in cold blood. This was, without question, the riskiest bet ever laid down at the Harvard Club. Ness, "a slight figure in a camel's-hair topcoat," simply strode forward, upright and resolute in the style of John Wayne or Gary Cooper—high noon in the suburbs of Cleveland.

For several moments, as Ness and his men passed through the pool of light at the front of the club, no sounds were heard apart from a low rustle of wind and the crunch of leather soles on gravel. Then, a tight, rolling murmur rose from the crowd of bystanders as Ness led his men up the short flight of stairs to the front entrance. At the top, Ness motioned to a couple of officers to rap on the steel door with their truncheons. A pair of eyes looked out from a peephole slider. Ness leaned in close. "I'm Eliot Ness," he announced. "I'm coming in with some search warrants." The slider closed with a snap, and a voice could be heard from behind the heavy door: "It's that goddam Eliot Ness." A moment later the bolts clicked as the door swung open. Ness pushed past a burly figure in a tuxedo and rushed inside with Cullitan close behind. "All right," Ness said to the prosecutor. "Let your men go in there and serve their warrants. We'll back them up."

Later, Oscar Fraley of *Untouchables* fame would put a hyperbolic spin on the scene, placing Ness at the center of a whirlwind of splintered door frames and jujitsu moves—"as quick as one of the six cats he had at home." In truth, as Ness had learned in Chicago, the hard part was over—he'd made it through the door. The job now was to push forward and mop up before any more of the club's staff and equipment could disappear.

Inside, the gambling parlor had fallen eerily silent. The raiders hurried through an empty lobby, passing a cigarette girl who sat placidly counting her tips, and made their way to the casino floor, a vast space measuring some ninety feet square. Earlier that night, hundreds of patrons had swarmed the gaming tables and roulette wheels. Now the room stood cavernous and bare, emptied out during the long standoff. Only a few baize-covered tables remained, along with a gigantic chalkboard covered with race results. The customers and employees had fled in such haste that a large number of felt hats remained behind, and a scattering of betting slips covered the floor.

Ness and the raiders fanned out in search of Shimmy Patton and Arthur Hebebrand, in the faint hope that the two operators might still be somewhere on the premises. The safety director's efforts drew an indignant challenge from a glowering "plug-ugly," one of the few remaining club employees. "Say, who do you think you are?" he asked, mistaking the youthful Ness for one of Cullitan's recruits. "You were only sworn in a few hours ago." Ness brushed past him. Looking up, he caught sight of the outlines of an overhead "strong room" that commanded a view of the gaming floor, complete with slits for machine gun barrels. The raiders quickly pulled down a folding ladder from the ceiling and forced their way inside. "Before that," Ness said, "we weren't certain whether we would be 'mowed down' as had been threatened."

As his men climbed down from the strong room, Ness sensed a change in mood. His off-duty officers had been held in check up to this point, he said, "just aching for something to happen." The emptiness of the club had settled over them as "something of an anticlimax to the tense hours of siege," as George Condon would write, and now their pent-up frustrations had them spoiling for a fight.

Soon enough, they got their chance. As Byron "Shorty" Filkins, a five-foot-two *Press* photographer, climbed onto a chair to get a better view of the room, a Harvard Club straggler rushed forward and pushed him to the floor, shouting that pictures were off-limits. Filkins's colleagues sprang to his defense. A cameraman from the *News* launched a "haymaker from around the knees," sending Filkins's assailant sprawling across a craps table. "Pandemonium broke loose," reported the *Plain Dealer*. "Fists flew and folding chairs were smashed as the club attachés pitched into the battle." Ness's off-duty policemen leapt into the fray, perhaps all too eagerly, though Ness himself would remain vague on this point in days to come. "Everything happened so fast," he insisted.

To Ness's surprise, the punch-up flushed Arthur Hebebrand out of hiding. As the fighting escalated, the casino operator appeared suddenly from a back room and attempted to wade in, only to be seized by a police sergeant. "Don't try to slug me," Hebebrand shouted. "If you do, you won't get out of this place alive!" When the brawl sputtered out, however, Hebebrand appeared to concede defeat. While Ness went looking for Shimmy Patton, Hebebrand shrugged his shoulders and told Cullitan that he would grab his coat and hat for the ride downtown. Cullitan stood politely waiting as Hebebrand drifted off to a nearby counting room. Once inside, however, Hebebrand suddenly turned and blockaded the door, sealing himself inside with a small crew of holdouts.

When Ness returned to the casino floor, an abashed Cullitan told him what had happened. Ness had grown weary of half measures by this time: "I told Cullitan I thought tear gas was what we ought to use." He made this suggestion in a very loud voice, apparently, because the door to the counting room flew open before the order could be carried out. As the men inside filed out, however, Hebebrand was not among them. Ness elbowed his way in and found the room empty. All that remained were four heavy floor safes stripped of their contents, their doors hanging open. Hebebrand had placed a chair on top of a table and crawled out through a high window, joining Shimmy Patton in making his getaway. The big fish had slipped through the net, just as they had earlier at the Thomas Club.

Ness was said to be amused, knowing that neither man would get terribly far. All that remained now was to load the confiscated gambling equipment into Cullitan's moving trucks. Facing reporters outside, Ness glossed over Hebebrand's escape, preferring instead to lavish praise on his off-duty volunteers. "Gee," he said, sounding more like a Boy Scout than ever, "this ought to do an awful lot for law enforcement in the city and county. I hope what happened here tonight is shown in its true light." Pressed for details, Ness diplomatically extended an olive branch to the feckless Sheriff Sulzmann. "It was a real victory and I hope the county people keep up their good work. With their co-operation my job of trying to keep Cleveland as free from crime as possible will be just that much easier." With that, Ness headed back over the city line to celebrate in his customary fashion, holing up in a downtown saloon with a few colleagues.

By the following morning, the story had gone out over the wires and made national headlines. A city that had grown weary and cynical now "blinked in surprise and pleasure," George Condon would recall. "All of a sudden, the contest between law and the lawbreaker, the good guys and the bad guys, had come alive. All of a sudden the issue was in doubt and Eliot Ness was the town hero. His timing was terrific. The city seldom had needed a hero so badly."

For all of that, the raid had accomplished very little in concrete terms. Cullitan's arrest warrants had not been served, and the Harvard Club would soon be up and running again in a new location, as would the Thomas Club. Even so, Cullitan took issue with any suggestion that the operation had fallen short. "Our objective was to close the place," he told a reporter, "and we did it." He posed for press photos brandishing a tear gas gun over the financial ledgers seized at the Thomas Club.

Whatever the immediate effect might have been, the night's events cemented a powerful alliance between Cullitan and Ness, with lasting consequences for both men. Together, as the *Plain Dealer* observed, the pair was destined to achieve great things, because Ness "has the courage and knowledge to fight for a cleaner city" while Cullitan "knows what to do with evidence." In other words, Ness would round up the bad guys and Cullitan would put them away. The raid also proved to be a decisive moment for John Sulzmann, the "alleged sheriff" of Cuyahoga County, who found himself cast as the villain of the piece for his failure to come to the prosecutor's aid. "He cooked his political goose blacker than a chunk of coal," one columnist observed, and in the next election, the sheriff would be voted out of office.

Though Ness could not have known it at the time, his own political prospects had also been scorched. It would later emerge that the notorious gangster Alvin Karpis, the FBI's current Public Enemy No. 1, may have been lying low at the Harvard Club as Cullitan's raiders arrived. The presence of Karpis, fresh off a daring $46,000 train robbery in nearby Garrettsville, Ohio, might well explain the unexpectedly stiff resistance to Cullitan's initial attempt to enter the club. In any case, Karpis was reported to have slipped away during the long standoff, much to the disgust of FBI Director J. Edgar Hoover. The gangster was probably long gone by the time Ness reached the Harvard Club, but Hoover blamed Ness for letting him get away, believing that dirty cops must have tipped off the gangster.

Hoover himself was on the cusp of an embarrassing public relations debacle at the time. In April of that year, he would be forced to admit, during a famously combative Senate hearing, that in spite of his towering reputation as a law officer, he had never personally made an arrest. Stung by the perception "that his manhood had been impugned," Hoover resolved to rectify the embarrassment by personally overseeing the capture of Alvin Karpis. When agents tracked the gangster to New Orleans, Hoover chartered a plane to be present for the arrest. "Karpis Captured in New Orleans by Hoover Himself," read a headline in *The New York Times*. "The timing was so dramatic," a columnist would remark, "that one might almost suspect a touch of stage direction."

Hoover's frantic efforts to repair his public image, coming on the heels of the lionization of Ness at the Harvard Club, can only have sharpened the edge of his resentment toward the "young, fighting safety director." Ness, for his part, was sensitive to the charge that one of his men might have alerted Karpis to the raid. He wrote to Hoover to say that he would fire the offenders if any evidence could be produced. Cleveland field agents assured Hoover that Ness was a "great admirer" and that he was "anxious to cooperate with you and the Bureau in every way possible."

Hoover would not be swayed. The director held fast to his belief that Ness "was not very cordially disposed to the bureau," and made a point of warning his agents to steer clear. At one stage, when an FBI official relayed a request for advice on dealing with the safety director, Hoover summed up his feelings in a cutting phrase:

"There is no advice I would give him," Hoover said, "except to beware of Ness."

8

THE TATTOOED MAN

The nude, headless body of a murdered man was found by searchers late today in Kingsbury Run, 1,000 feet from the spot where a head previously had been discovered.

Cleveland News, June 6, 1936

It was perhaps the worst decision that either boy would ever make, but that day—Friday, June 5, 1936—promised to be bright and balmy, too nice a day to spend in school. Thirteen-year-old Gomez Ivey and his friend Louis Cheeley, age eleven, set off a little before 8:30 in the morning and followed the New York Central Railroad tracks toward Lake Erie. Both boys carried fishing poles across their shoulders. No one saw them leave. With luck, they told themselves, their parents would never know they'd played hooky.

Their path cut through Kingsbury Run near a bridge at East 55th Street. As the boys trudged along a barren stretch near the Shaker Rapid Transit tracks, they spotted a ball of cloth beneath a willow tree. Stepping closer, they saw that they had found a discarded pair of brown pants. The two boys looked at each other. "We see the pants all rolled up and we think maybe there's money in the pockets," Ivey would recall. "So we take a fish pole and poke the bundle." If the boys hoped to dislodge some loose change, they would be sorely disappointed. As the bundle loosened and began to unfurl, a dark, round object rolled slowly into view. It was a severed human head.

"We're so scared we run straight home," Ivey said. "I wanted to ask my mother what to do but she wasn't home." Badly shaken, the boys spent the next eight hours lying low, waiting for Mrs. Ivey to return. When she finally came through the door at five, the gruesome tale came spilling out. Mrs. Ivey immediately took charge and had the boys repeat the story to a patrolman named Hendricks.

Hendricks made a brief effort to locate the head on his own, but apparently Ivey and Cheeley were unable to pinpoint the exact location. When his initial search came up empty, the patrolman radioed for assistance. Within the hour, the head had been located at a spot a few hundred yards from the nearest main road, Kinsman Road, having lain undisturbed for the entire day. By this time, a large number of officers had converged on the scene. Significantly, the group included several investigators who had also worked the Andrassy and Polillo investigations. Detectives Emil Musil and Orley May were among the first to arrive, along with Sergeant James Hogan.

Once the scene had been photographed, the investigators moved in for a closer look. The head had been cleanly severed at the neck, but no traces of blood were seen on the ground nearby or anywhere in the vicinity, suggesting that the decapitation had taken place elsewhere. Numerous articles of clothing, many of them bloodied and torn, were found crammed inside the legs and pockets of the brown pants. These included a white polo shirt, a brown-striped dress shirt, a pair of men's underwear, a black leather belt, and a dirty white handkerchief. A few yards away police also found a pair of oxford shoes tied together by the laces, with a pair of striped socks stuffed inside. An oil-stained brown cap also turned up nearby.

Police quickly established that all of these items, including the victim's head, had been dumped at the scene within the previous twenty-four hours. A railroad detective, who made regular patrols of the area for the New York Central, insisted that the ground had been clear the previous day. A late-model Cadillac had been spotted under a nearby bridge during the night. Perhaps, police speculated, the killer had driven as close as he could and carried his "ghastly cargo" into Kingsbury Run on foot, under cover of darkness.

Deputy Coroner Wilson Chamberlain began an examination of the severed head at the county morgue early the following morning. He noted that the victim had reddish-brown hair, brown eyes, a fair complexion, and a strong jaw and nose. The dead man was described as "strikingly handsome," with high cheekbones and fine features. He also had excellent teeth, the coroner's report noted, although several molars were missing. The head had been severed between the first and second cervical vertebrae, but little damage was evident to the face or scalp. The report estimated the victim's age somewhere between twenty and twenty-five. The time of death was fixed at roughly two days prior to discovery.

Already a major effort was under way to identify the victim. Investigators combed through missing persons reports and circulated photographs of the dead man's face. At the morgue, a startlingly lifelike plaster casting was taken to supplement the photographic documentation. Police chased down dental records and made an exhaustive canvass of local dry cleaners, working from laundry marks found on some of the discarded clothing. Incredibly, the coroner's office even arranged a macabre after-hours viewing for the general public, in the hope that someone in the crowd might step forward with a positive identification. The severed head was carefully cleaned and arranged on a metal gurney, swathed in plush fabric and angled in a manner that somehow gave an impression of tranquility, as if the young victim were luxuriating at a spa. As word of the strange spectacle spread across the city, a long line of people formed along 9th Street, many of them "merely morbidly curious," according to the *Press*, creating an atmosphere much like that of a midnight horror film. As many as two thousand people filed solemnly past the gurney. Some became nauseated by the spectacle; a few needed to be helped from the room. No one could offer a clue as to the unfortunate man's identity.

A breakthrough came on Saturday, June 6, as a pair of New York

Central Railroad workers came across a nude, headless body partially concealed in a cluster of thick brush near the East 55th Street bridge. Almost at once the fresh remains were established as a match for the severed head, which had been found only a few hundred yards away. Soon, the coroner's office would release a fresh round of details. The victim had stood five feet eleven inches and weighed roughly 165 pounds. There was alcohol in his system, and the contents of his stomach showed that he had eaten baked beans shortly before his death. Coroner Pearse told a reporter that "the youth probably was killed as he slept, his head severed by a blow from a butcher knife." One detail, the cause of death, carried an unsettling echo of earlier crimes: the man had died as a result of decapitation and the resulting shock.

Investigators managed to pull a clear set of fingerprints from the remains, raising hopes that they would soon learn the victim's name. In addition, it was now apparent that the young man had been enthusiastic—perhaps even fanatical—about tattoos. The body featured no fewer than six highly distinctive designs, all of them containing obvious clues that promised to help with the identification. On his right arm, he bore a heart pierced by an arrow, a set of crossed flags, and the initials "W.C.G." On the left arm, a dove fluttered over the names "Helen and Paul," while his shoulder presented a delicate butterfly. His right calf displayed a cupid and an anchor, while the left calf exhibited a likeness of the cartoon character Jiggs, complete with a cigar and checkered vest, from the popular *Bringing Up Father* comic strip. Surely, the investigators told themselves, the identity of a man with such a rich tapestry of tattoos would not be hard to uncover.

By this time, another crucial point had snapped into focus: the murder of the tattooed man, as he now came to be known, was not an isolated crime. The severed head had been discovered barely a mile away from Jackass Hill, where two other severed heads—those of Edward Andrassy and his still-unidentified companion—had been found nine months earlier. This chilling revelation would completely reshape the investigation. "The hand which removed from its body the head found in Kingsbury Run," announced the *Press*, "is the same hand which decapitated two men whose bodies were found in the same gully last September." The phrase "serial killer" had not yet come into use at the time, but a horrifying clarity now took root at Kingsbury Run. As Sergeant Hogan would tell the press, he and his detectives were on the trail of "a crazed killer with a flair for butchery."

The so-called Lady of the Lake, whose remains had washed up on the shore of Lake Erie some eighteen months earlier, had not yet entered into the calculations, but some investigators were inclined to list Florence Polillo among the victims, noting that her head, too, had been cleanly severed. Not all of the detectives agreed on this point, but the possibility introduced a perplexing layer of inconsistency. Perhaps the killer chose his victims almost at random, striking when the opportunity presented itself, without respect to gender. If so, police had been looking in the wrong places. In the case of Edward Andrassy, they had searched out anyone who might have harbored a grudge: a cuckolded husband or an angry hoodlum. With Florence Polillo, they had combed through the victim's history of prostitution and petty crime. Now, instead of hunting for suspects with a personal motive, investigators had to adapt to the possibility that this "mad torso slayer" might be driven by some compulsive bloodlust, a dark and unfathomable impulse toward murder for its own sake. In that case, there would almost certainly be more headless bodies to come. This emerging notion of a demon butcher running loose in the city brought a horrifying sense of urgency, intensifying an already massive police effort.

There were a number of crucial differences, however, between the earlier crimes and the most recent victim. Most notably, the body of the tattooed man showed no rope burns or other markings to indicate that he had been tied up and struggling at the time of death. Also, there would be no carefully worded references to "other mutilations" in the newspapers this time; the tattooed man's genitals were intact.

Other troubling inconsistencies became apparent as the crimes were considered in series. While Coroner Pearse routinely described the dismemberments as clean and precise, he and others also allowed for the presence of "hesitation marks" at some of the incision points, suggesting a less-practiced hand. At times the killer displayed a surgical knowledge and expertise, skillfully navigating the more troublesome joints and ligaments, while at other times he appeared crazed and savage, hacking wildly at his victims and even tearing them limb from limb. Similar contradictions hung over the dumping grounds where the body parts had been discovered. The tidy, almost prim manner in which Florence Polillo's remains had been gathered up into neat bundles indicated a cold and methodical killer. By contrast, the hideous clump of severed genitals tossed aside at Jackass Hill suggested a brutal recklessness. Perhaps these incongruities pointed to an accomplice in the crimes and their aftermath. Could one person acting alone have carried the bodies of Andrassy and his companion down the treacherous incline at Jackass Hill, or was there a second pair of hands to assist in the heavy lifting? Or perhaps, as some would theorize, the killer's personality encompassed both icy discipline and wild rage, veering from one extreme to other in the manner of Jekyll and Hyde.

Often these contradictions bubbled to the surface as the investigators spoke to the press. Charles Nevel, an acting detective inspector, described the murderer as "a maniac with a lust to kill" who had probably stumbled across the tattooed man sheltering in Kingsbury Run. "While he was sleeping this maniac attacked him," Nevel continued. "First he cut his throat. Then he hacked away at the neck. Then he undressed the victim." When a reporter asked what this last step had accomplished, Nevel hesitated. Possibly the question threw him off balance, or perhaps he felt reluctant to address the hazy outline of sexual sadism that had now crept in at the edges of the case. Either way, his answer did little to clarify the matter. "That's a maniac's trick!" Nevel insisted.

This opaque response reflected a general sense of disorientation. All at once, the police found themselves grappling with a crime that went beyond the experience of anyone on the force—nothing less than a modern-day Jack the Ripper. "Is there somewhere in Cuyahoga county a madman whose god is the guillotine?" the *Cleveland News* would ask. "What fantastic chemistry of the civilized mind converted him into a human butcher?" This was a question that the Cleveland police of 1936 were ill-equipped to answer. For all their hard work and sincere intentions, the men working the case had come up in the era of Murphy call boxes and leather truncheons; the "fantastic chemistry of the civilized mind" had no place on their duty roster. In the days to come, the city's detectives would throw themselves into the investigation with extraordinary drive and intensity, and push themselves toward a better understanding of the psychological underpinnings of the crimes. For the moment, however, they simply cast a wide net and hoped for the best. "Police today descended on a shantytown camp for homeless men," reported the *Press* on June 8, "and arrested 13 inhabitants in the hopes of finding among them the 'human butcher' believed to be operating on the Southeast Side."

When this raid and others like it failed to bring results, investigators reexamined the Andrassy and Polillo files, seeking a link between the latest victim and the earlier crimes. Other detectives pressed ahead with the effort to uncover the tattooed man's name. "He still has not been identified although hundreds of visitors continue to visit the Morgue," noted a reporter, "and although his body bore numerous distinguished tattooed figures and initials." If anything, the bewildering array of tattoos seemed to have clouded the issue. Was his name Paul, as suggested by the "Helen and Paul" design on his left arm? If so, what was the significance of the initials "W.C.G." on his right arm? Detectives sent inquiries to tattoo parlors all across the country, hoping that someone would recall the singular grouping of images, but no one did. Military records were also searched, on the theory that the anchor and crossed-flag tattoos might indicate service in the armed forces. Again, there were no results. Frustratingly, the fingerprints taken from the body also failed to shed light—they did not match any of the records in George Koestle's extensive catalog. As with the Jackass Hill and Florence Polillo cases, the trail appeared to be growing cold. "Until they identify the tattooed, beheaded body of his victim," noted the *Plain Dealer*, "police say they are helpless in finding the killer."

Meanwhile, in the pages of the three major newspapers, a circulation war gathered heat. The city's journalists now came to realize, some more reluctantly than others, that the so-called "torso killer" was good for business. With the discovery of the tattooed man, as Peter Bellamy of the *Press* would note, the hunt for the killer captured the city's full attention, and the population would henceforth be "divided into torso suspects, torso experts, torso victims and newspapermen praying to God that the next torso won't show up five minutes before edition time."

Almost at once, the coverage became disturbingly graphic. On June 6, the day after the tattooed man's head was found, a lurid photo gallery in the *Press* featured an image of Gomez Ivey superimposed over the spot where he made the discovery in Kingsbury Run, along with mug shots of Florence Polillo and Edward Andrassy. The tattooed man was also featured. "The *Press*," read a carefully worded caption, "in an effort to aid in identification of the victim, publishes a photograph of his facial features at the lower left." This was disingenuous at best. The "facial features" were apparent because the *Press* elected to publish a photo of the tattooed man's severed head, rather than a sketch or an image of the plaster casting taken at the morgue. An escalating cycle of sensationalism had begun. "My God," Bellamy would say of the unknown murderer, "how that man can sell newspapers!"

The same could have been said of Eliot Ness, who had yet to offer a public comment on the killings. Instead, as the drama surrounding the tattooed man captured the city's attention, Ness threw himself into another round of his anti-corruption campaign. He had dropped everything, for reasons that were not immediately apparent, to race across town and kick down the door of another "vice resort."

The Black Hawk Inn, in the Fourteenth Precinct, had been on Ness's radar for some time. It appeared to be an ordinary tavern from the street, but the back room housed a thriving gambling parlor. Whenever police appeared, a system of lookouts and warning buzzers allowed the operators to "turn the room," a lightning-fast process by which incriminating equipment was covered up, flipped over, or otherwise hidden from view, to be replaced by seemingly innocent games of Ping-Pong or canasta. Ness had no warrant when he forced his way into the place on June 6, later explaining that he "thought it imperative to enter." He and his raiders scooped up the club's owner, a well-known "night life figure" named Edward Harwood, who had been skirting the law for some time. More to the point, he was the son of Michael J. Harwood, a twenty-four-year police veteran who happened to be captain of the Fourteenth Precinct. The "flamboyant, two-fisted" Captain Harwood had been Ness's real target that day. The captain had turned a blind eye to illegal activities in his precinct, and his own son was one of the worst offenders. Worse yet, it had long been rumored that Captain Harwood had a healthy financial stake in his son's operations, including gambling and bootleg liquor. By the end of the day, Ness had given orders to relieve Harwood of his command. "I am the most misjudged man in Cleveland," Harwood insisted. "I am unqualifiedly honest and never took a dishonest penny." The claim proved difficult to sustain in the days to come, as Harwood stood trial on an impressive slate of graft charges under the "caustic, slashing" prosecution of Frank Cullitan. By the close of the year, Harwood would be behind bars at the Ohio Penitentiary.

The removal of Captain Harwood capped off a remarkable effort by Ness in the early months of 1936 as he worked to make good on his promise to clean up the city's corrupt police force. "A falling domino pattern began to develop," recalled Philip Porter. "One policeman told of payoffs and that led to another. Saloonkeepers began to phone Ness with tips. Wives of men who had squandered their paychecks in gambling joints gave him names and addresses." The city watched in amazement as several more officers were marched off to prison and many others resigned or opted for early retirement.

Ness made a particular specialty of taking down crooked precinct captains, an effort he likened to cutting off the head of a snake. The campaign climaxed with the shocking downfall of Louis J. Cadek of the Sixteenth, a captain said to be so powerful that "nobody went to the bathroom" without his permission. Like Harwood, Cadek appeared to have profited greatly from shady dealings on his turf. It emerged that the thirty-one-year veteran, whose annual salary topped out at $3,500, had managed to accrue savings of some $139,000, much of it stashed away in bank accounts under false names. Though the "thrifty captain" remained silent on how he managed this feat, tales of graft abounded. One story had Cadek presiding over a gathering of bootleggers who were expected to fill a barrel full of cash in tribute.

The turning point came when investigative reporter Clayton Fritchey of the *Press* brought evidence to Ness that placed Cadek at the center of a wildly ambitious pyramid scheme. The scam preyed on the city's immigrant population, selling shares in a plan that offered cemetery plots at grossly inflated prices. So many phony shares had been sold, said Fritchey, that "Cleveland's dead could be buried for 500 years." The dirt piled up quickly, leading to a conviction on four counts of soliciting bribes. "Nothing left now for the poor fellow but to go to prison," crowed the *Press*.

"Eliot Ness, with his boyish face and enigmatic manner, is well aware of what is going on in the department, and attending to one matter at a time," wrote Philip Porter. "The cops were at first inclined to scoff at him, but by now they are aware he knows his business. It is fairly obvious that he considers his business the rebuilding of a police force which has gone badly to seed. His greatest handicap is that he must investigate by himself and can trust so few others."

He wasn't doing it by himself. The general public remained unaware of the Unknowns, but the existence of Ness's private squad became an open secret at city hall, though steps were taken to shield their identities. According to Arnold Sagalyn, a recent college graduate who would sign on a few years later, most of the "small, crack team of civilian criminal investigators" worked outside of Ness's office because they did not want their faces to become too familiar. As a result, Ness, too, frequently abandoned his desk to work in the field alongside his team. During the summer months of 1936, he would vanish from his office for days at a time. "He is the world's original mystery man," wrote one observer, "and none of his associates is ever completely in his confidence. Employees who have worked for Ness since he became safety director are still in the dark about most phases of his temperament. They are almost never certain of his whereabouts and are uncertain as to his habits."

Some of the mystery would lift in a few months' time when Ness delivered an explosive eighty-six-page dossier on corruption in the police department. "The report was the work of his new Untouchables and his own investigative perseverance," wrote George Condon. "He had spent one hundred consecutive summer nights following the trail of police crookedness through some of the city's worst dives and some of the metropolitan area's nicest suburbs. He had talked with bums and degenerates and respectable community leaders on the same night about the same suspect."

This was the work Ness had hoped to do when he landed the job in Cleveland, translating the lessons of Capone into lasting reform. As the purge took hold, Ness seized on his soaring notoriety to build a case for his ambitious slate of police reforms. In a fresh round of public appearances, he argued for a bigger slice of the city budget so that he could hire more men and replace the city's ancient fleet of squad cars, upgraded to include modern two-way radios. He also urged an overhaul of the department's training methods, drawing on both the Vollmer system and the latest FBI guidelines. To be successful, Ness declared, a policeman had to be "a diplomat, a marksman, a memory expert, a boxer, a wrestler, a sprinter, and an authority on a wide variety of subjects." He pushed to establish an intensive three-month course that covered psychology, arrest procedure, criminal law, and first aid. Soon, an innovative police academy would be up and running in the Flats, with hands-on instruction in ballistics, fingerprinting, and photographic evidence. Trainees also tested their powers of observation in an elaborate "Murder Room," where a department store mannequin served in place of a corpse. One member of the original class of twenty recruits recalled that Ness handed over his private phone number and told the men to call immediately if anyone offered a bribe. Otherwise, he warned, "don't plan on being a police officer for very long."

Ness received a great deal of national acclaim for these efforts— "Nemesis of Capone Uses G-Men Tactics as Safety Director" read a typical headline—but he understood that he could succeed only with Frank Cullitan as his closer. The partnership they had forged on the night of the Harvard Club raid confounded the city's entrenched party operatives. Ness was now closely identified with the Republican mayor, while

Cullitan had been a "blue and true" Democrat for twenty-five years. Nevertheless, Ness would cross party lines to give stump speeches for Cullitan's next reelection campaign, declaring that the prosecutor was "so important to the community that no partisan political question should be involved." As one graft case after another came to trial, Cullitan made a point of consulting with Ness at the prosecution table, and the safety director's presence in the courtroom was taken as a signal that the axe was about to fall. "There is nothing about Ness's appearance to inspire fear," wrote Howard Beaufait in the *News*, "but the shadowy characters who sometimes drift into the Criminal Courts Building point him out with awe. 'There goes Ness,' they say as though they were indicating Wyatt Earp, the two-gun sharp-shooter of the gold rush days."

For Mayor Burton, whose recovery effort reached a critical phase in June of 1936, Ness had become indispensable: "Need Ness," the mayor would scrawl in the margin of an action plan. Burton had swept to victory seven months earlier promising to guide the city out of the shadow of the Great Depression. That summer he intended to make good, seizing the national spotlight with a string of high-profile events designed to jump-start the economy. This "gala of glory" would kick off with the 1936 Republican National Convention, at which Governor Alf Landon would be nominated to take on President Roosevelt in the fall presidential election. The GOP gathering had been lured to the city through the energetic efforts of Burton and a group of civic leaders known as the "Come to Cleveland" committee, many of whom were also bankrolling Ness and the Unknowns. Twelve million dollars had been spent sprucing up the downtown Public Auditorium, and now, as a massive horde of delegates began streaming into town, it was vitally important that nothing should go wrong.

Burton had taken pains to give Ness a highly visible role, welcoming important guests and helping to navigate the difficulties presented by an overcrowded city. Not everyone was impressed: "Gang's Nemesis Now Greeter at Cleveland," announced the *Chicago Daily News*. It might have seemed frivolous to some, but Mayor Burton wanted the safety director out front shaking hands, even if it meant pulling Ness away from day-to-day police business. Several other major conferences would follow the Republican convention over the course of the summer, climaxing in September with a massive gathering of the American Legion, expected to bring thousands of flag-waving "doughboy funsters" marching down Euclid Avenue. Ness would take a central role in all of these events. He accepted these duties as a necessary part of his job, but at the same time, he refused to slow down on his anti-corruption efforts, which kept him out until all hours of the night. For several weeks, he admitted to friends, he barely found time to eat or sleep. Inevitably, the strain began to show. As Burton's summer gala wore on, Ness could spare only a few moments here and there for the daily police docket.

This meant, to all outward appearances, that the city's safety director had taken no notice whatsoever of the murders in Kingsbury Run. For the moment, it would have seemed reasonable to Ness to maintain a watchful distance. Although Kingsbury Run had now gripped the public imagination, there was not yet an immediate sense of peril. In years to come, the entire city would recoil at the disappearance of ten-year-old Beverly Potts, the savage murder of sixteen-year-old Beverly Jarosz, and the shocking death of Marilyn Sheppard, wife of noted surgeon Sam Sheppard. These were crimes that struck close to home, uncomfortably so. By contrast, the Kingsbury Run victims had been transients and "police characters," not the sort who lived next door. "A remarkable feature of the killing is the fact that so many victims can disappear apparently without being missed, and with no outcry raised in any quarter," a *Press* editorial would note. "Grewsome as this fact is, it is sufficient to allay any sense of community hysteria. The killer shows his cunning. His method is to lure someone who will not be missed to an isolated spot in a fairly restricted area. Apparently there is no reason for alarm by any who keep themselves from fitting into this formula." The message was clear, if far from altruistic: respectable folks were safe.

Behind the scenes, however, Ness had set plans in motion, exercising the full weight of his new authority. He realized at once that the emerging theory of a single killer would put additional pressure on his investigators. Already Ness had replaced the ineffective head of the detective bureau with the hardworking Joseph Sweeney, and over the course of the summer an additional twenty-five detectives would be assigned to the Kingsbury Run case. Sweeney had an excellent record, and Ness had reason to hope that the extra manpower would allow his new chief detective to get some traction. In any other city, this would have been enough. The director of public safety wasn't expected to hunt murderers any more than he was expected to put out house fires or rescue cats stranded in trees. His job was to clean up the police department and create a more modern, more efficient force. By that measure, Ness had made spectacular progress in only six months. He was doing exactly what he was hired to do.

Unlike his predecessors, however, Ness had encouraged the public to expect more. He had come to city hall promising to lead from the front lines, and the raid on the Harvard Club had set a high bar. Now, as the city absorbed the news of a mad butcher on the loose, the safety director appeared to have subsided into bureaucratic banality, gladhanding at Burton's side in a series of staged photo opportunities. On the day that the headless body of the tattooed man was discovered, Ness and Burton were taking delivery of fifteen shiny white Oldsmobiles, specially modified to assist with crowd control during the Republican convention. Each car had an outsize bullhorn mounted on top and a crisp slogan splashed across the side: "Voice of Safety." As often as not during that long, hectic summer, the "fighting young G-Man" looked like a carnival barker.

There was one moment, however, when the demands of Mayor Burton's agenda intersected with the stepped-up effort at Kingsbury Run, allowing Ness to use his outsize bullhorn in service of the investigation. That summer, as a complement to Mayor Burton's ambitious slate of business gatherings, the city also mounted a lavish, hundred-day Great Lakes Exposition for tourists and the general public, conceived on a scale to rival the celebrated Century of Progress showcase at the 1933 Chicago World's Fair. Three thousand men had been put to work building new roads and bridges for the 135-acre fairground, at a cost of $25 million. The design spoke of soaring ambition, beginning with a row of seven monolithic pylons, each of them seventy feet tall, that spanned the entrance plaza like the pillars of an ancient temple. "Our city is just beginning to emerge from under an unfavorable cloud," wrote reporter Mary Hirschfeld, "and the Great Lakes Exposition affords an opportunity to prove to ourselves and to the nation that though we have been staggered a little, we are putting that behind us."

On June 27, some four hundred miles away at the White House, President Roosevelt pressed a button at his desk and a series of gates along the towering pylons swung open. Inside, visitors found a "magic city on the lakefront," with exhibition halls, carnival rides, and a symphony shell amphitheater. A tightly packed cluster of 150 buildings known as the "Streets of the World" featured German beer halls, Japanese pagodas, Swiss chalets, and more, representing some three dozen of Cleveland's varied ethnic cultures. Even the city's Hindu population, consisting of only seven people, was represented with a restaurant and tea shop. For three dollars, guests could get an aerial view from the Goodyear blimp. For groundlings, a faithful reproduction of the Globe Theatre waited on the Midway. Other forms of entertainment included guest artists such as Cab Calloway and Jimmy Durante, a troupe of 260-pound ballerinas, a snake show, and "Callipygian Beauties Treading Pavanes and Rigadoons in Diaphanous Garments."

Each day that summer, a long line of visitors streamed through a cavernous Hall of the Great Lakes, a seemingly colorless gathering of "historical, educational and cultural exhibits by federal, state and local governments." Under Ness's authorization, the Cleveland Police Department used their allotted space to showcase the latest techniques in criminology. Ness also arranged for a "finger-printing bureau," where thousands of people cheerfully pressed their fingers onto a well-worn ink pad, apparently untroubled by the fact that their prints would now be enshrined at the police records office.

In one corner of the exhibit, the plaster death mask of the tattooed man gazed out at the passing parade, like Banquo's ghost on the midway. It struck a jarring chord, wildly at odds with the cheery, wholesome Expo just beyond the pavilion walls. As with the macabre viewings of the unidentified victim's severed head at the city morgue, Ness and the detective bureau hoped that this unsettling display would justify itself if someone recognized the likeness and unlocked his identity. Hundreds of thousands of people would pause in front of the death mask over the next three months, but no one stepped forward with a name.

One seven-year-old boy would remember this "creepy freakshow" to the end of his life. "It was so lifelike that I thought I was staring at an actual severed head," he recalled more than seventy-five years later. "It looked like he was just sleeping. I was afraid that if I breathed too hard, I might wake him up."

9

LAKE TORSO

Police annals tend to prove that the most difficult murder cases to solve are those in which a solitary individual does away with a number of obscure people. The classic crime of this type is, of course, London's "Jack-the-Ripper" who terrorized the White-chapel district with a series of mutilation murders and then vanished from the eyes of the police. Such lone operators kill until they are sated or finally caught.

Cleveland Press, July 24, 1936

For a time during the summer of 1933, fourteen-year-old Marie Barkley of Hope Avenue, on the city's west side, seemed to go missing every time she left the house. In July, she pedaled off on her bicycle, staying away long enough to draw the notice of the police. Apparently she enjoyed the attention. The following month, she vanished again, this time on roller skates. A few weeks later, she engineered a third disappearance, making her escape on foot. Somehow these repeated episodes came to be regarded as a "girlish lark" rather than cause for alarm. When she bolted for a fourth time, having announced that she was on her way to Hollywood, the newspapers made light of her "fickle" behavior. "Persistence will win is the motto," declared one account, along with a suggestion for future adventures: "Next time an airplane."

Barkley's wanderings took an unhappy turn three years later, in late July of 1936. Now seventeen, she once again set off from home on foot, covering some four miles or so to reach a lonely, wooded stretch along the banks of Big Creek, a tributary of the Cuyahoga River in the suburb of Brooklyn Village. At about 11:30 that morning, as she made her way along a path beside the B&O Railroad tracks, Barkley stopped suddenly and fixed her eyes on a brownish, rotting mass a few yards ahead of her. Lying near the path, partially covered with brush, was a nude, headless male body. The head would be discovered about ten feet away, along with a pile of muddied clothing. The torso killer, it appeared, had struck again.

Cleveland police converged on the remote location within two hours, along with officers from the suburbs. An initial examination of the remains, lying chest-down in a gully beside the creek, indicated that the victim had been dead for two or three months, though the advanced state of decomposition made it difficult to be precise. There appeared to be traces of pooled blood in the soil near the torso's severed neck, suggesting that he had been killed where he lay. Unlike the body of the tattooed man, discovered less than seven weeks earlier, this victim had no obvious distinguishing marks, or at least none that remained apparent. Authorities judged him to be roughly forty years of age, about five feet five inches tall, weighing perhaps 145 pounds. The facial features were rotted beyond any possibility of recognition, though a great deal of thinning brown hair, worn uncommonly long, still clung to the scalp. He had good teeth, though three were missing. The long hair and missing teeth, together with the proximity of several hobo camps, led police to conclude that the victim had probably been a transient.

By mid-afternoon, officers had fanned out through the woods to look for additional clues. Many of the responding detectives—including James Hogan, Charles Nevel, and Orley May—had taken part in the earlier investigations. As soon as a police photographer had documented the scene, the detectives moved in to examine the pile of discarded clothing, some of which bore clear traces of blood. A dark gray suit jacket was found to have a knife slash on the right sleeve. There was also a light blue polo shirt, a leather belt, a pair of oxford shoes, socks, white underwear, and a black cap with gray stripes. As with the earlier crimes, police could find no wallet, papers, clothing labels, or other clues to help uncover the victim's identity.

The remains reached the morgue at the end of the afternoon, where the work of Coroner Pearse and pathologist Reuben Straus was made difficult by "innumerable worms and other forms of bugs in great numbers." Troubling contradictions emerged in the effort to establish the cause of death. Coroner Pearse officially ruled the death a homicide as a result of decapitation, but in a statement to the press, he appeared to say otherwise, claiming that he had found "nothing to indicate that there was any violence on skull or body." More confusion followed over the next two days. Pearse told one reporter that the head had been severed cleanly, indicating surgical skill and knowledge on the part of the killer, but he remarked elsewhere that the remains had been "so decomposed that it is possible for the head to have dropped off and to have been carried a few yards by a dog or other animal." Possibly the contradictions arose in the reporting, some of which was rushed and careless, or perhaps Pearse's conclusions about decapitation had been an extrapolation, building off the previous crimes and the knife slash found on the latest victim's jacket. Reuben Straus, for his part, appeared undecided on the matter. The pathologist had observed only smooth surfaces on the bones of the neck, without knife marks of any kind, prompting him to return a verdict of "probable murder" by an unknown method.

Although the hands were intact, Straus and Pearse were not able to get usable fingerprints owing to the state of decay. In the absence of prints and facial features, detectives combed through the department's missing persons reports, hoping to match the victim's age and general body type, but they made no headway. In spite of these obstacles, investigators seemed eager to share new theories of the case. Sergeant Hogan, in particular, emphasized the similarities between the Big Creek victim and the tattooed man. Both sets of remains had been found out in the open with a pile of clothing nearby, and both men were believed to have been killed at or near the spot where they were found. Though a distance of several miles separated Big Creek and Kingsbury Run, the two deaths appeared to have taken place within a few days of each other. Judging by the state of the remains, the Big Creek victim might have been killed first.

Fresh contradictions emerged when the two more recent crimes were considered alongside the earlier killings. The two bodies at Jackass Hill—Edward Andrassy and the still-unidentified older man—had been killed elsewhere and carried to the dumping ground, rather than butchered on the spot. Both of the earlier male victims had also been "otherwise mutilated," in the *Plain Dealer*'s delicate phrase, while the latter two had not. If Florence Polillo was included among the butcher's tally, as most of the investigators now seemed inclined to do, further inconsistencies became apparent. Even apart from the obvious fact that Polillo was the only female victim thus far, her case presented significant deviations from the pattern. Her body, as the investigators recalled all too vividly, had been divided into small parcels, wrapped in newspaper, and disposed of in bushel baskets. Unlike the other four victims, her head had not been discovered nearby—in fact, it had never been found at all. In spite of these many discrepancies, all three of the major local newspapers were now reporting the discovery at Big Creek as the unknown butcher's fifth victim, reflecting the prevailing view of the police. The Lady of the Lake, discovered some two years earlier, remained at the margins of the investigation.

New theories emerged to account for the inconsistencies. The *Press* reported that detectives were seeking "thrill-killers," echoing a notorious phrase from the trial of Nathan Leopold and Richard Loeb, the latter of whom had been murdered in prison earlier that year. Implausible as it might have seemed, the notion of young thrill-seekers offered a theory that accounted for at least some of the contradictions. If a group of opportunistic killers had set out to commit a "perfect crime," as the teenage Leopold and Loeb had sought to do, it might explain the range of victim types and variations in knife marks. The targets would have been chosen almost at random from the ranks of the homeless, a large pool of potential victims who were unlikely to be identified, and the butchering would have been done by more than one person.

Many enigmas remained. The previous month, in the aftermath of the tattooed man's discovery, acting Detective Inspector Charles Nevel appeared to stumble over a question concerning the undressing of the victim's body. Now, returning to the theme in the glare of Big Creek, he took another swing at it. Nevel declared that "a homicidal madman with a fondness for decapitation was responsible," rather than a group of thrill-killers. Although Nevel remained unconvinced that Florence Polillo had fallen prey to "the same villain," he now offered a string of conjectures about the four men. The *Press* reported his theories under the heading of "Fiend Beheads Living Victims":

THE killer is probably a pervert who lures his victims into lonely places. After cutting off their heads he assaults them.

DECAPITATION occurs while the victims are alive. Inspector Nevel deduces this from the fact that none of the victims has shown marks indicating they were killed before decapitation.

RATHER than a meat cleaver or butcher knife, he uses a large, razor-sharp pocket knife. This from the fact that in two instances it was necessary for him to make two cuts in order to complete the decapitation.

EITHER from study or experimentation, he possesses considerable knowledge of the structure of bones. The heads of the four men killed so far were severed by cutting the vertebrae apart at their joints.

Nevel had clearly chosen his words with care, but no amount of discretion could mask the dark turn that the investigation had taken. With the explicit references to the killer's "fondness for decapitation" and the assaults carried out after death, it was clear that Nevel and at least some of his colleagues now viewed the torso slayer through a lens of horrifying sexual depravity. Investigators had long believed that sexual gratification played a role in the crimes, but the exact contours of that impulse remained obscure. Did the killer's carnal urges govern the choice of victim? If so, was the butcher's sexuality elastic enough to encompass handsome young men like Andrassy and the tattooed man alongside a middle-aged female prostitute such as Florence Polillo? Or was it a mistake to include Polillo among the victims, as Nevel and others had proposed? Possibly the gender and physical attributes of the victims were beside the point. Perhaps the killer derived sexual gratification from the act of beheading his victims, as suggested by the deceptively bland phrase Nevel had employed: "fondness for decapitation." These were murky waters. Like the "razor-sharp pocket knife" Nevel had mentioned—large enough to sever a human head in two strokes but small enough to slip into a pocket—the killer's profile presented many paradoxes.

Once again, while his detectives grappled with the most recent of the butcher's outrages, Eliot Ness was across town engineering the downfall of yet another police captain. This time, on the very day that Marie Barkley stumbled across the remains at Big Creek, Ness was putting the finishing touches on the suspension of Captain Adolph Lenahan, commander of the Eighth Precinct, following an investigation spearheaded by the Unknowns. This latest effort centered on a notorious betting parlor on West 25th Street, in the heart of Rowdy Row, which had been operating "wide open" for more than ten years while Lenahan looked the other way. Ness had drawn up plans for a raid with the help of five rookie policemen, sworn in just a few weeks earlier, who were sent into the club posing as gamblers. When Ness and the Unknowns burst through the doors a few minutes later, the rookies were already in position. They drew their weapons and covered the exits as the raiders swept through, a maneuver hailed for its "G-man precision." That same day, as Chief Matowitz called Lenahan onto the carpet to account for himself, the captain proved unable to mount much of a defense, being drunk at the time. Ness accepted his resignation without public comment. Another tarnished "gold braid" was off the force.

Ness had yet to appear at Big Creek or any of the butcher's other crime scenes, but as the summer of 1936 wore on, he seemed to pop up just about everywhere else. One day he might be found at the Great Lakes Exposition exchanging pleasantries with Rudy Vallee, the celebrated crooner, and the next Ness was seen running tests on a new "drunk detector" apparatus designed to get impaired drivers off the road, or rolling out a special "camera-eye squad" to guard against pickpockets. More and more, however, the daily bulletins of Ness's doings seemed to bump up against grim reports of the Kingsbury Run investigation, a contrast that showed the safety director at a distinct disadvantage. A typical day saw side-by-side articles headlined "Clean Up City, Ness Orders" and "Hunt Fiend in 4 Decapitations." Ness received briefings from Joseph Sweeney and other detectives, but he made no public comment. There is no evidence to suggest that he or anyone else at city hall was attempting to put a lid on the coverage, but so long as Burton's summer gala remained in full swing, with swarms of out-of-towners crowding onto the Expo fairgrounds every day, no one would have been eager to draw attention to a homicidal fiend who continued to thwart the best efforts of local police. Not even the evangelical "Come to Cleveland" committee could have put a cheery spin on this story.

At the same time, Burton's gala had saddled Ness with a great many duties that could not be handed off to anyone else, and one obligation in particular absorbed much of his time that summer. In August, Colonel E. W. Starling, the "gaunt, patrician" chief of the White House Secret Service detail, arrived to lay the groundwork for a forthcoming visit to the city by President Roosevelt. Officially, Roosevelt was coming to take in the wonders of the Great Lakes Exposition, but he had a compelling political incentive to visit Ohio ahead of the November election. "President Roosevelt's re-election is by no means in the bag," as one commentator had written, pointing to lingering uncertainty over the struggling economy and New Deal programs. Then as now, Ohio's electoral college votes would loom large.

Downtown Cleveland had been buffed to a high gloss by the time Roosevelt arrived aboard a special train at 9:30 on the morning of Friday, August 14. Ness provided one thousand police officers and five hundred firemen to augment the president's security detail, calling for the "precision and order of a trained army." Secret Service men stood on the running board of Roosevelt's open-topped limousine as a six-car motorcade began a slow, meandering crawl through the city. Businesses along the Euclid Avenue corridor had shut down for the occasion, and people stood six-deep on the street, with thousands more leaning out of windows and crowding onto rooftops to give the "largest, noisiest and most enthusiastic" reception in city history. "The sky, gloomy to start with, was darkened by the deluge of ticker tape, paper and torn-up phone books," ran an account in the *Press*, "which floated down out of office buildings as the President's world famous smile flashed forth its greetings from his slowly moving car."

Stone-faced and rigid, Ness kept a vigil from the rear car, scanning the crowd for signs of trouble. At one stage, a woman darted forward to snap a picture, but before she could raise her camera, a swarm of police officers carried her back to the curb. Ness gave a tight nod of approval as his car rolled past. He had instructed his police cordon to stand facing the crowd, an unusual decision at the time. "Looking at the crowd, it is much easier to circumvent any trouble," Ness explained. "Those seconds are precious when a president's life is at stake."

At East 55th Street, a twelve-year-old girl named Marian Rohn pushed her way past a row of firemen and darted forward, clutching a bouquet of roses. Narrowly avoiding the hooves of a mounted patrolman's rearing horse, she got within a few yards of the motorcade before Secret Service agents lifted her off her feet. Noticing the disturbance, Roosevelt called out as his car rolled past. "Bring her back!" he shouted, waving his panama hat. The agents lifted the girl onto the limousine's running board, where Roosevelt accepted the flowers with a handshake and a smile. Afterward, Rohn seemed eager for a repeat performance: "Was I frightened at all the commotion? No, I wouldn't say that. The men all around were excited."

Mayor Burton, riding at the head of the motorcade beside the president, also seemed a bit on edge. At one stage, Roosevelt asked how many people were expected to turn out for the spectacle. Burton, evidently misunderstanding the question, estimated "about three million," a figure several times greater than the city's population. Roosevelt appeared bemused. "I congratulate Cleveland on its growth," he said.

There were, in fact, signs of growth everywhere, especially along the lakefront, where the motorcade paused to allow Roosevelt to admire a land reclamation effort carried out under the banner of the Works Progress Administration. "This is marvelous," the president remarked. "I remember this lakefront when it was a tin can dump."

At 12:30, after three hours of "courtly smiles and waves," the motorcade reached the pylon gates of the Great Lakes Exposition. The president was given a rapid-fire tour of the festival's high points, followed by a special performance of a water ballet. Afterward, in a radio address from the fairgrounds, Roosevelt lauded the Expo as a sign of America's resilience and returning prosperity. "I only wish," he added, "that I could stay with you for a whole week and see it all."

In fact, the president lingered barely long enough to eat an "Expo Cake" before departing on his special train, which had been diverted to a private spur on the fairgrounds. There would be a great deal of backslapping over a job well done as the train pulled away, but for Ness, the responsibilities of the day had not yet ended. One of Roosevelt's secretaries had been turned away from an official reception for lack of a ticket, and it fell to Ness to vouch for the man's identity and find him something to eat.

"You are doing a fine job here in Cleveland," the president had declared in his closing remarks, "a fine job for the nation." As August drew to a close, Roosevelt's praise served as a benediction on Burton's ambitious summer agenda. The Expo, in particular, had exceeded expectations, with a return engagement planned for the following year. For Ness, the end of summer signaled a return to police business, and perhaps even a vacation. He promised Edna that they would get away for a few days when his anti-corruption campaign cleared its next hurdle and he finally passed off his massive graft report to Frank Cullitan. Edna began making plans for a trip in October.

On the morning of Thursday, September 10, a young vagrant named Jerry Harris pulled himself into position on a railway abutment overlooking

Kingsbury Run, waiting to hop a freight train. From his perch along the East 37th Street bridge, Harris could see an "oily, coffee-colored creek" that flowed sluggishly through a stone culvert. As he stood and readied himself for the next train, Harris caught sight of a flash of white in the murky water. Straining for a better look, he glimpsed a section of a human torso floating lazily below. Startled and aghast, Harris ran to a nearby oil facility and alerted a clerk, who put in a call to the police.

Sergeant Hogan, the ulcer-plagued veteran, had been expecting something of this sort, having recently told reporters that he could almost sense the killer gathering himself to strike again. Hogan reached the scene within fifteen minutes, followed closely by Detectives Orley May, Emil Musil, and others. They could now see two large sections of human remains drifting in the fetid water, and when efforts to photograph them ended in frustration, Hogan had them fished out. A quick examination confirmed the objects to be "the torso of a white man, sliced in two with the skill that has marked each of the slayings." For Hogan, there could be only one conclusion. As the next edition of the *Press* reported, the detective "flatly said this killing was also the work of the butcher."

Nearby, within sight of the Nickel Plate Railroad and Shaker Rapid Transit tracks, the water flowing through the stone culvert formed a deep, stagnant pool. By all accounts, it was hideous—filled with jagged rocks and foul-smelling sludge—a cesspit for the dregs and debris of Kingsbury Run. Within minutes, a large team of investigators had spread out along the rim of the pool, on the theory that any additional remains of this latest victim would be discovered at the bottom. Soon, scrapings of human flesh were found clinging to surfaces at the edge of the water, an apparent confirmation of the hypothesis, and plans were made to drag the twenty-foot depths.

Almost at once, a team from the Cleveland Fire Department went to work with grappling hooks. When their initial efforts brought no results, they switched to longer boat hooks and quickly dredged up two more body parts from the muddy depths: the victim's lower legs and feet, severed at the knee joints. These were bundled up and sent to the morgue, where pathologist Reuben Straus had already begun an examination of the torso remains.

At the morgue, Straus estimated the victim's age at somewhere between twenty-five and thirty years, with a height of five feet ten inches and a weight of no less than 145 pounds. The head had been severed between the third and fourth cervical vertebrae by two strokes of a sharp blade, one from the back and one from the front. The torso had been cut in two above the navel, slicing through the stomach and both kidneys. The cutting had been notably forceful and precise, leaving few hesitation marks. Charles Nevel had theorized about a razor-sharp pocketknife after examining the remains at Big Creek, but Straus's findings pointed to a larger, heavier blade. "Judging from the character of the cut through the bone," Straus said, "it would require either considerable force with a heavy knife or some heavier instrument as a hatchet or cleaver to do this." In days to come, there would be talk of glittering scimitars and bloody hacksaws, but no single style of blade appeared to account for all of the incisions. In a new and particularly stomach-churning variation on the earlier crimes, the killer had returned to the type of mutilation practiced on Andrassy and his companion. The latest victim's penis had been severed with a sharp, brutal cut, leaving a one-inch stump behind.

Unlike the Big Creek remains, the body of the latest victim was fresh enough to yield conclusive insights. Coroner Pearse would declare the cause of death as "probable murder by decapitation and section of the body." Deputy Coroner Wilson Chamberlain added a chilling clarification, telling reporters that his examination of the heart showed that the victim had been alive when the dismemberment began. He does not appear to have specified between the decapitation and the bisection of the torso, but Chamberlain's finding raised the specter of a torture chamber along the lines of "The Pit and the Pendulum," Poe's story of a prisoner's torment during the Spanish Inquisition. If possible, the killings now took on an even darker and more depraved aspect.

Coroner Pearse confirmed the findings for a *News* reporter and summarized his conclusions. "The killer is apparently a sex maniac of the sadistic type," Pearse declared. "This is indicated by the condition of his victims. He is probably a muscular man. The slayer definitely has expert knowledge of human anatomy. The incisions of his knife are clean and were made in each case without guesswork. He may have gathered his knowledge of anatomy as a medical student. Or it is possible he is a butcher. The murders, with one exception, were committed some place other than where the bodies were found. While the killer is obviously obsessed and insane, he is also shrewd, works alone, and is clever enough to avoid detection indefinitely."

Many of these pronouncements had become accepted as fact through sheer repetition, but even at this stage, several of Pearse's conclusions remained open to debate. In particular, investigators appeared to waver on the question of whether the crimes were committed at the discovery site or in some "butcher's laboratory" where the killer could operate without fear of interruption. When a bloodied slab of stone turned up near the abutment where the remains were first spotted, some detectives believed they had found "the butcher block" used in the killing and dismemberment of the latest victim. From this, they extrapolated that "the human butcher kills his victims near the places where they have been found." Sergeant Hogan offered a loud dissent, telling a *News* reporter that he had "no way of determining if the victim had been killed at the scene—as indicated in four of the other killings—or had been butchered in some hidden murder laboratory and the torso taken to the Run." Even as the general outline of the crimes came into focus, investigators could not agree on the details.

At the murky drainage pool in Kingsbury Run, police still had hopes of recovering the victim's head and hands for purposes of identification. As the afternoon of September 10 wore on, however, Sergeant Hogan grew impatient with the slow progress of the dragging operation. Assuming there were any remains left at the bottom of the pool, every moment they stayed submerged made it less likely that they would retain any value for the investigation. Up to this point, the work had been maddeningly laborious; Hogan called it the most exasperating task he had faced in more than thirty years of police work. After several fruitless hours, investigators borrowed a small boat from the Coast Guard and resumed their efforts from the center of the pool, hoping that a fresh angle would yield results. Orley May and his partner, Gordon Shibley, reported striking "fleshlike objects" but were unable to bring them to the surface.

By this time, searchers had combed through the surrounding area and gathered up an assortment of discarded clothing that appeared to belong to the victim, another increasingly familiar sign of the killer's handiwork. One item in particular—a distinctive blue denim work shirt wrapped in newspaper—seemed to offer promising leads. The shirt had bloodstains as well as a patch above the right front pocket and a label above the left, stamped with the number five. "It had been cut at the neck," observed the *Press*, "apparently when the fiend decapitated his victim." As in the Florence Polillo case, police took careful note of the newspaper wrappings, which had been taken from a recent edition of the *Plain Dealer*, an apparent confirmation that the crime had occurred within the past day or two.

Along with the shirt, police also found a strip of faded green under-wear bearing a laundry mark with the initials "J.W." and a gray felt hat with a label from "Loudy's Smart Shop" of Bellevue, Ohio, roughly sixty miles away. The latter discovery produced a brief flicker of excitement when a man in Bellevue reported that his mother had given the hat to "a tramp who begged clothing two weeks ago." Police believed this transient must have been the butcher's latest victim until the man in question stepped forward, no worse for wear, having somehow mislaid the hat.

Over the next few days, police would struggle to place the slender clues they had gathered into the broader pattern of crimes. As in the case of the tattooed man, a railroad detective had patrolled the area on the day before the discovery of the remains. If there had been body parts any-where to be found, he insisted, he would have seen them. Investigators concluded that "the murder probably took place Wednesday," the day before the discovery, with the remains dumped at Kingsbury Run after dark. Two Nickel Plate switchmen had seen a vehicle parked nearby that night, perhaps at the spot where the body parts had been hurled into the pool. They had thought nothing of it at the time, they said, because the spot saw regular use as a lovers' lane. Police were told to be on the look-out for a "light roadster with a box-like rear compartment."

As the dragging operation continued on Friday, September 11, Ser-geant Hogan made arrangements with the fire department to bring in a metal hose and a high-pressure pump, hoping to blast through the sludge and dislodge any remnants that might have settled at the bottom. "There were old shoes, pieces of furniture and other rubbish," a reporter noted, "but nothing that was once human." The effort must have had some effect, however. When searchers resumed dragging the pool with hooks, they managed to recover the victim's right thigh, which "bore evidence of the careful surgery which has marked all the work of the slayer." The following day, planks were stretched over the water in an effort to drag the inaccessible areas, bringing up the left thigh. The head and hands remained elusive, and some officers, recalling the fruitless search for Florence Polillo's head, despaired of ever finding them.

A growing sense of frustration led Coroner Pearse to suggest us-ing dynamite to blow open a hole at the lower depths of the pool, in hope of draining it. Sergeant Hogan, meanwhile, put in a request for emergency funds, having hit on the plan of hiring a professional diver. Soon, a trained frogman named Richard Boyce was on the scene, pulling on a full-body submersion suit and helmet. Even the most experienced marine diver might have blanched at this assignment, which was little better than plunging into a septic tank, but those who had trained along the waterways of Lake Erie were made of sterner stuff. "We never see anything," one veteran remarked, explaining that he and his colleagues had learned to navigate the opaque waters largely by sense of touch. "If there are any more pieces of the body in the water," he insisted, "we'll find them." In all, Boyce would spend five wretched hours feeling his way across the bottom of the "murder pool," as it had now come to be called, even venturing into the adjacent culvert, but he found nothing.

One year earlier, small knots of anxious residents from the sur-rounding neighborhoods had gathered along the rim of Kingsbury Run to watch the drama at Jackass Hill. Now, with the discovery of the sixth headless murder victim in a year, it seemed as if the entire city had converged on the site, with a line of automobiles stretching for half a mile. Unlike the remote Big Creek location, the activity at this latest scene was unfolding along a well-traveled commuter route, and the weight of the crowd's expectations gathered an almost palpable force. "Pressing forward," the *Plain Dealer* noted, "eager to see but half afraid of what grisly objects might be brought to the surface, they waited, mothers with children in their arms, men who paused on their way home from work to witness the tedious search in the rusty water." One photo shows a sprawling group of onlookers seated on the muddy banks and leaning up against a chain-link fence, their faces grim and expectant. Some of these curiosity-seekers eventually made their way down to the morgue, hoping that the latest body parts would be displayed as the tattooed man's head had been. Coroner Pearse, realizing that none of them could possibly make an identification without the head, ordered the morgue closed to "tourists."

"The detectives have used all the ordinary means, and some extraordinary ones, in their efforts to get a definite clew," the *Press* reported, but it was clear that the options were narrowing. Inspector Sweeney pored through George Koestle's Bertillon records, even though he had no fingerprints to guide his search, looking for suspects classified with "sadistic tendencies." Others checked in with hospitals and mental institutions across Ohio and nine other states, hoping to find a possibility among the recently released patients. Volunteers were pressed into service to comb through the fields and swamps radiating outward from the drainage pool, while uniformed officers knocked on doors in the surrounding neighborhoods, "talking to housewives, boys, anybody who might have the slightest shred of information."

Many of the veteran detectives sounded despondent. Some of them had been on the case since Jackass Hill, and they could see the familiar signs of the trail growing cold. "With a blank wall of clewless mystery facing them, the detectives frankly have been baffled," reported the *News*, "their only hopes being that the fiend might some time be interrupted in one of his missions of death." A disheartened Sergeant Hogan acknowledged that he saw "practically no chance of identifying the victim" without the head or hands. Save for a lucky break of some kind, he admitted, the "chance of solving the mysterious murders is very slight."

At city hall, Mayor Burton read the newspaper stories with mounting despair. He knew that the police were chasing down every possible lead, but the public outcry had now risen to an operatic pitch. Burton felt additional heat as a councilman named Joseph Artl, a Democrat with mayoral ambitions, drew up a resolution offering a reward for information leading to the arrest and conviction of the killer. A page-one banner in the *Plain Dealer* lionized him: "Urges $1000 Torso Murder Reward."

For Burton, a political gauntlet had been thrown down. Thousands of commuters were getting a firsthand look at the so-called murder pool, showcasing the frustrations and slow pace of the investigation. An editorial in the *Press* made a blunt call for action: "Stop This Slaughter." The *News* jumped in to offer its own thousand-dollar reward, likening the murders to the "deepest, opium-maddened dreams" of Edgar Allan Poe:

> *Of all horrible nightmares come to life, the most shuddering is the fiend who decapitates his victims in the dark, dank recesses of Kingsbury Run.*

> *That a man of this nature should be permitted to work his crazed vengeance upon six people in a city the size of Cleveland should be Cleveland's shame.*

On Saturday, September 12, Mayor Burton summoned Eliot Ness to his office. From this point forward, Burton told him, Ness would take personal charge of the investigation. The butcher had to be stopped.

Ness must have known that this day would come. He had kept his distance from the investigation up to this point, perhaps realizing, as one crime historian has suggested, that Kingsbury Run was "a quagmire" in every sense, and "beyond his experience as a federal agent." Still, Ness had swept into office nine months earlier with bold claims that he would conduct his own investigations out in the field, and not be chained to a desk. Again and again, he had emphasized the importance of modern techniques, scientific training, and the principles of investigation laid out by his mentor, August Vollmer. Now, the moment had come to back it up, to see if the "scientifically-trained boy wonder" could bring in the mad butcher of Kingsbury Run. "He had to do something," Detective Peter Merylo would recall. "The mayor was on his neck; so were the Chamber of Commerce and the Come to Cleveland Committee and some of the people who rode home to Shaker Heights through the Run on the Rapid Transit. But so was the whole town, for that matter. It was getting to be something of a national disgrace, Cleveland's uncaught torso murderer."

Ness didn't want the assignment, but he was determined to face it head-on. "I'm going to do all I can to aid in the investigation," he announced. "I want to see this psycho caught."

10

VOODOO DOCTORS AND CHICKEN FREAKS

Safety Director Eliot Ness today took personal charge of the investigation of the mystery of the headless dead.

Cleveland Press, September 12, 1936

Ness had waited nine months to weigh in publicly on the Kingsbury Run murders. Now, as if to make up for lost time, he appeared determined to break the case open in a single afternoon. "As his first step he ordered a clean-out of the Kingsbury Run area where four of the decapitation murders have been done," noted the *Press*. "A small army of police moved into the run area from E. 24th Street eastward to bring in the score or more of 'permanent residents' there."

This bold stroke played well to the cameras, but it did not mark a radical change of direction. Inspector Sweeney, Sergeant Hogan, and others had been questioning shantytown residents for several months, but the order from Ness signaled a heightened resolve. Police rounded up thirteen men, most of whom would be released quickly after questioning about "what might have been heard along the hoboes' grapevine." None of them could provide any solid leads, but several reported hearing warnings about the butcher. All across the country, they said, the word had gone out to avoid Kingsbury Run. This information gave no help in catching the killer, but it did offer hope that the pool of potential victims could dry up, in which case the butcher might be drawn into the open or forced to abandon his killing spree altogether. For the moment, Ness's order had the desired effect, establishing that the manhunt had become an urgent priority. "Police Act on Order of Ness," announced a banner headline. "Clean Out Haunts of Mad Killer."

Even now, Ness made few public statements about the case, reverting to the "Facts First, Then Talk" policy that had characterized his administration from its first days. When he did offer a few words about the butcher, his thinking appeared rooted in presuppositions and tired biases. "This killer has great cunning," he remarked. "He certainly doesn't leave many, if any, clues. About all we have to go on is that one of the victims we've been able to identify was a pervert and another was a prostitute. This man seems to specialize in the sort of people nobody is likely to miss."

Hoping for fresh insights, Ness threw his weight behind an emergency "crime conference" organized by Coroner Pearse. A hastily assembled group of scientists and law enforcement officials came together in the ballistics lab of the Central Police Station on the evening of Tuesday, September 15, marking "a concerted effort to pull the hunt for the Kingsbury Run slayer out of the blind alley in which it has been groping." For Pearse, the strain of the investigation had begun to show. The previous day's headlines had announced the discovery of yet another set of remains, under circumstances that appeared to fit the familiar pattern. A pair of schoolboys walking through a vacant lot near the Nickel Plate Railroad tracks had stumbled across a headless female skeleton. The bones, examined by Pearse at the scene, appeared clean apart from "a bit of decayed flesh" clinging to one foot. Pearse noted that some of the vertebrae had been crudely wired together in places, and that several ribs were missing along with the skull. The remains were those of a woman of small stature whose death had come "about a month ago," he announced. In his view, this woman might well prove to be another victim of the butcher.

Pearse's findings sparked a brief but intense flurry of activity as investigators mobilized for a fresh effort. The following day, however, a schoolteacher came forward to identify the suspicious skeleton as a discarded medical specimen, owned by his family for more than fifteen years, bringing this latest furor to a thudding halt. Pearse, it now became clear, had mistaken an old classroom skeleton for a possible torso victim. The city's journalists chose to be diplomatic. They praised the coroner for making short work of the mystery, and discreetly refrained from mentioning the decayed bit of flesh Pearse claimed to have identified, or his baffling assertion that the remains were only about a month old.

Possibly the coroner had been distracted with preparations for his forensic conference, now informally dubbed the "torso clinic." The gathering brought together more than thirty people, including professors of anatomy and medicine, a court psychiatrist, the superintendent of a mental institution, and various other medical experts. Ness arrived with a team of police investigators that included Inspector Sweeney, Sergeant Hogan, Chief Matowitz, and several others. "It is hoped," said one observer, "that the conference may pull various expert opinions into a single channel and point the way toward a solution to the fiendish killings."

Here, Pearse's instincts were commendable. At a time when modern notions of criminal profiling had not yet emerged, the Cleveland panel took an ambitious swing at creating what they called a "synthetic portrait" of the killer. After two and a half hours of discussion and a slideshow of grisly evidence photos, the experts agreed upon a generalized outline of their quarry. They insisted that he represented a "new insane type" whose actions would not "fit into a recognized pattern." The killer worked alone, they said, and lived somewhere along the boundaries of Kingsbury Run, a vicinity he knew intimately. He was undoubtedly large and strong, they continued, and seemed likely to have acquired his skill at dismemberment as a butcher or a hunter rather than as a result of medical training, as had been previously assumed. He probably spent weeks or even months befriending his victims, they added, so as to lower his quarry's guard at the moment of attack. The panel also concluded that the killer maintained a butcher's laboratory or "murder studio" somewhere in the surrounding area, where he could "do his sanguinary work before taking his corpses to the Run." Possibly he operated more than one of these bloody workshops, as suggested by the Big Creek and Florence Polillo murders, both of which had taken the killer farther afield. The scientists and lawmen all agreed that the butcher preyed on transient or marginalized individuals because their absence would almost certainly go unnoticed, at least until the remains were found. Some of the body parts, they added, might never be recovered, because the killer "probably hung on to some of the heads for purposes of sexual perversion or cannibalism." For all of that, the clinic participants appeared convinced that the butcher was capable of hiding in plain sight, mixing easily with his neighbors and coworkers, and presenting a dull, ordinary facade to the outside world. "Aside from fatal moments of sadistic passion," noted one summary of the conference, "he may lead a normal life."

To a great extent, the crime conference simply put a light coat of varnish onto conclusions that had already emerged over the course of the summer. Other statements fell apart under scrutiny. It is impossible to know why the conference members rejected the notion that the killer possessed a surgical background, which had been a guiding tenet of Coroner Pearse's findings from the beginning. Possibly the medical men on the panel, all of whom were respected professionals and leading citizens, found it impossible to believe that a man capable of such depravity could pass unnoticed in their circles. At the same time, the details of the Florence Polillo and Edward Andrassy cases—the only two victims who had been successfully identified—contradicted the assertion that the killer focused on transients. Though Polillo and Andrassy were both rootless figures to some extent, both had fixed addresses at the time of their deaths, and their disappearances had, in fact, drawn notice before the discovery of their remains.

The other notable change of direction—the notion that the killer might have spent weeks or even months gaining the confidence of his victims— appears to have originated with Ness. The safety director had said little for much of the conference, but at one stage he piped up to "advance the theory that the slayer decapitated his victims in order to dispose of the heads." This might have been done, he added, "to prevent identification of men in whose company he had been frequently seen shortly before the murders." Ness does not appear to have ventured an opinion on the possibility of sexual perversion or cannibalism.

Clearly not all of the participants felt optimistic. "Gentlemen," said Sergeant Hogan at the outset, "tonight we're right where we were on the day the first body was found." Still, they appeared determined. A photo of the gathering shows a group of grim, resolute figures, most of whom had thrown off their suit coats and rolled up their shirtsleeves, listening to Coroner Pearse with rapt attention. Ness sits at the middle of the room with his suit coat primly buttoned, a stiff contrast in a double row of rumpled white shirts, looking like a Bible student who had somehow wandered into a strip club.

Ness had at least one kindred spirit in the room. The crime clinic offered a chance to forge an alliance with David Cowles, the guiding force behind Cleveland's emerging Scientific Investigation Bureau. As the era of George Koestle's Bertillon department faded under Ness's reforms, the thirty-eight-year-old Cowles had stepped in to modernize the force's criminal science labs, bringing "a sometimes balky, often skeptical department into the modern era." A gifted chemist, Cowles also excelled at fieldwork. He could be seen toiling away in the background at crime scenes, stooping low to gather a soil sample or peering through his round glasses at a bloodstain.

No one knew quite how this courtly, unassuming man had acquired his vast knowledge of forensics. Cowles had left school at the age of thirteen to help support his eleven siblings, but as a teenager, he somehow managed to provide himself with a comprehensive background in laboratory sciences. He landed a job as a chemist with the city's health department at the age of twenty-one, becoming the first non–college graduate to pass the civil service exam, but already he had set his sights on law enforcement. One night, police officers summoned him to an apartment stairwell where a man lay dead of a bullet to the head. A gun had been found on the stairs one level below, but officers could not be sure whether it had been dropped by the dead man or by an unknown assailant. They challenged Cowles to determine whether the man lying before him had been a murder victim or a suicide. Cowles made short work of it, noting the singed hair at the victim's temple and the residue of gun oil on the index finger. He confidently pronounced a verdict of suicide, a finding later confirmed by the coroner. Soon, Cowles found himself on the police department's payroll.

Ness would lean on Cowles as he waded into the Kingsbury Run drama. Cowles had been on the scene at many of the butcher's dumping grounds, including the White Front Meat Market, where Florence Polillo had been discovered, and, more recently, had carried out a minute examination of the discarded clothing found at the so-called murder pool. Cowles had also been at the center of the tattooed-man investigation, and is generally believed to have fashioned the plaster death mask displayed at the Great Lakes Exposition. Perhaps most important, Cowles shared the safety director's faith that a modern, scientific approach stood the best chance of bringing in this new type of killer, whose actions did not fit any "recognized pattern of insanity."

Others, like Detective Peter Merylo, a seventeen-year veteran of the force, favored a more traditional approach, attacking the problem with "shoe leather and night sticks." Like David Cowles, Merylo had been on the periphery of Kingsbury Run almost from the beginning. The previous year, he had been among the group of officers who informed Joseph Andrassy of his son's murder. "It's not fun to crowd into a man's home and confront him with the murder of his son," he recalled years later, "and ask him a lot of questions about his son's sex life." Perhaps not, but Merylo had a reputation for doing whatever the job required.

Shortly after noon on September 10, just a couple of hours after the floating remains were discovered at the so-called murder pool, Merylo received an urgent telephone call at home. The detective had been asleep at the time, having worked an exhausting overnight shift in the Roaring Third. Groggy after only a couple of hours in bed, he sounded incredulous upon being told that Chief Matowitz had a special assignment for him. "Again?" he groaned. "Another special detail?" He sighed, put the phone down, and began pulling on his clothes.

Arriving at the Central Police Station, Merylo was stunned to learn that Chief Matowitz had officially cleared his caseload in response to the latest discovery in Kingsbury Run. As of this moment, Merylo was told, he would work full-time on the torso slayings. Blindsided by the sudden reassignment, Merylo arranged a face-to-face meeting with the chief, wanting to know why he had been picked over any of the other detectives available, many of whom had logged more time on the killings. "I have faith in you," Matowitz told him. "If you don't find the killer, no one will."

Merylo's background and sterling record appeared to justify the chief's confidence. The detective, a Ukrainian immigrant, grew up speaking several Eastern European languages, which allowed him to mix easily with the city's enormous immigrant population. He joined the force in 1919 and advanced steadily, first as a patrolman and then on the police motorcycle squad, and put in long hours at the shooting range after work to become the department's reigning pistol marksman. By the summer of 1931, he had earned a spot on the detective bureau. "I am confident that you will make a wonderful Sherlock Holmes," a friend told him, but others saw him more in the mold of Inspector Lestrade, the detective's tenacious, if uninspired counterpart at Scotland Yard. "He was a hard worker," a colleague would say, "but he had no finesse. He was more of a plodder. He got hooked on one thing and that's all there was to it. But I'll tell you one thing: I'd hate to have Pete Merylo after me."

Two days after Merylo received his unexpected reassignment from Matowitz, news filtered down through the ranks that Mayor Burton had also responded to the latest killing, independently of the chief, and kicked the Kingsbury Run investigation over to Ness. Within hours, Merylo found himself summoned to the safety director's office. Both men had reason to be wary. In Merylo's eyes, Ness was soft, a smooth-talking upstart who somehow had the gall to go after Mike Harwood and other "gold braids." To Ness, Merylo looked like just another dim-witted Cleveland flatfoot, stuck in the past and probably shady. Chief Matowitz saw great potential in Merylo's record of laborious service, but Ness found only cause for suspicion.

Not surprisingly, the meeting went badly. No sooner had Merylo taken a seat than Ness demanded to know what progress the detective had made. Merylo was affronted. He'd been on the job for barely two days, and had spent most of that time holed up with a thick stack of case files, and already the boy wonder seemed impatient for a breakthrough. Merylo could answer only that he was still marshaling his facts, but he ventured his opinion that sex played a central role in the killer's motivation. In days to come, Merylo would often describe the butcher as a "sex degenerate," and once theorized that the butcher derived "sexual gratification while watching the blood flow after cutting the jugular vein of his victim."

Listening to the veteran detective's theories in his office that day, Ness appeared impatient. He asked a few perfunctory questions and then brought the meeting to an abrupt close, telling Merylo to keep him apprised of any progress. They parted on frosty terms. "You can't bring up Eliot Ness to Peter," Merylo's wife would recall. "He starts to get nasty. He did not like the man."

Merylo had a prickly temperament at the best of times, but in this case, his pique appears justified. The detective had rough edges, but he was a cunning and capable workhorse at a time when Ness badly needed one. If for no other reason, Ness should have made some effort to accommodate the man in whom Chief Matowitz had placed his trust. Instead, Ness appeared dismissive and sowed dissent. From this point forward, the investigation would proceed on two parallel tracks. Merylo soon became the public face of the effort, running down tips and rousting potential suspects, while Ness took a step back from the spotlight, pursuing a separate line of inquiry with the Unknowns. Some have suggested that this was a canny maneuver on Ness's part, letting Merylo serve as a kind of lightning rod while he and his team operated in the shadows. In truth, the situation only served to spotlight Ness's distrust of the officers he commanded. Caution of this sort was understandable while he rooted out crooked cops, but corruption played no part in the Kingsbury Run investigation. There was absolutely no one in the Cleveland Police Department, no matter how dirty, who wanted to see the killings continue. Ness had the entire force to command, but instead of uniting his men against a common enemy, he chose instead to operate exactly as he had in Chicago, an outsider instead of a leader, working in the dark.

If anything, Ness's curt dismissal served to energize Detective Merylo. Chief Matowitz had authorized him to pick his own partner and to work any hours necessary to crack the case. Merylo decided to pair up with Detective Martin Zalewski, a twenty-three-year veteran. Like Merylo, Zalewski had a reputation for hard work and he spoke several languages. He had also been a patrolman in the Jackass Hill neighborhood for several years. "This job will take endless patience and determination because there are literally no clues," Inspector Sweeney told the press. "But I know these men will work day and night without becoming discouraged."

Over the next few weeks, Merylo and Zalewski racked up a spectacular number of arrests, seemingly determined to bring in anyone who crossed their paths. The sprawling catalog of charges included assault, concealed weapons, larceny, forgery, immigration violations, robbery, child neglect, indecent exposure, and—perhaps the most serviceable—vagrancy. As with the general roundup Ness had ordered, most of these suspects would be released after questioning while others were detained on charges unrelated to the murders. "With the Kingsbury amphitheater their stage," wrote one admirer, "and anyone who set foot in it without valid excuse their quarry, the pair have combed out of the gully's three-mile expanse a veritable army of woebegone hoboes, addled knife grinders, broken down doctors and others of twisted behavior."

Merylo and Zalewski also made the rounds of the city's slaughterhouses, becoming convinced that no ordinary butcher could have committed the crimes, and called in at various laundries and dry cleaning establishments, asking to be notified whenever bloody articles of clothing surfaced. They even did some all-too-literal digging for clues at a local potter's field, disinterring some recent burials on the theory that grave robbery might be a factor in the crimes. "No stratagem," the *Plain Dealer* noted, "has been too bizarre for the officers to try." Merylo insisted that they had to follow up as many leads as possible, no matter how unpromising they might seem. "When anybody calls I always call their bluff and go meet them," he would tell a reporter. "Some time I may get something."

Ness, meanwhile, had issued a general order urging a department-wide acceleration of activity to bring in the killer "before he strikes again." The stepped-up efforts included a telephone tip line and random traffic stops late at night, designed to snare the killer on his way to the dumping ground. Ness also suggested that detectives "retrace their steps and examine exhaustively each clew," spurring investigators to take a fresh look at old case files.

One old case rose to the top of the pile. In December of 1928, police had been summoned to an apartment house on East 40th Street following the discovery of a headless corpse in the basement. Suspicion fell on a mysterious "voodoo doctor," arrested previously for practicing medicine without a license. Confronted by police, the suspect was shot in both legs while trying to escape. After treatment at a nearby hospital, he confessed to murder and supplied the identity of the headless corpse, only to have his supposed victim appear at the police station declaring, "I'm pretty much alive." Detectives were left to puzzle over the true identity of the victim, which remained obscure even after the discovery of a decapitated head in a basement cupboard. "If he didn't kill the man he said he killed," a detective asked, "then who did he kill?" The question could not be answered at the time, and according to some reports, the so-called voodoo doctor would eventually be released for lack of evidence. Now, realizing that this macabre story appeared to fit the template of the more recent crimes, Sergeant Hogan authorized a search of the suspect's old haunts. Hogan admitted, however, that he "placed little stock" in the undertaking, and the effort soon fizzled out.

As it happened, Hogan had not given up his grinding labors at the nearby "murder pool," where he would carry on the search for additional body parts for several more weeks. In time, Hogan received authorization to bring in heavy machinery that would drain off an estimated three million gallons of water, leaving roughly two feet of fetid sludge at the bottom of the pool. Detective Merylo, never one to shy away from getting his hands dirty, joined fellow officers and utility workers as they raked through the muck. "And nothing to show for it," Merylo would recall, "nothing but junk."

Meanwhile, the heightened police effort in and around Kingsbury Run brought in a remarkable variety of eccentrics. One of them was said to live under the Lorain-Carnegie Bridge, surrounded with some five hundred pairs of women's shoes. Another was known to perform acrobatics over the Run on a forty-foot wire, in the manner of Tarzan. He came to the attention of detectives because he took pleasure in strangling rabbits. Another denizen, a man "bedecked with beads and amulets," insisted that he possessed a secret that enabled him to transplant human heads from one person to the next. Under other circumstances, the claim would have been dismissed with a shrug, but investigators reasoned that any attempt at pursuing this goal, no matter how misguided, would likely produce a trail of headless corpses. Officers checked the story carefully but learned that the suspect had been in prison when the crimes occurred.

"Those were the days when every man was his own expert," Detective Merylo would say, "and the papers, with an eye to dramatic reading matter, quoted a lot of would-be experts." One of these experts was Michael R. Collegeman, head of the federal narcotics bureau office in Cleveland, who advanced the notion that the butcher's "unreasoning desire to kill" might be rooted in marijuana use. "Both the desire for a thrill and a homicidal obsession are easily induced by the loco weed cigarettes," he insisted. It bears mentioning that *Reefer Madness*, the wildly hyperbolic propaganda film, was released that year. Some versions of the film featured not only a man driven insane by a single puff of marijuana but also a pot-fueled axe murderer. Michael Collegeman's theory appeared to gain credence when police arrested a thirty-one-year-old "dope addict" found wandering aimlessly in Kingsbury Run, "apparently inflamed by marijuana." The suspect drew the attention of police after some garbled muttering to the effect that he had "cut a lot of meat." Detectives locked him up for the night and stationed officers nearby to overhear any "coherent mumbling that might connect the man with the case." None was forthcoming, and this latest suspect would soon be turned loose.

For a time, investigators benefited from a patch of unseasonably warm weather. In October, as the temperature climbed toward 80 degrees,

Merylo and Zalewski came upon a man hard at work near the Erie Railroad tracks, squeezing juice out of a can of cherries. In spite of the heat, he wore two pairs of pants, three suit jackets, two overcoats, and, as the detectives later discovered, woolen underwear. On his head, he sported a wet towel, topped by three different hats. The towel, he explained, "keeps my head cool while I'm thinking." Nearby sat a bushel basket filled with clippings from the financial pages of the local papers. "Just a few statements from my bankers," he remarked. "When I make my second million I'm going to marry a beautiful heiress." From one of his many pockets, he produced a photograph of "a duly enchanting beauty." Merylo and Zalewski soon discovered that his pockets also contained three razors, a homemade stiletto knife, and a hammer head wrapped in a pair of stockings. The detectives brought him in for questioning, but no link could be found to the slayings.

As the hunt continued, investigators began to improvise, finding ways to surmount the limits of their resources and the technology. Some of these jury-rigged efforts took a form that anticipated techniques of the computer age. At one stage, police went looking for a particular suspect who had "given evidence of degenerate tendencies." A seemingly insurmountable difficulty arose when no photograph could be found of the thirty-four-year-old man—apart from one taken at the age of twelve. Unwilling to let the matter drop, investigators brought in a local artist who projected the childhood photo onto a canvas. With the aid of descriptions from various sources, the artist altered and embellished the image to generate an approximation of the man's present-day appearance. Today, age-progression software has become commonplace; at the time, the determined investigators did their best with the materials at hand.

Detectives also quizzed prostitutes about clients who exhibited bizarre sexual tendencies, a line of inquiry that generated a distressingly large pool of candidates. Merylo and Zalewski spent weeks in pursuit of a "best and likely suspect" who manifested a notably gruesome fetish. Once a week or so, he would purchase a live chicken and carry it off to a local brothel. There he would pay anywhere from three to five dollars to have a prostitute cut off the chicken's head while he pleasured himself. Merylo and Zalewski believed that this form of sexual sadism might have propelled the man to darker crimes over the years. The detectives finally tracked him down with the help of a license plate number supplied by a call girl, but they found their quarry to be mentally challenged and likely incapable of carrying out the slayings. The detectives took fingerprints but turned the man loose. Encounters like this one had brought Merylo face-to-face with "people I never knew or believed existed," he would tell a reporter. "The man we want is stranger than any of them."

Many of the arrests made during this surge of activity were "catch and release" affairs, with police setting the suspects free after one or two rounds of questioning. In other instances, according to reporter Thomas W. Wolfe, the effort became "the instrument of retributive justice." People caught up in the torso sweep were quickly linked to other crimes, resulting in the closing of cases that had been on the books for weeks or months, and jail terms for the offenders. More than a few innocent people were also caught up in the net, including a blameless knife salesman who found himself briefly held for questioning. He came under suspicion simply because he carried his samples in his pockets rather than in a display case. At least some of these arrests led to confinement in a state hospital for the insane. At the time, these forced institutionalizations were reported as a positive dividend of the increased policing, getting "mental defectives" off the street. The point is debatable, at the very least, and Chief Matowitz preferred to focus on the criminal convictions. "Even though the torso killer has been able to evade capture with uncanny success to date," Matowitz declared, "there does seem to be some consolation in the fact that almost two dozen other serious law violators have landed in jail as a result of the Kingsbury Run case. But none of these additional arrests, of course, has caused us to let down in the slightest in the hunt for the torso murderer."

Even as the Kingsbury Run clean-out continued, Ness had begun looking farther afield. Some one hundred miles away in Pennsylvania, a potentially explosive breakthrough was taking shape. In mid-September, on the heels of the torso clinic, details came to light of a series of eerily similar crimes in the vicinity of New Castle, a small but thriving industrial city near the Ohio border. Just outside of New Castle lay a bleak, swampy stretch of several hundred acres that "always has been avoided by the timid," much like Kingsbury Run. A few weeks earlier, on July 1, a man living nearby had noticed several hawks circling above a string of boxcars on a siding belonging to the Pittsburgh & Lake Erie Railroad, about one hundred yards from the swamp. The boxcars had stood abandoned since 1930, but railway workers conducted regular inspections, the last of which had occurred a couple of weeks earlier. Now, alerted by the circling hawks, a pair of P&LE inspectors hurried to the scene and found an open door on one of the boxcars. As they drew closer, they became aware of buzzing flies and a heavy, putrid odor. Climbing inside, they discovered a nude, headless male corpse lying chest-down, partly covered by a burlap bag. The state of decomposition indicated that the victim had been dead roughly ten days. Bloodstained clothing turned up nearby, but the head was nowhere to be found. When police investigators arrived and shifted the remains, they found three sections of newspaper underneath, dated three years earlier. One of the papers, they noted, came from Cleveland.

For longtime residents of New Castle, the discovery carried a disturbing echo of past horrors. No fewer than four other dead bodies had been discovered in the swamplands dating back to the early years of Prohibition, and similar episodes had occurred across the state. For more than a decade police had been frustrated in their efforts to track a culprit, and it became widely assumed that these earlier victims had run afoul of local bootleggers or mobsters. The mystery intensified in October of 1925 when three mutilated bodies turned up within a few weeks of one another. Concerned citizens organized a thorough search of the swamp, but the effort yielded little of value, and despite the determined work of local police, the investigation quickly sputtered out. Over time, the gloomy thread of marshy land outside of New Castle became known as the "murder swamp."

Now, as the atrocities in Cleveland attracted national attention, the similarities between the two sets of crimes came to the fore. "The mystery of the headless dead went deeper today," reported the *Plain Dealer* on September 17. "The probability that Cleveland's mad butcher may have two or more scenes of operations was advanced." The theory had much to recommend it. Several freight and passenger train lines connected the two locales, and some of the bodies at either end had been dumped within sight of railroad tracks. If, as police had long theorized, the killer deliberately preyed on train-hopping transients, perhaps he himself also rode the rails, disappearing onto passing freight cars after committing his crimes.

In mid-September, Ness dispatched John Flynn, his executive assistant, to meet with New Castle officials for a briefing. Flynn, a dashing young lawyer with an Errol Flynn mustache, had become Ness's closest confidant over the previous months, often stepping in as the safety director's proxy during the hectic days of Mayor Burton's summer gala. Now, as his focus shifted to Kingsbury Run, Ness sent Flynn to determine if the situation in New Castle demanded a closer look. Some accounts claim that Ness himself joined Flynn on the trip. This seems unlikely as there is no contemporary mention of it, and Ness—never one to shy away from a camera—doesn't appear with Flynn in a photograph taken at the scene. In either case, Flynn toured the swamp, spoke with residents, and interviewed the two railroad inspectors who discovered the body in the boxcar. At least some of the Pennsylvania lawmen, Flynn learned, still believed that mob violence played a role. "The swamp is a handy place, evidently, to hide the victims of gangs," New Castle's police chief insisted. In spite of the many similarities, the Pennsylvania authorities were inclined to downplay a possible connection to the Cleveland crimes. Flynn seemed to agree. By the time he returned to Ohio and reported to Ness, the *Plain Dealer* was reporting that the hot lead in New Castle "blew up" under closer scrutiny. The earlier Pennsylvania crimes were found to have been "dissimilar" to the Kingsbury Run cases, and one detail in particular appeared to settle the matter: "None of the bodies were dismembered, as were those here."

"Flynn returned to Cleveland a little dubious about the New Castle torsos," Detective Merylo would remark. "He wasn't sure those murders had been committed by the same man." Merylo strongly disagreed. After traveling to New Castle himself, Merylo became convinced that the killer moved back and forth by rail and butchered at least some of his victims in boxcars. "I was sure," he said. The detective's certainty would deepen over time, so much so that he would spend a two-week vacation digging for leads in New Castle, and even brought his wife and two daughters out from Cleveland to get a look at the terrain. "I was convinced beyond any doubt that the murders in New Castle were identically the same as they were in Cleveland," he would say.

Then as now, opinions divided sharply on this point. A great deal hinges on the exact condition of the Pennsylvania remains, especially the earlier ones, but the surviving evidence is frustratingly limited and inconsistent. Though the *Plain Dealer* reported that the bodies had not been dismembered, it is apparent that advanced decomposition had clouded the issue, as it had in Cleveland's Big Creek case earlier that summer. A few accounts suggest that only some of the Pennsylvania bodies were headless and that one, in fact, remained entirely intact, but other sources make reference to the type of knife cuts seen in the Cleveland cases. At least one unverified statement referred to bullet wounds in some of the corpses, which would not only lend credence to the theory of mob violence but also mark a considerable divergence from the Cleveland pattern.

Merylo's insistence that the crimes presented as "identically the same" probably relies more on the veteran officer's gut instinct than hard evidence. Possibly Merylo investigated the irregularities and was able to discount them, or perhaps his intense focus blinded him to details that contradicted his assumptions. Either way, he held fast to his belief that a single killer stood behind both sets of atrocities. His conviction about the New Castle crimes would shape his future efforts, and served to widen the gulf between him and Ness. Merylo's low opinion of the safety director and his circle would not have improved when John Flynn weighed in with a further conjecture, positing that the Cleveland crimes might have been carried out by a woman. Others had speculated along these lines, and would do so again. It would have taken a woman of conspicuous strength to have performed the single-blow dismemberments and the heavy lifting apparent at Jackass Hill, but it was not an impossible notion. Still, Merylo refused to consider, even for a moment, any possibility that butcher might be a woman. "If she were," he commented in private writings, "and we never had the remotest indication it was a woman, she must have been a super-Amazon." This dismissiveness became Merylo's default position. Often in the days to come, when someone would venture a public opinion on the case, Merylo would offer a biting retort: "Was you there, Charlie?"

Though Merylo and Zalewski continued to push themselves as hard as ever, some of the other detectives working the case would be reassigned to their normal duties as the year drew to a close. Publicly, Ness appeared to have taken another step back. "As I've said before, we are investigating these homicides and doing everything within our power to bring the killer or killers to justice," he declared. "Just because a homicide investigation is under way doesn't mean we should drop all of our other work." The statement left a great deal unsaid. It had now become apparent that the intense concentration of effort in the wake of the "murder pool" drama would not flush out the killer, as Ness had hoped, and the inconclusive findings in New Castle added to his frustration. At the same time, he became preoccupied as his anti-corruption effort entered a crucial phase, with the trial of the disgraced Captain Michael Harwood set to begin in December.

In a further complication, County Prosecutor Frank Cullitan came up for reelection in November, and Ness could not risk seeing his vital ally voted out of office. In early October, the city's front pages showed Ness handing over his massive police-graft report to a smiling Cullitan, who promised to take action as soon as possible. The message was clear: Ness and Cullitan were a package deal. On November 3, as President Roosevelt racked up an astounding 98 percent of the electoral college vote, Cullitan easily cruised to victory on the Democratic slate.

Also on the ballot was Coroner Arthur Pearse, a Republican, whose popularity and distinguished record could not hold off the Roosevelt landslide. Pearse lost by a slim margin to Democrat Samuel Gerber, with immediate consequences for the Kingsbury Run investigation. The thirty-eight-year-old Gerber worked closely with the city's "worthy poor" as physician in charge of the Wayfarer's Lodge, a prominent relief organization for the homeless. He brought a renewed intensity to the torso murders, immediately undertaking a fresh examination of the evidence. "I inherited a lot of information from Dr. Pearse," he would say, "but we went back and did our own tests." Gerber took nothing at face value, even his predecessor's conclusions about decapitation as the cause of death. Gerber acknowledged that he found no other signs of fatal injury, but, he said, "death could have occurred in other ways. For instance, they could have been asphyxiated—smothered. It would have been very difficult, you know, to decapitate a living person." Gerber offered no conclusions about the Lady of the Lake, who had left "too few details," but he concluded that "the peculiar dissection of the bodies" in the other cases pointed to a single killer. "The possibility of a different operator having entered the series is slight," he insisted.

Ness was also looking for patterns, in keeping with his long-standing views of crime detection. "In crime, in accident, and in any series of events menacing public safety," he would write, "the cause, the why, is the thing to ferret out. As the pattern evolves, experience and intelligence point to a solution on the basis of those facts, and a course of action becomes crystal clear."

So far, in the Kingsbury Run investigation, nothing at all had become crystal clear. Though he appeared to have taken a step back publicly, Ness had quietly laid the groundwork to investigate personally. Clippings about the killings began to appear in his personal scrapbooks, in jarring contrast to the usual run of wholesome puff pieces. Reports on such things as his address to police academy graduates—"Buy Your Own Meals, Ness Tells Rookies"—were pasted in alongside bulletins on the case—"Police Learn Skeleton Not Murder Victim."

Ness had promised Edna a vacation after handing his graft report over to Cullitan, but he abruptly canceled the plans in October, adding to his wife's ever-expanding catalog of discontents. He declined to give an official reason, leaving the press to draw an obvious connection to a grand jury proceeding that opened the following day, involving the "parade of graft witnesses" named in his report. These proceedings absorbed much of his attention, but Ness had other reasons for staying close to home. He had now begun doing his own legwork on the Kingsbury Run case, though his usual retinue of reporters and photographers were conspicuously absent. Years later, the older sister of Peter Kostura, one of the two boys who stumbled across the bodies at Jackass Hill, would recall that Ness appeared at their home one day asking questions. The discovery at Jackass Hill had occurred three months before he took office, but Ness had undertaken a personal review of the earlier evidence and reports, just as he had urged his detectives to do. He said nothing about these efforts publicly, perhaps frustrated by his slow progress, but the work continued behind the scenes.

Soon, Ness took steps to expand his secret investigation. Although he and Edna still lived out in Bay Village, Ness had taken a small apartment downtown to comply with an ordinance requiring city employees to live within city limits. One night, away from prying eyes at city hall, Ness used the apartment to host a confidential meeting with David Cowles, head of the Scientific Investigation Bureau. Also present was an unnamed figure from the *Cleveland Press*, perhaps Clayton Fritchey, the investigative reporter who broke the story of Captain Louis Cadek and his scheme to sell cemetery plots. Fritchey had been working so closely with the Unknowns that Ness came to consider him a de facto member of the team, but some suggest that the unknown *Press* representative was none other than editor in chief Louis B. Seltzer, a man whose influence and civic-mindedness earned him the nickname of "Mr. Cleveland." Ness would have found a kindred spirit in Seltzer, who took a hard line on shady politicians. "No crook in public office has slept well in Louis Seltzer's regime," *Life* magazine would say of him, but Seltzer's memoirs are silent on the subject of Kingsbury Run.

Whoever the mysterious third figure was, he had the full weight of the *Press* behind him, and access to the checkbook. The three men had gathered in Ness's apartment to create yet another privately funded, independent squad of investigators. This team would have one job and one job only: to find the butcher. Cowles would select eight men, and Ness would coordinate the details, which involved probing underworld contacts for information not available to the official lawmen. Once again, Ness intended to fall back on the tactics that had served him so well as leader of the Untouchables. The handpicked task force would operate independently of official restrictions and oversight, bankrolled by the *Press*, and they would make use of the talents of reformed criminals who knew the terrain.

The existence of this secret butcher squad throws a fresh light on Ness's strained relationship with Peter Merylo, the standard-bearer of the official effort. Publicly, Ness would continue to put his weight behind the detective bureau, but the creation of the independent team must be taken as a sign that he was losing confidence. One can understand why Ness would reach for a familiar tactic, but the merits of this backroom approach are debatable. Ness could feel justified in creating his earlier Cleveland task force, the Unknowns, because the cloak of secrecy indemnified that team against the wide-scale corruption they hoped to stamp out. With this new team, however, he risked throwing barriers in the way of the official investigation and disrupting the flow of information. There is no indication that he ever briefed Detective Merylo on these sub-rosa activities. At a time when Ness was supposed to be restoring confidence in a battered system, he once again chose a course of action to subvert it.

Perhaps he felt he had no choice, given that his police reforms were still a work in progress, but a larger problem stood in the path of Ness's new elite force. The job of the Untouchables had been defined by a clear, highly visible target. Al Capone was the most famous man in the city at a time when Ness was entirely unknown, leaving the young agent free to move in the shadows. Now, the script had been flipped. Ness was the most famous man in the city, and his quarry had the advantage of anonymity, able to strike seemingly at will. Nothing in Ness's background had prepared him for this. To succeed, he would have to adapt.

For the moment, Ness could feel confident that the public would support him through whatever challenges lay ahead. As 1936 drew to a close, he found himself hailed as the city's "Man of the Year," somehow edging out Cleveland native Jesse Owens, the four-time gold medalist in that year's Olympic Games. "So great is Ness's public reputation and so secure his public confidence," the *Plain Dealer* noted, that any potential Democratic contender in the following year's mayoral contest "would do well to promise to retain Ness if elected."

That said, it was clear to all that there were storm clouds gathering. As the *Press* observed in the final days of that turbulent year, "Ness has his work cut out for him."

Eliot Ness as he appeared in 1931, during his initial burst of fame. "I was now receiving a great deal of newspaper publicity," he recalled, "and gradually becoming known as a 'gangbuster.'"

(Author's Collection)

CAPONE NEMESIS MAY GET CLEVELAND POST

Eliot Ness Considered For Safety Director.

By United Press.

CLEVELAND, Dec. 7.—Eliot Ness, former ace government sleuth in Chicago, may be Cleveland's next safety director. Mayor Burton announced he would discuss the position with Mr. Ness and a subsequent statement by Ness that he would accept the job if it was offered. At present he is investigator in charge of the federal alcohol tax unit in Cleveland.

Mr. Ness gained national attention several years ago when he gathered evidence which resulted in Al Capone being sent to prison for income tax evasion.

(Author's Collection)

"Most of the veteran policemen were cynical and didn't believe Ness was for real," said one reporter of Ness's appointment as Cleveland's safety director. "The politicians of both parties were sure he was an overpublicized tyro, a Boy Scout built up by the newspapers, who would soon fall on his face."

(The Cleveland Press Collection, Cleveland State University)

"We were beginning to be tagged as a city unable to enforce the law," declared newly elected Mayor Harold Burton, seen here with Ness. Burton provided his safety director with off-the-books funding for a small force of trusted men to clean out corruption within the police force—Cleveland's answer to the Untouchables.

(Author's Collection)

"If, outside of regular working hours, you can get Eliot Ness away from a handball court long enough, you may get him to tell you about his wrecking of Al Capone's breweries." As safety director, Ness often spent his lunch hour at the gym, stressing the importance of physical conditioning for police officers.

(The Cleveland Press Collection, Cleveland State University)

"Four-score armed men, led by the unarmed Ness, came marching forward in a solid phalanx." Ness, with his gold badge pinned to his lapel, to the left of County Prosecutor Frank Cullitan, on the night they raided the Harvard Club, a notorious gambling parlor.

(The Cleveland Press Collection, Cleveland State University)

Ness handing over a massive dossier on police corruption to Cullitan, the first step in an ambitious slate of reforms. "The report was the work of his new Untouchables and his own investigative perseverance," wrote journalist George Condon. "He had spent one hundred consecutive summer nights following the trail of police crookedness."

*(Cleveland Public Library/
Photograph Collection)*

The three Mrs. Nesses: Edna (left), Evaline (below left), and Elisabeth (below right). "Women threw themselves at Eliot," a friend remarked. "That was his trouble."

*(The Cleveland Press Collection,
Cleveland State University)*

As Notables Take a Ribbing in City Club's Anvil Revue

FRANK HERBERT AS
MAYOR BURTON

JAMES A. HAMILTON
AS CHIEF MATOWITZ

FRED P. STASHOWER
AS THE HIGH LAMA
OF BINGO

E. J. TYLER AS
CORDELL HULL

A. H. ZYCHICK
AS ROBERT H.
JACKSON

ALLISON LE PONTOIS
AS ELIOT NESS

Ness came in for a good-natured drubbing at the Anvil Revue, an annual program of political skits designed to "deflate notables of the stuffed shirt variety." One actor took the stage in a child's Buster Brown uniform (above left) to mock the safety director's youth and gee-whiz enthusiasm. "I'm the youngest safety director in the United States!" he declared. "I'd like to tell you in a few words how to rid the county of crime and corruption, jaundice, pyorrhea, toothache, and body odor!" *(Author's Collection)*

Ness gamely laughed along in the audience, drawing praise for his ability to "take it on the chin." *(Cleveland Public Library/Photograph Collection)*

The string of brutal murders ascribed to the butcher of Kingsbury Run touched off a lurid circulation war in the press. "My God," one journalist would say of the unknown killer, "how that man can sell newspapers!"

(Author's Collection)

"Do You Know This Room, Where Torso Victim Is Shown?" Detectives turned this photo over to *The Cleveland Press*, hoping that someone might come forward with information about Edward Andrassy, one of the Butcher's first victims.

(Author's Collection)

"Woman Slain, Head Sought in Coal Bins." The unfortunate Mrs. Florence Polillo, a "police character" whose remains were discovered behind a butcher shop.

(Cleveland Police Historical Society and Museum)

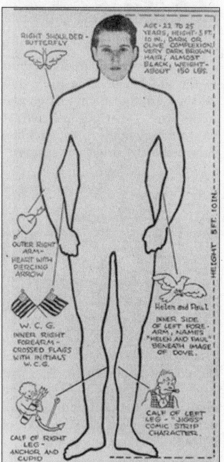

(Author's Collection)

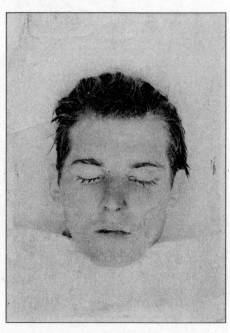

Hoping that someone might come forward with a positive identification, the coroner's office arranged for public viewings of the severed head of the victim known as "the tattooed man." A chart showing the placement of his many tattoos appeared in the newspapers.

(The Cleveland Press Collection, Cleveland State University)

The arrest of Frank Dolezal for the murder of Florence Polillo created a sensation. "He seemed just as normal as you or I, but his eyes seemed to stare right through you," a neighbor remarked. "They were like Svengali's eyes in the movies."

(Author's Collection)

Coroner Samuel Gerber (hatless) confers with investigators while gathering remains at the East Ninth Street dump. "He gives us one regularly every five months," a detective said of the killer.

(The Cleveland Press Collection, Cleveland State University)

Dr. Francis Edward Sweeney, the man Ness suspected of being the mad butcher of Kingsbury Run. In later life Sweeney delighted in showering Ness with "venomous, jeering" postcards, identifying himself as a "Paranoidal Nemesis" and making incoherent threats of "Legal Exaction."

(Cleveland Police Historical Society and Museum)

"Ness restored a sense of hope and pride to a beleaguered community," an admirer wrote on the day of his resignation as safety director in 1942. "Today, policemen no longer have to tip their hats when they pass a gangster on the streets."

(Author's Collection)

"Vote Yes for Eliot Ness." Ness hit the campaign trail during an ill-fated bid to become mayor of Cleveland in 1947.
(Cleveland Public Library/
Photograph Collection)

G433 ⚫ 35¢

The explosive, inside story of the Capone empire — as told by the man who smashed it

by ELIOT NESS
with Oscar Fraley

THE
UNTOUCHABLES

"Hair-raising"
— LOS ANGELES TIMES
"Unforgettable crime saga"
— BOSTON HERALD

(Author's Collection)

"Someday, you should write a book," Ness was told in his final years. "You might make some money with it." Ness did not live to see the publication of *The Untouchables.* *(The Cleveland Press Collection, Cleveland State University)*

11

STEEL AND BONE

CAN YOU HELP POLICE CAPTURE AMERICA'S GREATEST
MASS MURDERER, THE FIEND WHO KILLED TEN AND
LEFT NO CLEWS?

Official Detective Stories magazine, November 15, 1937

On New Year's Day 1937, Judge Carl Friebolin sat down, sharpened
a pencil, and began thinking of ways to ridicule Eliot Ness. By day,
Friebolin was one of the most respected legal minds in the city, and
a longtime federal referee in bankruptcy court. By night, he pursued
a second career as "Cleveland's Aristophanes," crafting a satiric production called the Anvil Revue, patterned on the famed Gridiron Club
Dinner in Washington, DC. Once a year Friebolin mounted a slick, high-
spirited program of skits and musical numbers designed to "deflate notables of the stuffed shirt variety." Anyone could become a target, and
being designated one of Friebolin's "goats" was taken as a signal that
one had risen to a level of social consequence. Each year as the curtain
fell on the latest production, an exhausted Friebolin would step forward
and declare that "this is positively my last show." In fact, he kept at it
for forty-eight years.

The previous year's Anvil Revue had been staged in the early days of
Harold Burton's administration, and Friebolin expressed disappointment

at the time that the mayor "hadn't yet made any mistakes worth joking about." He did, however, manage to take a healthy swing at Ness, parodying his gee-whiz enthusiasm and his cozy relationship with the press. Karl Heyner, an Anvil stalwart, took the role of Ness, wearing short pants and a child's beanie, and promising to rid the town of all crime and corruption—"if you'll let me tell the newspapers my story!" A second actor, portraying an exasperated Frank Cullitan, responded with his head in his hands: "Oh, you will, and to all the churches and clubs and ladies' auxiliaries . . ." But Ness had already turned away, raising a hand to his ear at the sound of an offstage police siren. "The call of duty!" he shouted. "I fly!"

The real Ness laughed along from his seat in the front rows of the Public Music Hall, and drew praise for his willingness to "take it on the chin."

As the formal invitations went out for the 1937 production, speculation mounted as to which of the city's "great and good" would be present to see themselves ridiculed. Reply cards, many of them featuring handwritten notes to the effect of "go easy on me," were pinned up on a so-called "goat board" backstage. "Some can take it," said one cast member. "Others can't." Burton and Ness, eager to show that they could take it, sat front and center when the curtain went up on April 10, along with *Press* editor Louis B. Seltzer, Senator Robert Bulkley, and other luminaries. Once again, Ness came in for special attention, with a portrayal that featured a pair of fluttering angel wings clipped to the back of his jacket. A chorus of police captains, each bearing a letter of resignation, joined in a tribute to the safety director's virtuosity:

Good Ness, gracious
Boy, but I'm couracious
Handsome and audacious
Greetings, meetings,
Take a lot of time;
I intrigue
The Junior League

You'll agree, man,
I'm a regular he-man
A-B-C-D-GEE, man!

By contrast, Mayor Burton saw himself rendered as a wistful figure-head, overshadowed by his headline-grabbing appointee:

Drab is the work of doing my duty;
Headlines are made by Eliot Ness . . .

Ah, Ness, you are my hero,
You are worth your fee.
Good Ness, all my career, oh,
I owe to thee.
Your gyrations are certain
To boost the stock of Harold H. Burton . . .

Possibly the joke cut a little close to the bone for Burton, who faced a reelection campaign later that year. Already there were backroom murmurs to the effect that the safety director would do well to run for office, perhaps even mount his own mayoral bid. Ness, who hadn't even had a clear party affiliation just a few months earlier, brushed aside all talk of elected office. "I still have the job I was appointed to do," he said.

Others were less circumspect. A few days earlier, Democratic Congressman Martin L. Sweeney of Cleveland's Twentieth District had fired a "double-barreled blast of his oratorical fury," criticizing both the mayor and "his alter ego, the great G-man" for their campaign against police corruption. Sweeney, a man who "fairly exuded belligerence," claimed that Burton and Ness had based their efforts on trifling charges that were long out of date, such as "taking $25 in graft money ten years ago." Though Sweeney stopped short of declaring his own bid for the mayor's office, he insisted that the "biggest task facing this community is to defeat Harold H. Burton."

The tirade might have passed unnoticed if he had left it there, but

Sweeney wasn't finished. Burton and Ness "were entertaining us with the prosecution of policemen," he continued, "when we have a Jack-the-Ripper in the city." Each day, the congressman insisted, it seemed that the city's front pages celebrated the news of another police captain booted off the force. "But," he said, "turn to page two and what do you see? Eleven unsolved torso murders in one year!"

Sweeney had exaggerated the number of killings to date, as reporters were quick to note, but he had accomplished his goal of dragging Kingsbury Run into the political arena, suggesting to voters that Ness's overzealous reforms had undercut the efforts of the detective bureau. For the moment, Sweeney's broadsides drew only condemnation. "No one belittles the importance of going after the killers," noted an editorial in the *Plain Dealer*. "It is, therefore, gratuitous and shamefully out of order for the Democratic insurgent to make this fling." The writer went on to chastise Sweeney for scoffing at the cleanup effort, calling his remarks "a new low in political morality even for the oft-elected gentleman." This was debatable. A few months earlier, Sweeney had roused himself on the floor of the United States House of Representatives to oppose a resolution of condolence on the death of Britain's King George V, shouting a vigorous "No" when the motion was put to a vote. His colleagues expressed embarrassment. "There are many ways of showing bad taste," a reporter noted, "but there is no excuse when bad taste is put on parade."

Ness could afford to brush off Sweeney's attacks. Even as the congressman railed against the "political prosecution of policemen," the public appeared united in praise as Ness brought another case to trial, resulting in the removal of Deputy Police Inspector Edwin Burns on graft charges. Sweeney declined to comment on the Burns case, drawing a taunt in the next day's papers: "Martin L. Sweeney Has Nothing to Say." Ness clipped the item for his scrapbook.

Sweeney would not stay silent for long, and to some extent his confusion over the tally of the butcher's victims underscored a growing sense of frustration among the investigators. The bodies found in New

Castle remained a subject of considerable speculation at the time, and a more recent discovery closer to home had thrown a fresh layer of uncertainty over the case.

On the afternoon of February 23, fifty-five-year-old Robert Smith had come down to the shore of Lake Erie, not far from the Euclid Beach amusement park, to check on a sailboat he had stored for the winter. The day was frigid and gray, and Smith took the opportunity to gather some driftwood to burn in his stove. As he neared the shoreline, he caught sight of a white object snagged in the shallow water. "At first I thought it was the body of a dog or a sheep," Smith told the *Plain Dealer*, but as he stepped closer he glimpsed the outlines of a human form—"part of a body," he said, "so I notified the police."

Lieutenant William Sargent reached the scene within minutes, followed closely by Sergeant James Hogan, who had only recently wrapped up his labors at the "murder pool." Inspector Joseph Sweeney and Detective Orley May were close behind, among others. While waiting for the others to arrive, Hogan alertly scanned the beach and noted only two sets of footprints in the sand, those of Robert Smith and Lieutenant Sargent. It seemed unlikely, therefore, that the killer had carried the remains to the shoreline and hurled them into the lake. Instead, Hogan reasoned, they must have entered the water at some other point, or perhaps from a boat. In light of recent weather patterns, Hogan concluded that the remains must have drifted toward shore recently, while the winds were relatively calm, rather than during the choppy weather earlier in the week. "The piece probably appeared in the last two days," the sergeant explained. "If it had floated up when the waves were high it would have been thrown far up on the beach." His conjectures were later confirmed; a pair of boys had been at the same spot a day earlier, skipping stones into the water, and had seen nothing.

After their brief scan of the scene, Hogan and Sargent waded into the icy water and pulled the floating object to shore. The remains, they now saw clearly, comprised the upper half of a woman's torso, with the head and arms removed. Hogan carefully wrapped the sodden torso in a blanket and dispatched it to the morgue. Next, as a squad of officers converged on the scene, he ordered a search of the surrounding area. Detectives combed the beach for a mile in both directions, but no further remains were found.

The veterans of the investigation were quick to grasp a special significance in this latest crime. The remains had appeared almost at the very spot where the so-called Lady of the Lake washed ashore two and a half years earlier. Up to this stage, there had been no official consensus over whether that earlier fatality should be counted among the butcher's victims, but no one could deny the similarities between this new discovery and the earlier one. If this latest victim could be definitively linked to the first, it might change the course of the investigation.

At the morgue, County Pathologist Reuben Straus began work almost immediately, with Samuel Gerber, the new coroner, adding his observations to the findings released to the press. "Coroner Gerber said the woman weighed about 120 pounds, but would not estimate her height closer than five feet five or eight inches," reported the *Plain Dealer*. "Examination further revealed that the woman had light brown hair." No evidence of drugs or alcohol was found in her system, and the state of remains suggested that she had been in the water for two days. Straus added that the condition of the lungs indicated that the victim had been a city dweller. Traces of sand and weeds were noted, a sign that the body might have rested on the ground at the time of the dismemberment. Gerber also told reporters that he believed the victim had given birth, perhaps more than once. Straus dissented on this point, insisting that it would take at least three days of testing to be certain.

Both men agreed on a verdict of murder, but it remained unclear to them whether this was definitively the work of the butcher. Straus acknowledged that the dismemberment of the body followed the pattern of at least some of the earlier slayings. "A sharp, heavy knife was used to lop off each arm in two slashing cuts," reported the *Plain Dealer*. "Decapitation was accomplished with multiple cuts at the root of the neck. The lower cut was a single stroke across the abdomen, just below the lower ribs." There were, however, several deviations from the established pattern, one of which seemed especially significant. Straus reported the presence of coagulated blood in the remains, signaling that decapitation had not been the cause of death, as it had in most, if not all, of the earlier cases. This latest victim's head had been removed after her heart stopped beating. Even so, the papers lost no time in raising the specter of the butcher. "Find New Torso Killer Victim," declared a banner headline in that afternoon's edition of the *News*. "Fear Kingsbury Fiend is Amuck Again as Lake Yields Body."

Gerber clarified his views after closer study, declaring that the knife cuts in this latest case were consistent with those of the Kingsbury Run victims. Moreover, the killer showed himself to be "highly intelligent in recognizing the anatomical landmarks as they were approached," suggesting formal medical training. Gerber also added some general observations about the series of crimes. He remarked that sexual perversion likely did not play a role in the crimes, or so he believed, since the killer targeted both genders. Instead, the coroner concluded, some combination of drugs and alcohol probably served to unleash the butcher's murderous impulses. Gerber's findings marked a contrast to the conclusions of Dr. Pearse, his predecessor, at the torso clinic just five months earlier. The clinic participants had backed away from characterizing the killer as a medical professional and had also leaned heavily on the likelihood of sexual perversion. Gerber, just a few weeks into his tenure, had moved decisively to put his own stamp on the findings, disagreeing not only with the previous coroner but also with many of the lead investigators. Soon, Philip Porter would note, "a little undeclared war" would break out between the coroner and the Cleveland Police Department, as Gerber began writing articles and making speeches about the killings. "This has miffed the cops," Porter wrote, "who feel somewhat properly that they have done a lot of hard, though fruitless work on the cases, and that the coroner was not intended by law to be a detective bureau." It could not have eased tensions when a pulp magazine published a lurid "as told to" piece under Gerber's name, encouraging readers to compete for cash prizes by supplying their own solutions to the "The Mystery of Cleveland's Headless Cadavers," in two hundred words or less.

At the morgue on Lakeside Avenue, the disagreements multiplied and compounded. Gerber omitted the earlier Lady of the Lake from his calculations, but Straus, the pathologist, saw a clear link between the two Euclid Beach victims, in spite of the two and a half years that separated the crimes. Straus declared that "the severance of the victim's trunk was identical in method and result with that of the earlier victim." He also pointed out telltale similarities to the remains found in Kingsbury Run. "He said the severance of this victim's head was almost identical with the severance in the other cases—a clean, bold stroke between the third and fourth vertebrae, a stroke resembling the skill of a surgeon," the *Plain Dealer* reported. Unlike Gerber, Straus would not specify whether drugs or sexual impulses had driven the killer to act, saying only that "whatever motivated the other crimes motivated this one."

Strikingly, Inspector Sweeney and Sergeant Hogan would insist that the two Euclid Beach victims stood apart from the Kingsbury Run series, if perhaps linked to each other. Sweeney maintained that the dismemberment in this latest case "was not marked with the same skill displayed in the others." Hogan agreed, later telling a reporter that the two women "were not victims of the mad butcher of Kingsbury Run." Even so, the pair were determined to gather more evidence, in the hope of clarifying the issue. "With the lake rolling the way it has," Hogan said, the search area would be wide, adding that there might even be additional body parts lodged in a breakwall some six miles to the west. He ordered a search, but it brought no result.

Hogan also directed attention to a pair of storm culverts that emptied into the lake close by. Although the culverts were blocked by snow and ice, Hogan consulted blueprints to plot out the entry points, on the theory that the dead woman's remains might have washed down to the lake during a heavy storm on the previous Sunday and left traces behind. "We believe the torso was either put in one of these culvert entries or was deposited in the lake from a boat," Hogan said. "The latter is less a possibility because boats in the lake these days would attract notice." Inevitably, Detectives Merylo and Zalewski had entered the fray by this time. When the blocked culverts became passable on Saturday, February 27, Merylo and Zalewski

made their way into a brick tunnel opening, accompanied by sewer workers. In all, they covered some ten miles underground, pushing ahead even
as the tunnel narrowed and forced them onto their hands and knees. The
big and bulky Zalewski had to climb out through a manhole cover when
the space grew tight, but Merylo pressed on even as the tunnel walls closed
in, "prepared to prod every inch." In the end, they found nothing.

By that stage, another possibility had captured their attention. On
February 25, a local pastor wrote to Merylo to draw his attention to a
suspected "refuge for unwed expectant mothers" thought to be operating somewhere in the area. Merylo took the information to Hogan, who
ordered his men to scour the neighborhood. A banner headline in the
Press seized on the lurid details: "Baby Farm Is Torso Clue." Hogan admitted that the hunt offered only a slim chance of a breakthrough, but
he couldn't ignore the possibility that this latest young woman "may
have been the victim of an illegal operation or may have died after child-
birth." If so, the hypothesis might also shed light on the fate of the earlier Lady of the Lake. Hogan reasoned that "the operators of an abortion
clinic or baby farm, having once disposed of another victim in this manner, might again take exactly the same steps." Coroner Gerber's earlier
pronouncement—that the victim had given birth—now took on added
significance, but Dr. Straus remained openly skeptical. The pathologist
told reporters that he did not believe the latest victim had borne a child,
or that she had been the victim of an abortionist. As he told a reporter,
"if the woman had died after an illegal operation, infection would be
present in vital organs." He had found none.

Merylo and Zalewski, meanwhile, appeared to have uncovered a
hot lead. While searching the neighborhood, roughly half a mile from
the place where the remains were discovered, the detectives came upon
a large bloodstain spreading across a pavement. Nearby, red splotches
led away in a pair of meandering trails, heading in the general direction
of the lake. Merylo speculated that two men had driven to the spot looking for a place to dispose of the latest victim.

David Cowles arrived to take a sample while Merylo laid plans
for a search of the shallow waters nearby. "It is the theory of Detective

Merylo that the stains are blood from the dissected body parts," a reporter explained. "The zigzagging which marks the trail was probably the path taken by the two men in their effort to avoid detection by residents." Merylo's theory that two men had produced these separate trails contradicted many of the prevailing assumptions about the case, notably that the killer operated as a lone wolf. Even so, the detective pursued the lead with his customary vigor, confident that it would provide a big break. A short time later, a newspaper delivery boy stepped forward to say that he had seen a dog struck by a car at the spot. The injured dog had limped away "yipping and howling," the boy said, leaving the crisscross pattern of blood that Merylo had attributed to two men. Officers confirmed the story by tracking down the dog's owner, according to the *Press*, which effectively "destroyed the hopes of detectives." Merylo's hopes were not so easily destroyed. A deeply obstinate man, Merylo refused to let go of the idea that the bloodstains would eventually connect to the butcher.

As this lead and others faded, however, an editorial in the *Press* captured a growing climate of despair:

> Eight dismembered human bodies found within two and a half years—and still no clew to the maniac or maniacs behind it all. Bewildered and outraged as the chilling discoveries mount, Cleveland faces a dilemma which holds the nation disagreeably fascinated.
>
> We ardently hope that yesterday's torso discovery will be the last.

Five months had passed since Mayor Burton put Ness in charge of the Kingsbury Run investigation, and this latest discovery was the first to occur on his watch. The city expected forceful, decisive action from its top lawman, but instead Ness's response to the latest discovery was utterly deflating: he was out of town at the critical moment. While Hogan waded into the icy waters of Lake Erie and Merylo prepared to crawl through storm drains, Ness was far from home, interviewing candidates for the post of city traffic engineer. This time, the hero of the Harvard Club appeared to have missed his big moment.

Ness had received reports directly from Gerber and Cowles, but the public wanted more from him, and he knew it. Had he wished to do so, Ness easily could have signaled a more active role. His search for a traffic engineer had taken him to his old Chicago stomping grounds, where he consulted with the Evanston Police Department, nationally recognized for its efforts in accident prevention, as well as the Northwestern University Traffic Institute. While there, he almost certainly would have stopped in at Northwestern University's famed crime lab, where he had spent a great deal of time as a young Prohibition agent, studying up on the latest crime prevention techniques and forging alliances with forensic experts. Now, as he grappled with Kingsbury Run, Ness and his secret butcher squad had begun making moves behind the scenes that would draw on the resources of the Northwestern crime lab, and he probably consulted with his old colleagues while on campus. It would have been a simple matter, when he returned to his desk at city hall, to have a quiet word with a friendly reporter, if only to say that he had a plan coming to a boil. Instead, Ness adhered rigidly to his "Facts First, Then Talk" policy, speaking only of traffic safety and his determination to "stop the slaughter on the streets." When he clipped the latest *Plain Dealer* headline for his scrapbook—"Ness for Traffic Engineer at Once"—he had to snip off the banner headline that had overshadowed his effort: "Quiz East Sider in Torso Mystery."

By that time, hopes of a breakthrough had faded. It would be three months before any further leads surfaced, and even then the response was muted. In early May, as the city prepared for the second season of the Great Lakes Exposition, a concessionaire testing a "swan boat" near East 30th Street spotted "another grisly trophy of the work of Cleveland's head-hunter" floating nearby. Members of the Coast Guard were summoned to retrieve an object that proved to be the lower half of a female torso. At the morgue, Coroner Gerber confirmed that the remains, remarkably well-preserved by the icy lake water, formed a perfect match with the section found earlier at Euclid Beach. Unfortunately, the find shed no light on the identity of the victim apart from prompting Gerber to revise his estimate of her age to "nearer 35." The general climate of pessimism now deepened. Gerber announced plans to test the remains for poison, but he and Hogan agreed that the latest find offered "no other new avenue for investigation." There seemed to be nothing to do but wait. Detective Orley May summed up the frustration in a gloomy remark made at Euclid Beach: "He gives us one regularly every five months."

The second season of the Great Lakes Exposition got under way at the start of June. New attractions included Billy Rose's Aquacade, a spectacle that "brought Broadway to Lake Erie" on a floating Art Deco stage, with a cast of hundreds of swimmers and divers, including Olympic champions Eleanor Holm and Johnny Weissmuller. That week also saw famed aviator Amelia Earhart embark on her second attempt at a 29,000-mile round-the-world flight. "I have a feeling there is just about one more good flight left in my system and I hope this trip is it," she declared before taking off from San Juan with navigator Fred Noonan. "Anyway, when I have finished this job, I mean to give up long-distance 'stunt' flying."

On Sunday, June 6, a fourteen-year-old boy named Russell Lauer made his way home from the movies on a route that took him underneath the massive Lorain-Carnegie Bridge. Overhead, a steady line of cars clattered onto the eastern approach of the long span that would carry them over the Cuyahoga River. The shadow of the hulking sandstone figures adorning the bridge, the *Guardians of Traffic*, fell across a trash-strewn lot below. Lauer had hopped off a bus before his usual stop so as to watch a Coast Guard detail at work on the river. A tugboat crewman had gone missing two days earlier, and the guardsmen had launched a dragging operation. After a few minutes, when this spectacle failed to generate any immediate excitement, Lauer continued on his way. About ten feet from the base of a towering bridge abutment, a flash of light caught his eye. Lauer drew closer. Bending down, he saw a human skull grinning back at him, with gold bridgework glittering in the late afternoon sunlight. "I didn't know what it was until I saw the gold teeth," he would tell a policeman. "Then I ran and told some men who were near the river what I had found."

Once again, James Hogan was among the first to respond, along with Orley May and others. Searchers fanned out beneath the bridge and quickly discovered an old wool cap, a remnant of a woman's dress, and a clump of crimped hair that appeared to be part of a wig. Crouching down, the investigators carefully brushed dirt away from the spot where the skull lay, uncovering a filthy burlap sack tied with a length of rotting hemp rope. Inside was a scattering of skeletal remains: ribs, pelvic bones, shoulder blades, and vertebrae. Even at a glance the investigators realized that the skeleton was incomplete—the arms and legs were missing. The sack also contained a grayish strip of some indistinct material and a scrap of newspaper from the *Plain Dealer* with details of a "Girls Review" that had appeared the previous year at Keith's Palace Theater on Euclid Avenue.

Already, this cursory inventory showed hallmarks of the butcher—a head separated from its body, missing limbs, discarded clothing, and a burlap sack of the type that had figured in the Florence Polillo case. After all the false alarms and dead ends of the previous months, however, investigators proceeded with caution. At the morgue, Gerber and Straus sought a consultation from Dr. T. Wingate Todd, a professor of anatomy at the Western Reserve University Medical School who had participated in the previous year's torso clinic. Soon, the coroner's office reported "definite knife marks" and "evidence of hacking and cutting" on the vertebrae. Gerber now felt justified in announcing that a link to the butcher had been established, adding that the victim had been "expertly dissected."

Other details would emerge in the days to come. Chemical tests revealed that the burlap sack bore traces of lime, a particular that recalled the original Lady of the Lake nearly three years earlier. Further testing, along with the presence of rusty hairpins, led Straus to conclude that the wig-like clump of hair found at the scene was actually a section of the victim's scalp, and that the grayish strip of indistinct material found in the burlap sack was likely decomposed human tissue. Gerber and his colleagues now concluded that the victim was "probably a colored woman," about five feet tall and weighing roughly a hundred pounds, perhaps in her thirties. The state of the remains indicated that she had been dead for more than a year.

The familiar problem of identifying the victim seemed all the more challenging in this case, given that the clues amounted to little more than a scattering of bones. Nonetheless, detectives set to work on scouring missing persons reports and canvassing the neighborhood. Orley May, working off the fragment of newspaper found in the sack, even took the trouble to question the manager of the Palace Theater, on the chance that a member of the "Girls Review" had gone missing the previous year.

Russell Lauer's attention had been drawn to the skull by sunlight flashing off the dead woman's dental work, which featured a distinctive bridge and three gold crowns. Peter Merylo and other detectives now hoped that a wide-ranging search of dental records would provide a match. Soon, a similar pattern of work surfaced in the records of a dentist in Cincinnati. The patient, forty-year-old Rose Wallace, had gone missing in Cleveland the previous summer.

This hopeful development quickly bogged down in contradictions. Coroner Gerber insisted that the victim had been dead for more than a year, but Rose Wallace had been seen alive at the end of August, barely nine months earlier. Matters became cloudier still when it emerged that the Cincinnati dentist who performed Rose Wallace's work had died fifteen years earlier, making a definitive documentation impossible. Gerber was reported to be skeptical of the identification, and some of the investigators admitted that it amounted to "no more than a good guess."

Not surprisingly, Peter Merylo ran with it. Merylo acknowledged the uncertainty, but he pressed ahead with his usual energy, determined to see where the identification might lead. Soon, a number of tantalizing possibilities surfaced. On the afternoon of August 21 of the previous year, Wallace had set off for a bar at the corner of East 19th Street and Scovill Avenue, in the Roaring Third, to meet an unidentified man. Later, she reportedly headed for a party on the city's west side, and was

subsequently seen riding in a car with three white men. She never returned to her home, also on Scovill Avenue, where a load of laundry
had been left soaking in a tub. According to one source, the pattern of
the tattered dress remnant found beneath the Lorain-Carnegie Bridge
appeared similar to the dress she wore at the time of her disappearance.

Like Florence Polillo, Rose Wallace had occasionally worked as a
prostitute, drifting through a world of "ephemeral loyalties and peculiar
friends," in *Press* reporter Peter Bellamy's delicate phrase. As detectives
dug deeper, it became clear that Wallace's orbit had intersected with Polillo's at various stages, opening a fresh and intriguing field of speculation. The bar where Wallace had gone on the day of her disappearance, it
seemed, had also been one of Polillo's haunts. Stranger still, Wallace had
regular dealings with One-Armed Willie, the man with whom Polillo
reportedly argued shortly before her disappearance. One-Armed Willie,
who the *Press* winkingly described as a "boyfriend" of both victims,
had been jailed for a week and questioned at length during the Polillo
investigation. Nothing had come of it, but now, if he could be found,
police would subject him to another round of grilling. Merylo told the
Plain Dealer that Wallace had "disappeared in the same circumstances"
as Polillo, and he felt certain the two crimes were linked.

By this time, a young man had appeared at the Central Police Station
asking to see the report on Rose Wallace's dental work. After explaining
his special interest in the matter, he received access to the file. "That's
my mother," he declared after a moment. "That was Rose Wallace."
Even now, the identification remained contentious. Merylo's conviction
strengthened, but many others expressed wariness. In either case, the
Rose Wallace angle had not brought any clarity to the investigation. If
anything, it had put another crack in the foundation. Already the killer
had defied conventional thinking by targeting both men and women.
Now, if this latest identification proved accurate, he appeared indifferent
to race as well as gender. Each new piece of information somehow had
the effect of drawing another veil across the face of the killer.

Eliot Ness's office at city hall was less than two miles away from
this latest crime scene. He could have walked there if he'd been feeling

energetic, but there is no record of the safety director putting in an appearance, much less dirtying his hands beneath the bridge. Possibly the early confusion and skepticism expressed by Coroner Gerber and Sergeant Hogan persuaded him that it wouldn't be worth his time. Perhaps, once Peter Merylo began running with the ball, Ness thought it best to keep his distance. The Rose Wallace story had broken at a politically sensitive moment, with Mayor Burton gearing up his reelection campaign. Of all the crime scenes to date, this one had been the least promising from the outset. Ness might have wished to avoid raising expectations in an investigation that stalled in its first moments, leaving himself open to attacks from Martin Sweeney and others. His caution would have been understandable. To this day, there is no consensus as to whether this victim actually was Rose Wallace, or whether she died at the hands of the butcher. Ness would have been sure that David Cowles and the butcher squad did their due diligence with the new findings, but in the end, he made no public comment. Privately, he was said to have expressed doubt over the identification, in spite of Merylo's assurances.

At the same time, Ness had a second, more immediate crisis brewing at city hall that week, one that would soon bring the city to the brink of martial law. At the end of May, members of the Steel Workers Organizing Committee, an early incarnation of the United Steel Workers of America, voted to go out on strike against Cleveland-based Republic Steel and other major independent producers, a group known as "Little Steel." In early June, as Hogan and his team were digging for clues at the Lorain-Carnegie Bridge, Burton and Ness were conferring with Ohio Governor Martin Davey in an effort to facilitate negotiations, a process that broke down almost immediately.

Although Burton declared a policy of "strict neutrality" in the escalating standoff, he saw that dramatic steps were needed to head off violence. As the effects of the strike took hold, Republic Steel made use of a small airfield on St. Clair Avenue to make airdrops of food and other necessities at their mills, bypassing the picket lines. On June 9, Burton went before the city council to revoke the company's permit to operate the airfield. The entire place, councilmen were told, had become a military-style compound with armed guards and barbed wire fences. "Is this the city of Cleveland in the twentieth century," a labor attorney asked, "or a feudal barony?"

At the end of the testimony, Burton and Ness decided to head out to the airfield to see for themselves. Burton rode in one car with a pair of officials while Ness followed in a second car with an airport commissioner. Reports of what happened next are fragmented and contradictory, but it is apparent that tensions ran high as the two cars neared the airfield. Striking workers had converged at the gates, spoiling for a fight. As Burton's car drew up, dozens of angry men rushed forward, apparently expecting a confrontation with strikebreakers. "Unaware of his identity, 30 or 40 pickets surrounded the automobile containing the mayor," reported the *Plain Dealer*, "and were apparently proceeding to overturn it." In some accounts, Ness is said to have intervened by brandishing a firearm to quell the violence, but the newspapers record only that the situation was defused.

Afterward, Burton waved off the incident as having "no importance," but he understood that more serious violence would likely erupt at any moment. Over the next three weeks, the crisis deepened with brutal clashes resulting in fatalities elsewhere in Ohio and in Illinois. Suddenly, at the beginning of July, Republic Steel announced that the strike had been "licked" and that four mills would reopen. Burton, anticipating further trouble, called an urgent meeting with Ness and Sheriff Martin O'Donnell to discuss emergency measures.

The atmosphere would have been frosty. A few days earlier, the Democratic Sheriff O'Donnell sparked a frenzy among "a couple of hundred rumor-carriers" by meeting secretly with Republican power brokers. The subject, it emerged, concerned labor leaders "who don't like Mayor Burton and Safety Director Eliot Ness." O'Donnell, a close friend and ally of Congressman Martin Sweeney, Ness's belligerent critic, appeared to be testing the waters in hope of mounting a challenge to "the boy scouts" in the fall election.

Now, with the "Little Steel Strike" building to a fresh crisis, political enmities had to be set aside. Emerging from the conference with Burton and Ness, O'Donnell issued an emergency order "establishing military rule in Cuyahoga County." On Monday, July 5, the city learned that "peacekeepers" were on the way. "This afternoon," readers of the *Plain Dealer* were told, "army trucks will roll into Cleveland bringing troops that will be stationed at the four plants to permit workers who wish to return to their jobs." Within hours, heavily armed National Guardsmen had taken up positions at "danger zones" in the Flats.

For some of these young guardsmen, the deployment soon took an unexpected turn. Shortly before dawn the following day, members of the 147th Infantry Regiment reported sightings of peculiar objects floating in the murky waters of the Cuyahoga River. Once again, the coverage was strangely muted, reflecting the urgency of the labor unrest and the degree to which the spotlight had shifted to a second, fast-developing news story reflected in that day's *Press* headline: "'Help—Sinking,' Amelia Radios."

Over the next several days, another scattering of human body parts would be fished out of the river—two halves of a man's torso; various segments of arms, legs, and hands; and a chunk of a human lung. Some of these grim parcels came in familiar wrappings of burlap and newspaper. "There is no doubt," Sergeant Hogan declared. "This is another of the series of torso murders." According to Coroner Gerber, this latest victim had been dead for perhaps forty-eight hours. Investigators speculated that the remains might have washed into the river, possibly from Kingsbury Run, following recent heavy rains. Reuben Straus, as he began literally putting the pieces back together at the morgue, concluded that the victim had been a muscular man about forty years of age, who stood five foot ten or under and weighed somewhere in the neighborhood of 160 pounds. A pair of old scars on the victim's thumb and a bluish, cross-shaped mark on the left leg were the only distinguishing features.

Alarming new developments came to light as Gerber and Straus probed further. Although this latest victim's genitals remained intact, the internal organs had been sliced and ripped out, which suggested an escalating level of savagery. Straus also observed "considerably more hacking than seen in the previous torso cases," along with hesitation marks indicating that the murderer's knife might have dulled with use. In spite of these variations, Gerber and Straus had no doubt that this was work of the butcher. "The killer leaves his signature every time," Gerber said.

Gerber and Straus managed to pull a set of usable fingerprints off the recovered hands, but found no match in police records. The burlap sack that had held one of the torso segments, originally used for chicken feed, yielded up a stray black-and-white dog hair, several strands of blond human hair, and a silk stocking with a run it. Detectives worked every possible angle, but none of these clues led to a breakthrough. Undaunted, David Cowles carried out experiments with ultraviolet light, an unfamiliar technology at the time, in an effort to lift fingerprints from the newspaper wrappings found with one of the body segments. Although the wrappings had soaked in river water for at least two days, Cowles hoped that his "flickering block of violet light" might bring out latent prints from perspiration salts absorbed in the grain of the newsprint. Nothing came of the effort.

In the meantime, Merylo and Zalewski doggedly worked their way through a fresh wave of tips and phone calls, many of them anonymous. Police took a middle-aged ambulance driver into custody following a barroom boast of his skill at "cutting people up." No one put much stock in his claim that he knew "all about the torso murders," but officers locked him up anyway, on the off chance that further questioning might produce something useful. In August, Coroner Gerber even mounted a reprise of his predecessor's torso clinic, presenting an elaborate gallery of morgue photos at a convention of the National Association of Coroners. It brought no results.

Many investigators felt a deflating sense of déjà vu as the leads went cold, but a *Press* reporter named Omar Ranney tried to make a virtue out of their energy and persistence, filing a glowing report on the round-the-clock efforts of the detective bureau. "This is the inside story of the greatest manhunt in the history of Cleveland," Ranney began. "The story of what Cleveland police and detectives have been doing to trace the mad butcher rivals any crime detection thriller." Sergeant Hogan gave the reporter a sampling of some of the leads he was chasing down, and displayed several filing cabinets bulging with letters, telegrams, and notes on telephone tips that had come in from all forty-eight states. Some were from fortune-tellers, mediums, and "other cranks," Hogan admitted, but he projected a reassuring confidence. "It's been a night-and-day job since the first torso was found," he said, "and it would seem like a pretty hopeless situation. But the cards are stacked against anyone who has killed 10 persons. We'll get him."

This optimism was typical of the coverage in the *Press*. Nevertheless, at a time when the paper's upper management was bankrolling the secret butcher squad, some reporters began turning on Ness. In his long-running "Most Anything" column, Jack Raper started taking potshots at the safety director's "exaggerated heroics," and deriding him as "Never-was G-Man Ness." It seemed to amuse Ness, judging by the number of these barbs preserved among his clippings, but the notices took on a sharper edge after the discovery of the latest remains in the Cuyahoga River. Raper now suggested, pointing to the National Guard's role in quelling the labor troubles, that perhaps Ness and Chief Matowitz might persuade the militia "to remain in town long enough to solve the torso murders."

Impatience with the sputtering investigation began to spread, throwing a shadow over Mayor Burton's bid for a second term. As the fall campaign heated up, Burton's Democratic challenger, John O. McWilliams, saw an opportunity to shape the contest into a referendum on Ness's "failed, pointless" efforts as safety director. McWilliams railed against "the myth of the super-sleuth, the great detective," while insisting that the city had become a "carnival of crime," with a police force demoralized by trumped-up graft charges. "What's the use of maintaining the Ness myth," voters were asked, "when it is not bringing results?" Congressman Martin Sweeney, Ness's most ardent critic, took to the hustings with claims that the safety director's reputation had been wildly overblown. "He was a prohibition agent, and he never caught Capone," Sweeney told one crowd. "His only claim to fame is that in Chicago he and his squad happened to run into a brewery where some old man was tending a still. They found out later that Capone had an interest in it."

The attacks grew darker as election day approached. Only a few months earlier, Sweeney had been excoriated for his efforts to drag the Kingsbury Run slayings into the political arena, but the public's mood had shifted as the investigation bogged down. Now, with Sweeney throwing his energetic support behind McWilliams, the butcher's crimes resurfaced as a direct challenge to Burton. "How was it possible," asked a spokesperson for the McWilliams campaign, "during your administration for the torso murderer to continue the most horrible series of crimes ever committed in any city under any administration?" McWilliams himself stopped short of placing the full blame on Ness—"I don't want to be a bit personal," he said—but his supporters encouraged voters to connect the dots. "Ten headless dead are crying out for vengeance," said Andrew Hagan, a former police captain and deputy inspector. "Who will be the next victim of this modern Dracula?" Along with the torso murders, Hagan claimed, armed robberies were on the rise, and women were no longer safe on the streets. "I charge that if the police department were allowed to run itself instead of being meddled with by theorists," Hagan told a McWilliams campaign rally, "it would solve this crime."

For a time, Ness tried to ignore the attacks, but Hagan's charges couldn't be brushed aside. As the race tightened in the final days, Ness called a press conference to refute the claims, producing a report to show that crime rates had in fact gone down under Burton's administration. Later, in a radio appearance, Ness avoided being drawn into a discussion of the torso murders, but addressed Hagan's statements about rising crime. "During the entire period in which he alleges that crime was riding rampant over the city, Andy Hagan made just two arrests, that of a drunk and that of a suspected gambler," Ness said. "The gambler was later released for lack of evidence." Burton himself gave unequivocal support, pointing out that the city had come too far to give up on the safety director's reforms. "I am asking the public not to let Eliot Ness down," he said.

In the end, Burton won reelection handily on November 2, but his opponent's criticisms had been galling to Ness. He had made extraordinary strides in cleaning up the city, and he believed that he was doing everything that could be done in the hunt for the butcher, but the public's support appeared to be wavering. For two years, Ness had been immune to the vagaries of politics. Now, for all the good he had done, his fortunes had become tethered to Kingsbury Run.

Five days later, on November 7, Ness received word that his seventy-three-year-old mother had died of heart attack in Chicago. The previous year, a *Press* reporter had traveled to Chicago to interview the "kindly and unassuming" Mrs. Ness, who shared stories of her son's adventures as a freckle-faced youth and declared that he had always been "prepared for anything that came along." He was not prepared for this, it seems. Outwardly, Ness absorbed the news with his usual stoicism. He made a grateful acknowledgment of the many public expressions of sympathy, which included an official "Resolution of Condolence" from the city council. Privately, he admitted to feeling deeply shaken.

His mood darkened as he and Edna made the long drive to Chicago. There had been a time, early in their marriage, when Edna took to waiting outside his office door in Chicago at the end of the workday, to make sure he made no detours on the way home. She had given up trying to exercise any control over his working hours in Cleveland, and often went for days at a time without catching sight of him. The marriage had come under additional strain in recent months, especially during the steel strike, which had brought a series of death threats. Edna accepted that long hours and a certain amount of danger came with the job, but she could no longer ignore that most of these late nights ended with liquor on her husband's breath and, occasionally, lipstick on his collar. Edna never commented publicly, but one suspects that she and her husband had a great deal to talk about on their drive to Chicago, given how little time they had spent together in recent months, or perhaps the marriage had reached a stage where they had nothing further to say.

Returning to Cleveland a few days later, Ness found that national coverage of Kingsbury Run had ascended to a new level, with a fresh wave of stories in "magazines which exist by appealing to morbid tastes." *Official Detective Stories*, a true crime pulp, published a lengthy breakdown of the investigation in its November issues, highlighting the most lurid aspects of the case:

> *One theory gaining approval is that the fiend is inspired by sexual jealousy. . . .*
>
> *He picks up his victims on the streets, finds them willing to submit to his perversion, takes them into his murder laboratory and prevails upon them to disrobe. He does likewise. Then, the stage set, he moves up in back of them, but instead of the degenerate act they are expecting he suddenly gashes their throats with his scalpel and indulges his unholy orgy while they bleed to death.*

One aspect of the magazine's coverage would have seized the attention of Ness and the detective bureau. *Official Detective Stories* offered a five-thousand-dollar reward to any professional investigator or private citizen who could supply information that enabled the magazine to be the "first to publish" information leading to the arrest and conviction of the killer. "It is the fervent hope," the editors wrote, "that this reward offer, and this complete summary of the man's hellish crimes, may hasten that day when the good citizens of Cleveland can live and breathe in security." This noble sentiment obscured a troubling reality: the investigation might well be subverted if a potentially useful tip went to a biweekly magazine rather than the Cleveland police.

Other magazines threw a spotlight on the frustrations of the detective bureau, and the repeated failure to locate the butcher's "blood-soaked abattoir." An account in *True Detective Mysteries*, purportedly written by Coroner Gerber himself, insisted that the investigators were utterly demoralized, and expecting worse things to come:

> The killer's laboratory has not been uncovered! And judging from past experiences, we feel fairly certain that another ghoulish product of this indescribable fiend will be discovered soon by some unsuspecting person.
>
> The question is: Who will be NEXT?

12

DO YOU KNOW THIS ROOM?

Don't ever veer from the path of strictly normal behavior in this town. One slip, and an inquisitive detective may come visiting.

Cleveland News, September 9, 1938

Decades later, David Cowles would receive an unwelcome telephone call at his new home in Florida. The former head of the Scientific Investigation Bureau had retired, reluctantly, in 1957, after twenty-eight years of service, but he never lost his passion for forensic science, and he kept tabs on the goings-on in his old department. "Dad never stopped reading Cleveland papers," his son recalled, "especially the police news. He stayed current and wanted to talk about it."

There was one case, however, that he never talked about. For several days, he had been fielding calls from a true crime specialist named Marilyn Bardsley, pressing him for details about the mad butcher of Kingsbury Run. In particular, Bardsley hoped to flesh out a vague but persistent rumor about a secret suspect known as "Doctor X," who was said to have come to the attention of Eliot Ness and his butcher squad in the early months of 1938. Bardsley had already spoken to several people with intimate knowledge of the investigation, and had pieced together some details about this mysterious, sadistic figure: a discredited doctor with a history of mental problems. The suspect not only fit the profile, but also appeared to take a perverse delight in being a target of investigation, and liked to thumb his nose at his pursuers, especially Eliot Ness. "He used to get drunk and call Eliot frequently at his office to taunt him," Bardsley was told. "He'd tell Eliot things that only the killer could know."

Over the course of a series of calls, Bardsley pushed Cowles as hard as she dared, hoping that she might gain his trust and perhaps even learn the identity of the mysterious doctor. Cowles was polite, but his answers were clipped and guarded. He confirmed some of the details she had gleaned from other sources, but he refused to give the suspect's name, honoring a promise he had made long ago.

Finally, after weeks of digging, Bardsley believed she had uncovered the identity of Doctor X, having teased out disparate pieces of the puzzle from various other sources. Hoping for confirmation, she gathered herself to make one last run at David Cowles. She dialed the phone and—without preamble of any kind—spoke three words into the phone.

"Who gave you that name?" Cowles demanded, and he slammed down the receiver.

On the afternoon of April 8, 1938, a thirty-five-year-old Works Progress Administration worker named Steve Morosky spotted something caught among a cluster of wooden pier pilings in the Cuyahoga River, at the foot of Superior Avenue in the Flats. For a few moments, Morosky poked at the object with a stick, thinking it was a dead fish. He soon realized otherwise and ran to call the police.

Within moments, investigators recovered the lower half of a human leg, severed at the knee and ankle—unmistakably the work of the butcher. For the veterans of Kingsbury Run, this fresh discovery would have been especially unwelcome. There hadn't been any "gruesome bundles" since July of the previous year, and the long interval had encouraged some to hope that the intense manhunt had sent the torso killer into hiding.

From the first moments, this latest discovery sparked confusion and debate. David Cowles, examining the find at the scene, could not even be certain of the sex of the victim, though the general contours suggested a woman. Cowles also took note of six long blond hairs, perhaps from the head of the victim, that had somehow adhered to the skin. The limb had surfaced at the mouth of a storm sewer, igniting a debate as to whether it had washed into the river from a distance, perhaps from Kingsbury Run, or whether the killer dumped it directly into the Cuyahoga. Witnesses reported seeing "a heavy-set man" walk into a storm sewer nearby a short time earlier, but Inspector Sweeney doubted that the limb had come through a drainage channel. The skin showed no signs of abrasion, he said, as one would have expected to see if the limb had tumbled through the sewers.

After a brief examination at the morgue, Coroner Gerber weighed in to confirm that the butcher had struck again. The dismemberment had been "expert," he said, perhaps performed with a surgeon's scalpel. The thirteen-inch length of the limb, he added, suggested someone who stood about five feet two inches. The absence of significant decomposition indicated that the victim had been dead less than a week, and that the limb had been in the water for no more than three days. "Crude knife marks," the coroner said, "indicate the slayer was in a hurry."

Gerber's findings seemed straightforward, but a series of turf battles broke out as the various detectives pressed ahead with their individual, often conflicting theories of the case. Many of these clashes took root in an incident that had passed largely unnoticed a few weeks earlier. On the night of March 3, a man named James Macka, an attendant at an oil refinery pump house in the Flats, saw a man get out of a car and throw a large bundle from the Jefferson Avenue bridge, near the Cuyahoga. From his vantage, Macka couldn't get a good look at the man, but "the car looked expensive," he said. Macka phoned the police, who began searching the area that same night. Officers found a large dent in the corrugated tin roof of a shanty under the bridge, indicating that a heavy object had struck the roof and perhaps rolled into the water. The next day, police and firemen dragged the river with grappling hooks, and even expanded their search into Kingsbury Run, but they found nothing.

Now, in the light of the new discovery, some investigators wondered if Macka had caught sight of the butcher disposing of his latest victim. Coroner Gerber did not take kindly to the suggestion. As a *Press* reporter explained: "Gerber's belief the leg was cut only two or three days ago would have to be reconciled with the date, March 3, when Macka reported this occurrence." Detectives were quick to offer a possible explanation for the discrepancy. If the bundle had become lodged in the mud at the bottom of the river, they said, the icy water might have preserved it uncommonly well. The leg might have dislodged and come to the surface only recently, in the heavy runoff of recent storms.

The dispute might have been resolved quietly if not for a clumsy intervention from the safety director's office, where a new executive assistant now served as Ness's proxy. A few months earlier, as the anticorruption campaign gathered momentum, Ness had been forced to accept the resignation of John Flynn, his previous assistant, who had become known as something of a political fixer, "the fellow to see to get a little phenagling done." Ness replaced Flynn with Robert Chamberlin, a rising young lawyer who "grew to think of Eliot much as I would my own brother." Chamberlin soon became so indispensable, the *Plain Dealer* would observe, that the job of safety director became "a two-man position."

Like Flynn before him, Chamberlin did a great deal of fieldwork on Ness's behalf to keep him current on the Kingsbury Run investigation. He kept a low profile whenever possible, and when he arrived at the Central Police Station following the discovery of the latest remains, he told reporters that "he would make no statement." His presence might have gone unremarked, but Chamberlin immediately ruffled feathers with a request that experts from City Hospital or Western Reserve University examine the severed limb, so as to verify the victim's time of death. The implication was clear: Chamberlin was attempting an end run around Coroner Gerber. Gerber refused to cooperate and, according to one source, physically blocked the door of the morgue to prevent access.

In theory, Chamberlin's request should not have raised Gerber's hackles. In the past, the coroner had consulted quite peaceably with outside experts, including Dr. Todd of Western Reserve the previous year. In this instance, however, Gerber took the request as an attack on his competence, in spite of Chamberlin's assurances to the contrary. "I mean no reflection on the Coroner," Chamberlin insisted, "but since there is a possibility this might even be the missing leg of the 10th victim found last July, the time of death is very important and I thought Dr. Gerber wouldn't mind other experts corroborating his findings."

In attempting to mend fences, Chamberlin had made things dramatically worse. His bewildering mention of the "missing leg of the 10th victim," referring to the remains pulled from the Cuyahoga the previous summer, called forth a fresh wave of indignation from Gerber. The earlier crime had occurred at least nine months prior, whereas Gerber had placed the more recent victim's time of death within the past week. It was possible, certainly, that Gerber had erred, but he was unlikely to have made a mistake of the magnitude implied by Chamberlin's request. More to the point, both of that earlier victim's lower legs had been recovered at the time. Setting aside the possibility of a three-legged victim, Chamberlin appeared to have bungled the facts quite spectacularly. Gerber believed that Chamberlin was trying to twist the details to suit a pet theory. "I refused to let Chamberlin send in a person to examine the leg," he said, "because I want someone who is absolutely impartial."

On Tuesday, April 12, as the squabble between Gerber and Chamberlin continued, Peter Merylo rolled out a further complication in the pages of the *Cleveland Press*. A curious and unsettling gallery of photographs spread across the top of an entire page, under a headline that posed an intriguing question: "Do You Know This Room, Where Torso Victim is Shown?" The four photos showed Edward Andrassy, elegantly attired in a dark three-piece suit, as he struck a series of dramatic poses, gazing moodily into the middle distance. Behind him a garish assortment of objects and wall hangings could be seen—a Japanese lantern, delicate ceramics, ornate wall sconces, and framed prints of nude women stood out against a heavy floral wallpaper. Andrassy's poses seemed to reflect the odd tone of the room. In one shot, he had thrown off his jacket to recline on a bed, with his hands on his hips and his head propped up against an elaborate headboard. "Where was Edward Andrassy, torso murder victim, when these pictures were made?" the caption asked.

Two and a half years had passed since the discovery of Andrassy's dismembered body and severed head at Jackass Hill. In that time, investigators had combed through every scrap of available evidence many times. Even so, Merylo and Zalewski had gone back to the Andrassy home a few days earlier and asked to take yet another look at the dead man's belongings. Incredibly, while going through an old trunk, the detectives uncovered film negatives of the four mysterious photos, which had somehow been previously overlooked.

Merylo and Zalewski realized at once that they had stumbled across an important new lead. Hoping that the distinctive background of the images might jog someone's memory, they handed the photos over to the *Press*. "Detectives so far have been unable to learn where the pictures were made, or who made them," readers were told. "If you recognize the settings, the furniture, the pictures on the walls or the decorations, call or write the Cleveland Police Department or *The Press* city editor."

The following day, a man named John Moessner stepped forward and identified himself as the person who took the photos. Moessner, a fifty-six-year-old bachelor, was described in the *Press* as "a small, thin, hook-nosed man with piercing dark eyes." At the time the photographs were taken, some seven or eight years earlier, he had been living on West 28th Street. Andrassy had visited him there, he said, "five or six times." The two had met at Brookside Park, Moessner recalled, not far from the Cleveland Zoo. "Have you got a match, fellow?" Andrassy had asked. "I've got a bad toothache and need a smoke." Moessner recalled Andrassy as a "nice boy" with whom he had quickly struck up a friendship. On one of Andrassy's visits, he brought along a camera and asked Moessner to take the photos that Merylo and Zalewski had found.

Moessner had moved away from West 28th Street in the intervening years and now lived quietly with his two sisters on Fulton Road, not far from the home of Andrassy's parents. His new residence, a reporter noted, was decorated in the same "indescribably bizarre" style as the room in the photos. Aside from his odd taste in furnishings, however, there seemed to be little about Moessner to rouse suspicion. For some years, he had been the head usher at Public Hall, and had also worked as a food inspector in a restaurant. His sisters told police that he "never, never had visitors" and was always home early in the evenings. Moessner had come forward now, it seemed, in a sincere effort to assist the police in their investigation.

Even so, Merylo and Zalewski began probing Moessner's background with their usual energy. Matters took a dark turn when a young man came forward, having recognized the room in the *Press* photographs, claiming that Moessner had plied him with alcohol and made unwelcome sexual advances. Further digging revealed that Moessner had been convicted of petty larceny over the theft of some linens in 1929, nearly a decade earlier. Moessner protested that the charge had been a "frame-up" arranged by a parlor maid; she became enraged, he said, when he refused her romantic overtures.

In the eyes of the investigators, however, Moessner now made a startlingly rapid transition from helpful citizen to prime suspect. A search of his room on Fulton Road turned up sixty-seven pieces of silverware, apparently filched from various restaurants and hotels, though Moessner claimed they had been given to him by employers who owed him money. Soon, suspicious dark stains came to light in various places—on the floor of the attic, on two pairs of Moessner's trousers, and, perhaps most damningly, along the edge of a "discolored, long-bladed knife."

Investigators readily admitted that the stains on the knife were probably just rust, but the gathering doubts about Moessner now took on an irresistible force. Merylo grew even more suspicious when the search of Moessner's room turned up a photo of a young naval officer who bore a strong resemblance to another of the butcher's victims, the tattooed man. Under heated questioning, Moessner claimed that he could not remember the man's name. He had met the young officer "long before prohibition," he said, while tending bar in downtown Cleveland. If Moessner's recollections were correct, the man in the photo would have been considerably older than the tattooed man, who was thought to have been in his mid-twenties at the time of death two years earlier. Given how much

time had passed, Moessner expressed doubt over whether the man in
the photo could be traced. "I don't think you will ever find him," he told
Merylo.

Merylo's answer, as reported in the *Press*, showed a rising level of
frustration. "I don't think I will ever find him either," the detective said.
"But if he is alive, I have got to find him. If he is dead I have got to know
how he died. There is too much resemblance between this man and the
one whose severed head was found in Kingsbury Run in June of 1936.
The bulging forehead, the bridge of the nose, the ear—all the same."

Meanwhile, a technician from David Cowles's Scientific Investigation Bureau took scrapings of the stains found in Moessner's attic. Preliminary tests came up positive for blood. Moessner's sisters rushed to
his defense; their brother suffered frequent nosebleeds, they said, and
had recently come home bleeding heavily after falling off a streetcar.
Even so, Merylo believed he had all he needed. By the end of the day—
the same day that Moessner came forward voluntarily—Merylo took
him into custody on an "investigation" charge. Moessner strongly protested his innocence, but Merylo insisted he had cause. "Detectives believed that even if the man had no connection with the chain of murders
he might supply information," the *Plain Dealer* reported, "which would
give them their first positive clews on which to work."

Moessner's treatment raises unsettling questions over the degree
to which blinkered attitudes regarding "sexual deviance" shaped the
investigation. Any doubt over Moessner's sexuality would have been
dispelled almost immediately when police discovered a bundle of
"mash notes" from young men in his room. The detectives assigned to
the Kingsbury Run case were dedicated, experienced, and hardworking
men, for the most part, but their actions were undoubtedly colored by
the prejudices of the time. Merylo, in particular, was the product of a
long career working vice crimes, having once declared that "in Cleveland today there are 20,000 perverts running loose." Over the course
of the long investigation, Merylo and Zalewski received a great deal of
praise for the number of arrests and successful prosecutions they made
while pursuing the butcher. A large percentage of these were "good

pinches" that put known criminals behind bars, but there were also a vast number of men prosecuted on sodomy charges. Later, a homicide detective named David Kerr would recall Merylo as "sex nuts," meaning that he saw nearly all crime through the lens of sexual aberration. Kerr added that Merylo once had Zalewski strip to his shorts and run along beside some railroad tracks, in the apparent belief that he was setting out a lure for "perverts." If Merylo's biases were perhaps an unavoidable expression of his era and circumstances, it should also be noted that he made a sincere effort to educate himself on the subject of sexual behaviors. He studied the available literature and tried to apply it to the Kingsbury Run investigation. "I am of the opinion," he once wrote, "that the murderer is a sex degenerate, suffering from NECROPHILIA, APHRODISIA, OR EROTOMANIA." Many of Merylo's attitudes seem outdated and regrettable at a remove of several generations, but as always, he had put in the work.

In the case of John Moessner, Merylo's single-mindedness took its toll. Soon after Moessner's arrest, a small notice appeared in the *Press*. "There is another torso murder victim today—the friendship between Detective Peter Merylo and Martin Zalewski," the account began. "Smoldering dissension between the veteran detectives broke out into the open when Zalewski served notice he didn't want to work on torso cases any more and he didn't want to work with Merylo." The two men had disagreed loudly over how to proceed with Moessner. Zalewski argued for letting him go free under surveillance, but Merylo insisted on having him booked and questioned at Central Station. Angered by his partner's obstinance, Zalewski announced that he was "washed up." Instead of working long into the night, as had become routine over the course of the investigation, the detective went home at the end of his shift—an event so unusual that it drew comment in the newspapers. Merylo, meanwhile, dug in his heels at the station house, subjecting Moessner to a grueling round of questioning that lasted until three a.m. When reporters pressed him for details of the disagreement with his partner, Merylo sounded petulant. "Any recommendation he wants to make will be okay with me," he said. "Maybe I'll get a partner who'll work."

John Moessner spent at least two days in prison answering questions about his involvement with Edward Andrassy. Soon, tests on the suspicious stains found in his home would come back negative and the case against him would fall apart, but the ugly saga did not end there. By the end of the week, newspapers reported that Moessner had now been "charged with a sex crime." On May 21, a notice appeared in the *Plain Dealer*: "Torso Figure is Sent to Prison." Moessner, who had come forward five weeks earlier to volunteer information in response to a public appeal, received an "indeterminate sentence in the Ohio Penitentiary."

Looking back on this shabby episode now, even setting aside the inexcusable treatment of Moessner, one wonders what impact this widely reported incident might have had on the investigation. The message was clear: if you come forward with information, the police might stitch you up. Seen in this light, Ness's heavily defended secrecy is better understood. Ness had sent his butcher squad to circulate among the city's criminal element. The Moessner story would have had a chilling effect on potential informants. Anyone with an unorthodox background, much less a criminal record, would think twice about cooperating, knowing that they could well be charged with some unrelated crime. To a great extent, the butcher squad's prospects for success depended on staying undercover and off the books.

Ness had an even more compelling reason to keep the lid on his secret operations as the Moessner story broke. On April 9, during the flurry of activity that led up to Moessner's arrest, a stark headline appeared in the *Cleveland News*. It read: "Hunt Ex-Doctor as Torso Killer." The story, which did not appear in either of the other two major papers, revealed that a "once-prominent Clevelander, described as a physician in disrepute with his profession, is under suspicion." Although many other disreputable physicians had come and gone over the course of the investigation, this one stood apart. Coroner Gerber told the *News* that the suspect had been under suspicion for many months, but he declined to give a name. "The man, said to have discontinued his practice, is middle-aged," the account continued, "has some surgical skill and is described as being a powerfully built chronic alcoholic with apparent sadistic tendencies." In other words, he ticked all the boxes.

There was a reason the story had broken at this moment. A few days earlier, in mid-March, a dog emerged from the woods near Sandusky, about sixty miles west of Cleveland, with a severed human leg clamped in its jaws. "The leg shows as neat a job of amputation as I ever saw," the local coroner announced. "From the appearance of the bone it looks like a professional job, and I am sure a surgeon's saw was used." The leg, with its foot still attached, had apparently lain in the woods for months, preserved by cold weather and snow. Cowles and Straus were reported to be on their way to investigate. Robert Chamberlin, Ness's assistant and confidant, joined in a search of the area.

No records survive to document any conclusions that the investigators might have drawn from the severed leg. Behind the scenes, however, the discovery in Sandusky had galvanized the butcher squad. Their focus had now turned to a shadowy suspect known as Doctor X, an occasional resident of the nearby Soldiers' and Sailors' Home, a facility that attended to the needs of wounded and disabled veterans.

Doctor X had been drifting in and out of the frame of the torso investigation for several weeks. Some investigators had dismissed him as a possibility because his periods of treatment at the Soldiers' and Sailors' Home appeared to provide an alibi for some of the crimes. Now, following the discovery of a severed limb nearby, Cowles and the butcher squad felt that the broken-down doctor warranted a closer look.

The suspect was born in Cleveland on May 5, 1894, the fifth of six children. His mother died soon after his ninth birthday, and by the time he turned sixteen, his father had been confined to a sanatorium for treatment of tuberculosis, later transferring to a state mental hospital. Two of his brothers had also died by the time he turned eighteen. In 1917, he joined the army and shipped overseas, where he spent much of his two-year hitch working in medical supply. In August of 1919, he received an honorable discharge along with a designation of "25% disabled," entitling him to benefits under the World War Adjusted Compensation Act, or

"Bonus Act." Sources vary as to the exact nature of the disability. Although it was not combat related, some accounts indicate a head injury. Others claim he was exposed to mustard gas.

Returning to Cleveland, he enrolled at the School of Pharmacy at Western Reserve University, supplementing his spotty scientific credentials with courses at John Carroll University. Bright and ambitious, he secured a place at the Saint Louis University School of Medicine in 1924. In the summer following his junior year, he married a nurse in Cleveland. Following his medical school graduation in 1928, he began an internship at Cleveland's St. Alexis Hospital, and by the following year, he had won his surgical credentials. Soon, he and his wife settled in Garfield Heights and began raising two sons.

The young doctor appeared set for a life of conventional prosperity, but both his marriage and his medical career collapsed within a few years. His wife filed for divorce in September of 1934, charging violent behavior, heavy drinking, and unexplained absences lasting for days at a time. By this time, she had also expressed public concern over her husband's sanity, filing an affidavit that resulted in a brief committal for observation at City Hospital. Eventually she would gain custody of the children and revert to her maiden name.

The doctor, meanwhile, was "going down and down and down with the booze," as David Cowles would say. His medical practice dwindled, and he did not appear to have a fixed address. He became reliant on barbiturates and was said to write prescriptions using assumed names to keep himself supplied. Court records refer to heavy drinking, hallucinations, and possible mental illness. There would be four competency hearings stretching over a five-year span from 1933 to 1938, but in each case the charges were dismissed.

"The suspect was a middle-aged man from a respectable family," one of Ness's investigators would recall. "A medical report that included a psychiatric examination stated that he had a 'frustrated desire to operate,' and this mental condition, combined with his surgical experience and evidence that he had been in the vicinity at the time when each murder occurred, made him a suspect who needed to be kept under surveillance."

From the first moments of this surveillance, the butcher squad took every possible precaution to keep their operation under wraps. Ness would have been appalled, on April 9, to see the *News* break the story open with its "Hunt Ex-Doctor as Torso Killer" headline. The suspect went unnamed in the accompanying account, however, which presented a thorny mishmash of details, apparently conflating specifics from earlier phases of the investigation with the more recent focus on Doctor X. The confusion mounted as Coroner Gerber weighed in, eager to assert his prominence in the investigation. "This man has been a 'hot' suspect for the last two years," the coroner said, adding that the ex-doctor had been under surveillance since the discovery of Edward Andrassy and the still-unidentified second body at Jackass Hill. Gerber's statements seem implausible and must be treated with caution, not least because the Jackass Hill murders occurred long before he became coroner—and before Ness and Chamberlin arrived on the scene—at a time when it was not yet clear that a connected string of murders was under way. Doctor X might well have drawn notice at the time, but Gerber wouldn't have had any part in it, and a prolonged surveillance effort at that early stage is unlikely. Gerber's comments were reported on the same day as his blowup with Robert Chamberlin over the so-called "missing leg of the 10th victim." It seems likely, in Gerber's comments about the "hot suspect," that personal animosity toward Chamberlin made the coroner even more territorial than usual.

Chamberlin's comments also caused an ill-timed headache for Ness. "Yes, we are watching him," Chamberlin said of the new suspect, but he quickly added, perhaps aware that he had said too much, "as well as two or three others." Ness, who had been tight-lipped about Kingsbury Run for months, was now flushed into the open. On a day that he would otherwise have spent talking about traffic safety and repairs to the Detroit-Superior high-level bridge, Ness instead found himself pressed to clarify Chamberlin's remarks. Speaking to a *Plain Dealer* reporter, Ness

appeared ruffled and defensive. He expressed hope for "an early solution" in the investigation but declined to elaborate, saying only that his
office had been more directly involved than previously disclosed. "We
have been doing intensive work for almost a year, but very quietly," he
declared. "I hope it will lead us to the end of the chain of killings." Following this brief statement, Ness retreated behind his wall of silence,
leaving his usual retinue of journalists confused and dissatisfied. The
story of the ex-doctor burned hot for one day and then, deprived of oxygen, sputtered out completely.

Ness had revealed almost nothing, but he would have grudged saying even this much. At that moment, he had only just begun to grapple
with the implications of the identity of his "once-prominent" suspect. It
would be many years before the real name of Doctor X became generally known, confirmed by the slamming of David Cowles's telephone in
Florida. In an interview from 1983, given after his conversations with the
true crime specialist Marilyn Bardsley, the eighty-six-year-old Cowles
approached the topic with unflagging caution. "I won't mention any
names," Cowles said. "A relative of his was a congressman," he added,
"and we had to be very careful how we handled him."

This remark, made almost half a century later, has launched a thousand conspiracy theories. The suspect's name, as Bardsley had discovered, was Francis Edward Sweeney. His "respectable family" included a
very prominent cousin: Congressman Martin L. Sweeney of Cleveland's
Twentieth District, the frequent antagonist and political rival of Harold
Burton and Eliot Ness. The irony of it strains belief. Congressman Sweeney had more than once attempted to gain political traction over "the
Ness-Burton failure to solve the torso murders." Now, Ness believed, his
butcher squad had not only solved the case, but they had identified the
killer as Congressman Sweeney's own cousin. One might have expected
Ness to unfurl a banner from the top of the Terminal Tower. Instead, at
least for the moment, he swore his colleagues to silence. He needed evidence that tied Francis Sweeney to the torso slayings, and he didn't have
it. He needed to bring proof to his ally Frank Cullitan that would stand
up in court. Otherwise, even a whisper of an accusation would backfire

spectacularly. Ness would be accused of political grandstanding, and Congressman Sweeney's family would close ranks, impeding further progress with the investigation.

Ness did not have the evidence he needed to make a move on Francis Sweeney, but he had a plan to get it.

PART III

WHO IS THIS MAD TORSO KILLER?

13

GAYLORD SUNDHEIM

Anything I whisper to a friend comes out in the newspapers the next day as if I'd shouted it from a megaphone on Public Square.

Attributed to Eliot Ness

The "Hunt Ex-Doctor" story had caused a one-day sensation, but the press fell silent as Ness clamped down. Even so, Ness had shown his hand, however briefly. Francis Sweeney, better known as Frank, had evidently recognized himself as the "chronic alcoholic with apparent sadistic tendencies" described in the *News* account. Strangely, he gave no sign of alarm. Instead, the attention seems to have delighted him.

According to Arnold Sagalyn of the Unknowns, who was occasionally pressed into service with the butcher squad, Sweeney soon came to enjoy playing "hide-and-seek games" with the men who kept him under surveillance whenever he was out and about in Cleveland. He took particular delight in tweaking their efforts to remain inconspicuous. On one occasion, he stopped short in the middle of the street, turned to the man tailing him, and formally introduced himself. Another time, after trolling through the downtown area for quite a while, he burst into a saloon that catered to the city's African American population and cheerfully ordered drinks for himself "and my white shadow." Sagalyn recalled an even more disconcerting moment, on one of his first assignments for Ness, when Sweeney shook off his pursuit by abruptly leaping off one streetcar and onto another that was passing in the opposite direction, leaving the inexperienced young operative stranded. "His maneuver exposed me, which was an embarrassing beginning to my career as a detective," Sagalyn recalled. Worse yet, when he returned to headquarters, Sagalyn found that Sweeney himself had already phoned to report the incident: "That young kid you had following me wasn't very good," Sweeney said. "If he wants to try again tomorrow, tell him I'll be in the men's department at Higbee's Department Store at 2 p.m."

Although it can't be proved one way or the other, Sweeney may also have begun prank calling Detective Peter Merylo. On April 10, the day after the "Hunt Ex-Doctor" piece appeared in the *News*, a report in the *Plain Dealer* noted that Merylo had been roused by a ringing telephone at four a.m. The man at the other end of the line promised "something for your investigation," but the tip proved to be nothing more than vague details of a "sexual irregularity." By this time, Merylo had been receiving phone calls of this type for many months, and apart from the unusual hour, this one did not seem to merit special attention. In the cold light of day, however, it seemed possible that the caller, who declined to identify himself, had been the butcher himself. As the *Plain Dealer* speculated, the slayer might have called Merylo at home "to learn of his whereabouts, knowing, probably, that the detective had been working at all hours of the day and was likely to appear in any section of the Kingsbury Run area."

In days to come, David Cowles would receive anonymous envelopes filled with newspaper articles about the torso slayings, along with a notation that they should be put "in my file." A drawing of the front door of the morgue also arrived, featuring a sign reading: "No More Bodies." Ness, too, found himself showered with curious items in the mail, including a photograph of a tree in an open field, along with a notation that advised him to "dig here." Sagalyn reported that leads like this one were always followed up, in spite of the suspect's known tendency for prankish behavior. "The tree in the photo was found and dug up," he recalled, "to no avail."

There were other suspects, as Chamberlin had indicated, but Sweeney had risen to the top of Ness's list. Some investigators were inclined to rule him out because of his periodic residencies at the Sandusky Soldiers' and Sailors' Home, which appeared to give him an alibi for some of the crimes. In fact, as the butcher squad had now discovered, Sweeney was able to come and go as he pleased much of the time. Years later, a visiting law enforcement professional would recall a night when Ness took him to a seedy bar and pointed out a drunk sitting by himself. "That's the man," Ness said, "we suspect is the torso murderer." Ness might well have been making a joke, pointing out a random bar patron and indulging a strain of dark humor that had developed in these years. But it is equally possible that he took his colleague to get a glimpse of Sweeney himself, who remained under constant surveillance while Ness brooded over the lack of clinching evidence.

By May of 1938, with public pressure spiking, Ness had decided on a bold plan of action. "This killer must be caught for the peace of mind of the city," the *Press* would note, "and its good name abroad." Ness, impatient with his lead suspect's cat-and-mouse games, gave the order to grab Sweeney off the street and bring him in for questioning.

Ness knew that he was on shaky legal ground, and he planned accordingly. He could have taken Sweeney into custody on an "investigation" charge, as Merylo had done with John Moessner, but even this flimsy legal pretext would have drawn too much attention. Instead, he had Sweeney brought to a specially reserved suite at the Hotel Cleveland on Public Square. There, Sweeney would be subjected to days and days of intense questioning at the hands of a small group of trusted officers, sweating it out under the watch of Ness, Robert Chamberlin, David Cowles, and a court psychiatrist named Royal Grossman.

It started badly. Cowles would recall that Sweeney "had been drinking heavy" when he arrived at the hotel, and Grossman added, perhaps fancifully, that it took three full days to sober him up so that questioning could begin. Ness didn't care how long it took. He had police guards stationed round-the-clock in an adjoining room, ready to intervene if Sweeney gave them any trouble. The arrangement allowed Ness and his colleagues to come and go when necessary, without any letup on Sweeney. They planned to wear him down with a rotating cast of interrogators, hammering away at his defenses, exposing cracks and contradictions in his story, and finally drawing out a confession. "We played on him for a long time," Cowles would say.

As Sweeney sobered up, Ness and the others caught sight of the malicious gamesmanship that the suspect had employed under surveillance. As the interrogation began in earnest, Sweeney flicked the questions aside with gibes and evasions. Instead of buckling under pressure, he appeared to gain strength as the barrage intensified, weathering the ordeal for the most part with detached amusement. He made lengthy digressions, at one stage inquiring after someone called "Slap-Hap McCord," presumably one of the men who had been tailing him. Some accounts report that he took special delight in squaring off against the slick, polished Ness, and sneered at the safety director's youth and inexperience. At other times, Sweeney seemed to grow despondent, complaining about his ex-wife's extravagances and worrying about pains in his hands and feet. Each time the interrogators tried to pin him down on the subject of the murders, Sweeney framed his answers so as to dodge any admission of guilt, but he pointedly avoided a direct denial. Instead, he sidled right up to the edge of confession and gave a wink.

The grilling continued without letup—"Possibly a week or two," Cowles would say—in sessions lasting eight hours at a stretch. It is a mark of Ness's frustration that he resorted to such strong-arm tactics. "Intelligence," he had declared the previous year, "must supplant brutality." Robert Chamberlin likewise insisted that Ness had phased out measures of this sort. The third degree, Chamberlin announced, "does not exist in Cleveland." Ness would have been acutely aware that his mentor, August Vollmer, disapproved of such methods, having taught his students to distrust confessions obtained under duress. Ness set his principles aside in this case, turning his back on due process. The investigation had brought him low.

Every so often, Sweeney's mask would slip and the air of amusement gave way to naked fury. During a moment when Ness happened to be alone with the suspect, Sweeney fixed him with an expression of such undisguised rage that Ness instinctively backed away toward the door to the adjoining room, in case he had to call the officers stationed there. Only then did Ness realize that the other room was empty. Sweeney's sudden anger had coincided with a change of shift, leaving Ness without backup. He admitted to feeling thoroughly unnerved.

Toward the end of the ordeal, Ness's methods swung back in line with August Vollmer's teachings. As David Cowles would recall, "We had Keeler come in with his lie detector from Chicago." This was Leonarde Keeler, a pioneer in the use of the polygraph, who was fast becoming the public face of this "new miracle of criminology." Ness had come to know Keeler at Northwestern University's Scientific Crime Detection Laboratory during his Chicago days, and followed Keeler's early work with "the Emotograph," as he originally called it. Though lie detector evidence was not admissible in court, Vollmer had become a vocal advocate. Ness's mentor is credited as the first to use the device in police work, and Vollmer had come to regard Keeler "with the affection that a father would a son."

Now, in answer to Ness's summons, Keeler flew to Cleveland carrying an up-to-the-minute portable version of his device. Somehow Ness made the arrangements in utter secrecy, at a time when Keeler's face was in the news for his role in prosecuting a hammer-wielding maniac. Sweeney is reported to have been amused at the arrival of the specialist, and he submitted cheerfully as Keeler wired him up with an array of rubber tubes, straps, and sensors. By this time, Keeler had administered tens of thousands of polygraph examinations, gauging subtle variations in blood pressure, pulse, respiration, and galvanic skin response, but it is unlikely that he'd ever presided over a session quite like this one.

Even a pro forma request to state his name sent Sweeney off the rails; he reportedly identified himself as "Gaylord Sundheim" before collapsing in a fit of spiteful laughter.

As Sweeney recovered himself, the polygraph session began in earnest. With calm deliberation, Keeler worked his way through a sheet of questions prepared in collaboration with Ness, keeping an eye on the sweep and pulse of the mechanical inkers that scratched across a scrolling strip of paper. Sweeney answered with the self-satisfied air of a man who believed he had total control of the situation. One witness suggested that the suspect seemed to think he and Keeler had established a fine rapport.

Sources differ as to how the session ended. Years later, Ness himself would give a brief sketch of the encounter to Oscar Fraley, his collaborator on *The Untouchables*. In time, Fraley would include a highly embellished account in a second book called *4 Against the Mob*, in which the suspect is shown studying Ness with "extremely calculating eyes" while fingering a razor-sharp steak knife from his lunch tray. "I think you did those killings!" Ness shouts in Fraley's telling. "Prove it!" Sweeney answers with a contemptuous laugh. "I happen to know that those lie detector tests are not admissible evidence!"

David Cowles's account makes no mention of steak knives or shouted accusations, but he did recall a dramatic pronouncement from Keeler as he packed up his equipment. "When Keeler got through, he said he was the man, no question about it," Cowles recalled. He quoted Keeler as saying, "I may as well throw my machine out the window if I say anything else."

Even now, Ness sought a second opinion, bringing in John Larson, an expert who was known to be even more clinically rigorous than Keeler. Larson was the first policeman in America with a PhD, and he is also credited as the inventor of the polygraph in the form widely in use at the time. Larson and Keeler often diverged in their approaches; if their results agreed in this case, Ness could feel confident of the verdict. Larson arrived shortly after Keeler's departure and carried out a second examination, finding "disturbances indicative of guilt" in Sweeney's responses. Cowles would report that Larson "gave us the same opinion" as Keeler had.

In the end, it made no difference. Ness believed wholeheartedly that he had unmasked Sweeney as the mad butcher of Kingsbury Run, but everyone present, including Sweeney himself, knew that he had nothing that would stand up in court. Everything in Ness's experience told him that the evidence had to be bulletproof. In Chicago, he had watched in despair as District Attorney Johnson struggled in vain to assemble a Prohibition case against Al Capone, resorting instead to tax evasion charges. In Cleveland, Ness's successful partnership with prosecutor Frank Cullitan, forged on the steps of the Harvard Club, rested on the unanswerable force and clarity of the evidence Ness presented, best exemplified by his eighty-six-page dossier on corruption in the police department. Now, after some two weeks spent hammering away at his suspect, Ness had nothing apart from the lie detector results and a gut feeling. He knew he was on thin ice.

Weary and exasperated, Ness ran through his options. No fewer than three of his closest colleagues would recall him saying that he was convinced he had the right man, but could do nothing about it. For a long moment, Ness stood at the hotel window staring out into the street. Finally, his gaze swung to the man in the chair. Sweeney, by all accounts, looked crumpled but defiant, ready to go another round. It can only have been a crushingly bitter moment for Ness, after days and days of grueling effort. He sat down across from Sweeney and spoke in a flat, clipped tone, warning the suspect that he would be under surveillance from that point forward, possibly forever. Then, sighing heavily, Ness stood up and gave the order he had no choice but to give. Sweeney walked free.

Ten years later, in the movie *Call Northside 777*, Leonarde Keeler would appear as himself in a pivotal scene alongside James Stewart, administering a lie detector test to a criminal suspect. Keeler begins the session with a set of simple yes-or-no questions to establish a baseline for the accuracy of the responses. Surprisingly, the suspect appears to stumble over one of these basic questions: "Are you married?" Afterward, Keeler explains that the suspect, a devout Catholic, considers himself a married man even though his wife has divorced him, creating a wrenching internal conflict that registered as a lie on the polygraph. It is a pivotal moment that humanizes the man wired up to the machine, who had previously been only an object of suspicion. Stewart's character claims to have found "a whole new way of looking at this thing."

Nothing quite so tidy and cinematic occurred during the Sweeney interrogation. It is significant, however, that the scene played out at a moment when Ness himself grappled with a wrenching internal conflict. During the weeks he spent sequestered at the Hotel Cleveland, Ness's cheeks still showed the fading glow of a recent trip to Florida with his wife. Few people knew, however, that Edna had remained behind to initiate divorce proceedings. As he faced Sweeney, Ness was quietly brooding, at a time when divorce still carried a heavy stigma, over the potential damage to his career. Friends would recall that he considered resigning to avoid embarrassment for the mayor.

In a different time and place, Sweeney might have offered Ness a cautionary glimpse of the road ahead. Sweeney's wife had shut out her ex-husband completely when she divorced him four years earlier, reverting to her maiden name and avoiding any acknowledgment of the marriage. In time, Edna Ness would do the same. Decades later, even after her former husband had become a household name on television, she avoided any mention of him. "She lived incognito," a friend said of her. "Nobody found out until she was bad off."

It is too much to say that any shared experience might have humanized Sweeney in Ness's eyes. If, however, they had found themselves side by side on a pair of barstools instead of an interrogation suite, Ness might well have found "a whole new way of looking at this thing."

Roughly three months later, on the afternoon of August 16, three men—James Dawson, James McShack, and Edward Smith—went scavenging for stray bits of scrap iron, hoping to sell whatever they found to a junk dealer. They spread out across a sprawling, fetid garbage dump anchored at the base of East 9th Street, hemmed in by the Pennsylvania Railroad tracks and the newly completed Lake Shore Drive. Swollen with debris from the dismantling of the Great Lakes Exposition, the dump spilled out over several acres. Depending on the direction of the lake breezes, it sent regular blasts of foul vapor as far as Public Square and East 26th Street.

At around four, Dawson stepped away from his two friends to retrieve a wheelbarrow. "I was getting ready to gather some of the iron together," he said, "when I passed a little gully and saw what looked like a coat sticking out from the rocks." As Dawson climbed down into a five-foot hollow, tripping over jagged stones and broken concrete, he became aware of an insistent buzzing of flies. Drawing closer, he could see that the "coat" was actually a bundle of ragged cloth weighted down by a pile of rocks. "I took a couple of rocks off the bundle," he recalled, but after a moment he reared back, noticing a sharp, peculiar odor that cut through the general stench. Realizing that something was seriously wrong, Dawson called for his two friends.

Edward Smith, the oldest of the three, cautiously approached the weighted cloth, picked off a few more rocks, and lifted up a corner of the fabric. Underneath, he spotted a tangle of human bones.

As always, James Hogan arrived in the first wave, along with Peter Merylo, Coroner Gerber, and a large complement of detectives and uniformed officers. The bones proved to be a badly decomposed female torso, wrapped like a Russian nesting doll in a strange series of layers—a tattered quilt, a man's blue suit coat, and heavy brown wrapping paper. Nearby, police found three more grim parcels: first, a pair of severed thighs held together by a rubber band and covered in brown paper; next, another brown paper bundle containing the desiccated remains of the victim's head, with a short length of silky brown hair still attached; and, finally, a makeshift cardboard container that held segments of the arms and lower legs.

From the first moments, this one felt different. All agreed that the butcher had struck again, but not since Big Creek, more than two years earlier, had investigators found an entire body, including the head, in one place. At the same time, the remains had come bundled up in wrappings that appeared almost willfully distinctive, as if throwing down a bald challenge to the detectives. The quilt that formed the outer covering of the torso was colorful and homemade, a one-of-a-kind item. The blue suit jacket had a label that police would, as always, make every effort to trace back to its owner. The brown cardboard container had been fashioned from two separate boxes, each clearly stamped with a manufacturer's mark. One had held biscuits made in Cleveland and the other frozen haddock shipped from Boston. Even the heavy brown paper, used in place of the usual newspaper wrappings, seemed to carry a pointed message. It was the coarse, sturdy paper found in shops across the city to wrap meat and fish: butcher's paper.

A pair of burlap sacks and a crumpled page from a March issue of *Collier's* magazine added to the strange jumble of clues. The location of the remains, too, appeared to mark a break in the pattern. East 9th Street was almost literally in the shadow of the Terminal Tower at the center of town, a far more open and public space than any of the previous dumping grounds, so much so that a massive crowd of rubberneckers arrived almost in tandem with the police. The mob would eventually number in the thousands, with scores of cars clogging the adjacent roads. Not since the "murder pool" in September of 1936 had the police carried out their efforts so directly in the public gaze.

The autopsy began within two hours of discovery. The victim had been a white, light-haired woman between thirty and forty years of age, five foot four, weighing about 125 pounds. She had been dead not more than six months. The organs were missing, but Gerber and Straus could not be sure whether they had been removed or had simply decomposed. There were knife marks on the "articular surfaces" where the joints had been separated, a clear sign of the butcher's handiwork. The pattern of decay, together with the leathered condition of the remaining tissue, led Gerber to wonder if some of the body parts had been stored in a cooler or freezer of some kind. "Portions of it were dry and hard, as if preserved," the coroner said, "and looked as if they might have been kept in a refrigerator." Attempts were made to draw usable prints from the hardened flesh on the left hand, to no avail.

Little remained of the facial features, so the best hope of identification appeared to rest with dental work that included two silver crowns and a distinctive porcelain tooth.

Sergeant Hogan did not seem optimistic that anything more would be learned at East 9th Street. "But the hunt will go on," a reporter insisted, "and if the surface gives no clew, police probably will attack again with picks and shovels in the faint hope of finding something." As darkness fell, the crowd of spectators showed no sign of abating. Some, like thirty-nine-year-old Tod Bartholomew, appeared determined to make a night of it. Bartholomew, a metalworker, had passed the site on his way home from work at 5:30, and decided to return around seven with his wife and a friend. As they jockeyed for position among the swelling crowd of onlookers, Bartholomew became aware of a foul smell rising from somewhere nearby. He stepped toward the source and found himself peering down into a hole in the ground. Inside were the bones of a second victim. For some investigators, this seemed to sum up the three-year ordeal: the butcher had now killed so many people that bystanders were tripping over bodies.

Some of the lead detectives, including Hogan, had already left to begin tracking the slender leads gleaned from the first victim's remains. Now, as darkness fell, they found themselves recalled to the scene to process a second discovery site. As the investigators mapped out the new search area, fading light and the swarming crowd made their work all the more difficult. Gerber, who had barely started work on the first victim, returned from the morgue and began gathering up the second set of bones, anticipating a long night ahead.

Crime scene protocols were far less rigid in this transitional era of forensic science. A photograph taken at the scene appears to show Gerber gripping a skull with his bare hands, rather than using protective gloves. Sergeant Hogan, too, seems to have been working with casual haste, scooping up a large collection of bones at the spot of Bartholomew's discovery. Hogan's report relates that he "found the pelvis bones, ribs and vertabraes [sic] of a human being lying on the ground next to a can." What the report does not say is that he picked up the discarded can, which had once held forty pounds of plum butter, with the idea of using it—rather than some form of evidence bag or sterile container—to carry the bones to the morgue. When he glanced down into the can, however, he found a human skull rattling around inside. Hogan's reaction to this gruesome surprise is not recorded. One suspects, after weathering so many unpleasant discoveries of this kind over the span of three years, that he felt a mix of shock and exasperation. Even so, he carried on with his usual diligence. Soon, he assembled a large team of detectives and uniformed officers to search the entire sprawl of the dump, all the way to the lakeshore and railroad tracks. He supplemented the official force with some one hundred volunteer "torso detectives," a team of civilians who willingly took on the task of rooting through the city's rotting garbage.

Soon, Gerber and Straus were able to report that the second victim had been a white male, somewhere between thirty and forty years old, weighing roughly 150 pounds, who stood about five foot eight. They estimated that he had been killed between seven to nine months earlier, as opposed to the four-to-six-month time frame for the female victim. The dead man had a good set of teeth, there were signs of a broken nose, and police found scraps of newspaper from May editions of the *Cleveland News* scattered among the bones.

The chance of identifying either set of remains appeared remote, so the investigators concentrated much of their attention on the strange collection of wrappings found at the scene, with particular emphasis on the tattered quilt, the plum butter can, and the distinctive cardboard boxes. "Meager as the clews were, they were the most promising yet obtained," insisted a *News* reporter. Merylo seemed energized at the prospect. "He's changing his technique," the detective said. "Why, I don't know. But for the first time since the two bodies were found in September of 1935, he has left two victims together. And, again, changing his method, he left heads of these last two." To Merylo, this suggested that the killer had become careless. "He's smart but he's gonna slip up," he insisted. "I know it."

Most of the other investigators joined Merylo in offering their opinions, with one conspicuous exception. Once again, the latest atrocity found Eliot Ness away from the city, attending yet another conference on traffic safety. Even as thousands of Clevelanders kept a grim vigil at East 9th Street, the United Press reported that their "sprightly young Safety Director" had unveiled plans for a series of safety lanes where motorists could have their brakes checked. It was not the message that Ness's public wanted to hear. The man at the top of the police department appeared oblivious and aloof.

In fact, as Ness made his way back to the city, plans were under way for dramatic action in Kingsbury Run. First, there were pressing questions that had to be answered. Was Frank Sweeney responsible for this latest atrocity? David Cowles would state publicly that the dissection in both of these new cases "matched the technique of the previous murders." If Coroner Gerber was correct, however, their deaths were likely to have occurred before Ness's interrogation of Sweeney at the Hotel Cleveland, though the remains were almost certainly dumped afterward. Had Sweeney somehow eluded the butcher squad's surveillance in order to place the remains at the dump? If not—if someone else was responsible—had Ness's team been tracking the wrong man all along? Robert Chamberlin, Ness's right-hand man, scrambled to get answers. A photo taken at the scene shows Chamberlin hovering over Coroner Gerber as he probed some debris. As they waited for results, Ness remained determined to keep the lid on his pursuit of Sweeney. Already, however, in the coverage of the findings at the dump, there were fleeting references to a suspect "subjected to lie detector tests." Ness saw that he wouldn't be able to keep it quiet much longer.

Detective Merylo, who had now patched things up with Martin Zalewski, began running down the clues left at the dump site. The pair tracked the plum butter can to a company on West 9th Street, but several hundred identical cans had been sold in the previous year, and the detectives realized that it would be impossible to get any specifics on the can found at the dump. Next, the focus shifted to the two cardboard containers found with the female victim's limbs inside. Both sections of the makeshift box, investigators learned, had arrived in Cleveland two months earlier, in June. Since the female victim had been dead for at least four months, this raised knotty questions about the sequence of events leading to her discovery at the dump. The cardboard container segments showed little damage from exposure to the elements, suggesting that they had not sat outside for more than a few days. Perhaps the killer had carried the remains to the dump in the burlap sacks found nearby, and then, seeking to postpone discovery, concealed the body parts with wrappings found at the site. Or possibly he had scavenged the containers from downtown markets and bundled up the remains elsewhere. In either case, the female victim had been killed months before the cardboard containers ever arrived in Cleveland. It stood to reason that her body and, almost certainly, the body of the male victim had been stored elsewhere for a considerable time without detection. Once again, the detectives launched a round of speculation over a secret "murder laboratory" located somewhere in the vicinity of Kingsbury Run. "Where in this densely populated part of the city," asked the *Plain Dealer*, "is there a place the decapitation slayer can keep the lifeless bodies of his victims for several months before disposing of them?"

Merylo and other detectives believed that the so-called "murder quilt"—the distinctive, homemade covering found with the first victim—might guide them to the secret laboratory. Unlike the plum butter can and cardboard cartons, the quilt was unique. If it could be traced, it might yield insight into the killer's movements. The *Press*, echoing the plea for information about John Moessner's oddly decorated room, ran a photo of this "flag of terror fluttering over the city" and invited readers to "Help Identify Torso Killer's Quilt!"

After a wide-ranging canvass, detectives tracked the quilt to the Scovill Rag & Paper Company, a junk shop in the heart of the Roaring Third. This was the neighborhood frequented by two earlier victims, Florence Polillo and Rose Wallace. In fact, the Scovill Avenue shop stood only two blocks from the White Front Meat Market, where the baskets containing Polillo's remains had been found. This could not be a coincidence, police reasoned. "Detectives are confident the torso slayer has centered his bloody operations there," reported the *News*.

The quilt, police learned, had come to the Scovill Avenue shop earlier that summer by way of a junk dealer. William Blusinsky, the shop's owner, could not recall having seen it, and seemed baffled as to how the quilt could have found its way into the killer's hands. He explained to Sergeant Hogan that he had not sold anything at all lately; demand had dropped in recent weeks, and he was waiting for prices to rebound. Blusinsky saw no signs of theft, and it seemed unlikely that any of his employees could have taken the quilt, since he kept a close watch on the operation and made a point of standing at the door each day as his workers left the building. In spite of these assurances, Hogan detained six of the employees for questioning and ordered a search of their homes. Nothing incriminating came to light.

Blusinsky speculated that the quilt might have been stolen from the receiving platform outside the shop before it could be bundled it up with other rags. If the killer lived or worked in the neighborhood, as the detectives now believed, perhaps he passed by the receiving platform on a regular basis. Police crews made a sweep of the neighborhood "in the hope of finding the slayer's death house." At the same time, plans were made for a roundup of two hundred of the city's junk peddlers.

Even as the search of the Roaring Third intensified, veterans of the case continued to puzzle over why the killer had shifted to a fresh site for the disposal of his victims. Possibly Kingsbury Run had become too risky with Merylo and others constantly on the prowl. The 9th Street location, investigators noted, offered many of the same advantages. There were no houses anywhere nearby, but the central location, as the *Plain Dealer* observed, "requires only a short trip by automobile to arrive at, and a dark trip, too, that avoids the danger of being seen." In the early hours of the morning, "there would be no witness to an automobile stopping at the roadside or the dark shadow of a man carrying a bulky bundle for disposal."

This much was true, but privately, some wondered if there was another, even more sinister layer of calculation in the selection of the spot. The East 9th Street dump lay within sight of city hall. In fact, as several commentators would note, the spot where the bodies were recovered might even have been glimpsed from the window of Ness's office. For the butcher squad, a disturbing possibility took shape: If this was, in fact, Frank Sweeney's handiwork, had he chosen this dumping ground to thumb his nose at their efforts? Was Sweeney demonstrating how easily he could shake off the best efforts of Ness and his surveillance team, perhaps using a confederate to do his dirty work?

There would be a further complication in the days to come. Soon, the unclaimed remains from the East 9th Street dump would transfer to the Western Reserve University Medical School, in accordance with Ohio law, where they came to the attention of Dr. T. Wingate Todd, the anatomy professor who had consulted on the torso case previously. Dr. Todd examined the remains and reached a potentially explosive conclusion, which he immediately shared with David Cowles. The female victim's remains, Todd believed, had been embalmed. That being the case, he continued, it seemed doubtful that she could be counted as a butcher victim at all. Although earlier victims had shown signs of exposure to chemical preservatives, Todd believed that this body, and perhaps that of the male victim, had undergone the more conventional processes associated with morticians, rather than some improvised treatment applied in the butcher's laboratory. If Todd's observations were correct, it meant that Gerber and Straus had completely botched their examination, calling their competence into question and casting doubt on the many conclusions based on their findings, not only in the current instance and but also in the earlier phases.

It is difficult to believe that either Gerber or Straus, both respected and experienced professionals, could have made such an enormous and consequential mistake. It bears repeating, however, that Gerber's predecessor Arthur Pearse had once mistaken a classroom skeleton for a butcher victim, demonstrating that mistakes were possible, at least in the more heated moments of the investigation. Possibly the earlier clash between Chamberlin and Gerber over the "missing leg of the 10th victim" sprang from qualms of this type. In any case, Todd and Cowles chose to keep quiet about their suspicions. Even so, Gerber became aware of the anatomist's views at some later stage and responded angrily, accusing Todd of unprofessional behavior. At least some of the lead detectives caught wind of the contretemps. Peter Merylo, in particular, came to regard the East 9th Street bodies with skepticism. In later writings, Merylo would omit the female victim from his tally of the butcher's crimes.

There would be no independent verification of Todd's assertion, and no official records concerning the incident have survived. Various threads of speculation persist, however, one of which has proved especially durable. As far back as the finding of the first Euclid Beach body in September of 1934—the original Lady of the Lake—investigators raised the possibility that grave robbery had been a factor in the crimes, or that a "prankishly inclined" student had carried out a ghoulish stunt with medical school cadavers. Was it possible, as some would suggest, that the bodies placed at the East 9th Street dump had been someone's demented idea of a practical joke? Or perhaps a copycat had entered the frame? Either scenario would have gone a long way toward explaining inconsistencies that continued to plague the investigators. More than one source would suggest, however, that the butcher himself might have placed the remains at East 9th Street in any case, even if those individuals had not met their deaths at his hands. Both Gerber and Cowles took note of knife marks consistent with those found in previous remains. If the intention had been to send a message to Ness, perhaps any body would do. The theory does nothing to prove or disprove the involvement of Frank Sweeney, however, and like so many other aspects of the case, the controversy over the possible embalming of the remains raises more questions than it answers.

A steady accumulation of frustrations had now brought Ness to a turning point. As an anxious mood gripped the city, the United Press told readers across the country that "the mad butcher of Kingsbury Run was as far away from capture today as at any time in his four-year reign of torso murder terror." The public had not been appeased by Ness's vague assurances of working "very quietly" behind the scenes. "What about the torso murders?" wondered reporter C. William Duncan in an otherwise flattering survey of the safety director's accomplishments. "How can the people praise Ness so highly with all those unsolved crimes on his hands?" When this challenge was put to Ness directly, his response left the reporter underwhelmed. "Director Ness refused to become excited over the torso murder question," Duncan remarked. "It is said he never is excited about anything." Ness appeared to feel justified in this tranquil approach, the reporter continued, because the killer preyed on vagrants rather than prominent citizens. "Of course Ness wants to catch the torso murderer and his men will get the killer in time," Duncan said flatly. "But Ness refuses to get excited."

Just after midnight on August 18—two days after the bodies were found at East 9th Street—a long line of squad cars rolled past Collision Bend, a sharp, coiling turn on the Cuyahoga River. The eleven-car convoy made its way to a darkened parking lot outside a fire station overlooking Kingsbury Run. Two paddy wagons and three fire trucks waited at the edge of a hill leading down into the Flats. Twenty-five men, including David Cowles and Robert Chamberlin, climbed out of the cars and circled up for a briefing. Some of the men carried hammers and truncheons; others held flashlights and carbide lamps. At the center of the group stood Ness in a crisp blue suit with his gold badge glinting on the lapel, slapping a wooden axe handle against his palm. He looked excited.

The fire station stood alongside the massive Central Viaduct, one of the high-level bridges that stretched across the looping river. In the distance, as Ness paced back and forth reviewing his plans, the men could see flickering campfires from the city's largest shantytown. Ness would describe this hillside encampment as the most miserable group of squats he'd ever seen in his life. "I've seen terrible hovels in Chicago," he insisted, "but I've never seen the likes of that spot."

"The shantytown became the target of investigation," a reporter would explain, after the cardboard boxes found at East 9th Street were traced to the nearby Central Market. "Inhabitants of the area, typical of the homeless men and women who have fallen victims under the mad slayer's knife, are known to frequent the market district and carry off rubbish." Ness felt certain that the butcher operated in the vicinity, he said, because "the contents of the stomachs of some of the victims have been mostly fruit and vegetables, indicating they live off refuse picked up around the markets."

This was a very slender pretext for what Ness had planned. On short notice, he had cobbled together a team of raiders comprised mostly of uniformed policemen and plainclothes detectives to supplement his butcher squad. Under cover of darkness, they would strike hard and fast, swooping into the hillside encampment to roust the inhabitants and sift through their meager belongings in search of clues. Perhaps, if the stars aligned just so, they might discover something that would unmask the butcher.

Ness designed this bold stroke to send a message. For many of the men huddled on the hillside that night, it marked a welcome return to form, a reminder of the resolute figure who had faced down the gangsters at the Harvard Club. It had been six years since Ness drove a truck through the doors of a Capone brewery. Tonight, as he barked out orders with a heavy wooden axe handle in hand, it seemed as if the leader of the Untouchables was back in action.

Frank Sweeney was not mentioned by name as Ness gave his instructions, but the raiding party included most, if not all, of the small circle of men who had taken part in the Hotel Cleveland interrogation. These men understood the full weight of the pressures that had brought Ness to the hillside that night. In Chicago, he had been unable to hang any evidence around the neck of Al Capone. Instead, he weakened Capone by striking at the source of his power. Tonight, if all went to plan, he believed he could achieve much the same effect at Kingsbury Run.

Just after one a.m., a group of ten men led by Sergeant James McDonald stealthily made their way down the incline of the Eagle Street ramp, taking up positions along Commercial and Canal Roads to intercept anyone fleeing the encampment. Moments later, Ness led a second, larger group down the hill to the edge of the shantytown, sweeping the ground ahead with the beams of their lamps and flashlights. Pausing at the door of a corrugated tin shack, Ness sent a signal to the fire trucks above, then shielded his eyes as a bright burst of powerful arc lights illuminated the scene. Squaring their shoulders, Ness and his raiders charged forward, banging on the doors of the shacks and dragging the men inside out into the light.

"The place was thrown into an uproar of cursing and protesting men and howling dogs as the detectives proceeded methodically to enter all the 30 or more huts," the *Plain Dealer* would report later that morning, "bashing in doors when admission was refused. Several of the men appeared to be in a drunken stupor and had to be carried from the shacks." In theory, the raiders were hunting for clues, but it was difficult to see much detective work amid the chaos. They tore through the camp with swinging clubs and pounding hammers, battering away at cardboard, tin, and tar paper, and scattering the few possessions found inside the ruined hovels.

As the night wore on, Ness veered between extremes of compassion and brutality. At one stage, he could be seen comforting a vagrant who appeared distraught at the loss of his modest shelter. Moments later, when another hobo charged toward him with a shovel, Ness dropped to the ground and narrowly avoided a blow to the head. Policemen rushed forward and subdued the attacker with their truncheons, leaving him bruised and bleeding.

Shortly before two a.m., two smaller bands of raiders broke off and regrouped for a second assault on two smaller hobo jungles, both adjacent to sites where victims of the butcher had been found. One group headed west toward an encampment at the Lorain-Carnegie Bridge, near the spot where the remains of the woman identified as Rose Wallace were discovered. Within moments, they scooped up another ten vagrants. The other group moved off toward East 37th Street, alongside the notorious "murder pool," where they seized roughly a dozen unfortunates sleeping on concrete slabs beneath a railroad bridge.

Everything had been meticulously planned. At least sixty men were bundled into the waiting paddy wagons and carted off to Central Station, where they would be fingerprinted and locked up for the night. Ness even arranged for wardens from the Animal Protective League to round up the homeless men's dogs and cats. At the base of operations beneath the Central Viaduct, detectives picked through a pile of odds and ends pulled from inside the ruined shacks. If Ness hoped to find evidence of the butcher—a bloody knife, perhaps, or a stained rag or scarred chopping block—he would have been disappointed. Instead, a sad harvest of threadbare clothing, makeshift bedding, and worn-out shoes lay at his feet.

As dawn approached, Ness had one last duty to perform. So far as the next few moments were concerned, it really didn't matter whether Frank Sweeney was the mad butcher or not. Ness had resolved to scorch the earth and deprive the killer of his hunting grounds. Using thick cables and a power winch, Battalion Chief Charles Rees directed two companies of firemen to drag the remnants of tin and cardboard dwellings to the bottom of Commercial Hill, where they were soaked in coal oil.

Surveying the ruins, Ness gave the most controversial order of his career.

"Burn it," he said. "Burn it to the ground."

14

MISGUIDED ZEAL

Safety Director Eliot Ness' personally-supervised raid upon the packing box homes underneath the Eagle street ramp may contribute something to the capture of the torso killer. We doubt it.

Editorial in the *Cleveland Press*, August 19, 1938

For years afterward, people on both sides of the river would claim to have watched Kingsbury Run burn on the morning of August 18, 1938. The column of flame, they said, could be seen for miles. "Of course I remember the fire," a longtime resident recalled seventy-five years later. "You could see a dark cloud covering the east side—a greasy, dark cloud. It looked as if downtown was going up in smoke."

For a time, it seemed as if Eliot Ness's reputation had also gone up in smoke. Reactions ranged from stunned disbelief to outright hostility. By razing the shantytowns, Ness hoped to bring the killings to a halt by depriving the butcher of his prey. Critics dismissed the strategy as cruel and misguided, leaving the killer at large while scores of blameless men suffered the consequences. "The net result of the director's raid seems to have been the wrecking of a few miserable huts and the confinement of the occupants," the *Press* would remark. "We can see no justification for the jailing of the jobless and penniless men."

The criticism intensified as Ness subjected the displaced men to interrogation and confinement. About a dozen were found to have criminal records and were turned over to various authorities for prosecution. Those few who could demonstrate employment or family support were eventually released, but the vast majority, nearly fifty men, were sentenced to lengthy terms in a workhouse.

Ness claimed to have acted out of concern for the shantytown residents, but detractors felt that he had used the Kingsbury Run investigation to justify a politically expedient course of action. Cleveland had a long-established reputation as a haven for vagrants, with generous civic resources and abundant handouts from kindhearted residents, but many complained that the swelling homeless population presented a threat to public health. Ness charged that the shantytowns were riddled with disease and filth, violating innumerable city ordinances. "If you want that thing to continue," he snapped at one critic, "you had better repeal your ordinances."

The hard-nosed approach came as a surprise to many. In happier times, Ness had been "the easiest of marks," a friend said of him, always ready to help anyone who needed "a quarter for a bite." Now, speaking to the press, he appeared coldly indifferent to the plight of the city's transients. "Henceforth," he said, "such men will have to stay at the Lodge, where there are ample facilities for them." This reference to the Wayfarer's Lodge, a charitable concern devoted to assisting the "worthy poor," made light of the vast scale and complexity of the problem. By every measure, there were more homeless people in the city than any one place could accommodate, even one on the scale of the Wayfarer's Lodge, which featured a six-hundred-seat chapel. Even if this had not been the case, many of the city's vagrants resisted the stringent requirements of the Lodge, which included lock-ins and eight-hour work shifts. "I do not like to stay at the Lodge," said Adolph Jacoby, one of the men swept up in Ness's raid. "There are so many men and so much noise." Jacoby insisted that he much preferred to take his chances at a shantytown. "The torso killer—bah!" he told a reporter. "We're not afraid of him."

One voice stood out in opposition to the chorus of censure. The editors of the struggling *Cleveland News*, always eager to distance themselves from the two more prosperous papers, had been pushing Ness to "clean out the jungles" for months. Whatever reservations they might have felt about the severity of his methods, the editors now doubled down on their support. "Good work, Eliot!" ran a typical editorial. "The *News* urges him not to spare the ax and the hose, and not to let these camps for floaters and morons redevelop." The shantytowns had been allowed to multiply "in defiance of sanitation, safety and morals," another article insisted, "and in collusion with the degeneracy which produces torso murders."

One detail in particular kept the controversy churning. Ness made a point of emphasizing that the displaced men had all been fingerprinted at Central Station, so as to allow for ready identification if any of them fell prey to the butcher at some future date. This apparent focus on tagging potential victims rather than tracking the killer brought a fresh storm of criticism. The *Press*, in particular, raked him over the coals in a blistering editorial entitled "Misguided Zeal."

> Director Ness himself did not believe that any of the transients arrested in this raid and two similar ones was the butcher who has slain and dismembered 13 persons. He said he was convinced that it was from such transients that the killer selected his victims and that he hoped that the fingerprinting of those arrested might aid in the identification of possible future victims.

> To most of us, the arrest of the mad butcher would seem more important than the completing of arrangements for the identification of a possible corpse.

In fairness, the fingerprinting of any group of men rounded up in a police raid was largely a matter of routine, and no one had offered so much as a whisper of complaint when thousands of visitors passed through Ness's "finger-printing bureau" at the Great Lakes Exposition. In this charged atmosphere, however, Ness had made a grave miscalculation. He appeared to be conceding the inevitability of future murders and handing out cardboard toe tags instead of hunting the killer.

Ness might have blunted some of this criticism by having a quiet word about Frank Sweeney with a friendly reporter or publisher. Instead, he maintained his blackout silence on this piece of the equation, though Sweeney remained under close surveillance. One week later, on August 25, the landscape shifted once again as Sweeney made a formal request for residency at the Soldiers' and Sailors' Home in Sandusky.

It has become customary to observe that Sweeney took this step to place himself out of Ness's reach. His removal to the Soldiers' and Sailors' Home, coming so hard on the heels of the shantytown raid, is generally reported as the equivalent of committal to a mental institution to avoid prison, another cunning maneuver by Sweeney to slip out of Ness's grasp. There is much to support this interpretation. In time, as Sweeney passed through a series of veterans' hospitals, he would be diagnosed as a "schizoid personality" and subject to enforced confinement. "He is also a known drug addict with addiction to barbiturates," a later report noted. "He is considered incompetent by the Veteran's Administration."

In 1938, however, Sweeney's residence at the Soldiers' and Sailors' Home was voluntary. He had already established himself as a familiar presence in Sandusky, and he was free to come and go as he pleased. He might have removed himself from Ness's jurisdiction, but it is too much to say that he had locked himself away in a place where the law couldn't touch him. Ness knew this perfectly well. Later, a notation would be discovered in Sweeney's file indicating that police in Sandusky and Cleveland were to be notified whenever he left the premises. Ness would not have relished the thought that Sweeney's cat-and-mouse games might well continue in the absence of ironclad evidence. At the very moment that Sweeney bundled himself off to Sandusky, however, a report crossed Ness's desk that promised "the first real clue to the identity of the arch murderer."

Four years earlier, in the winter of 1934, Emil Fronek had been living rough in Kingsbury Run. Fronek had come to the city to try his luck in the rail yards and loading docks, but work was scarce and soon he was reduced to going door-to-door asking for handouts. On one particularly cold, wet winter day, he found himself near the intersection of Broadway and East 55th, within sight of the dark brick facade of St. Alexis Hospital, which saw to the needs of workmen from the surrounding factories and railroads. Close by, Fronek came upon a two-story building that he took to be a medical office of some kind. He knocked at the back door, and a man who "looked like a doctor" answered. Fronek judged him to be about forty years old, with a fair complexion and light hair that showed traces of gray at the sides.

"He looked me over and invited me in," Fronek would recall. "I was invited to sit down. He said he would give me some shoes. He told me first he would give me something to eat." The doctor disappeared into another room and soon returned with coffee and a plate piled high with meat and potatoes. This, Fronek would say, was "the finest handout ever offered me."

Scarcely believing his luck, Fronek bent over the plate and began shoveling food into his mouth while the doctor looked on with approval. "Then, suddenly, I began to feel sick," Fronek said. "I told this man about it and he said he'd get me some whisky. He went into the other room again but I was getting suspicious."

As the room began to spin, Fronek's instincts kicked in. He struggled to stand but found his vision growing dark at the edges. "All I could see was the door," he said. "I jumped up and ran out." As he stumbled from the building, Fronek heard a voice calling from behind: "The doctor said, 'wait a minute, wait a minute! Let's have some more to drink!' But I kept going."

Fronek staggered toward some nearby train tracks and managed to find an empty boxcar standing on a siding. Climbing aboard, he collapsed in a heap on the wooden planking. "Some other men found me there three days later," Fronek told the police. "I had been out all that time." Gathering himself, Fronek realized he'd been drugged. "I went back to find the doctor—to fix him," he declared, but the doctor was nowhere to be found. Later, as his indignation faded, Fronek took stock of what had happened. "In my jungle life I've never been afraid of any-thing else," he said, but in those moments before losing consciousness, "I believed that man in Cleveland would kill me."

More precisely, as Fronek soon realized, he'd been lucky to escape in one piece. As he moved on and took a job in Chicago as a dockworker, Fronek began to hear stories of Cleveland's torso killings. His encounter with the doctor, he now believed, had brought him face-to-face with the man responsible for those crimes. "Hundreds of other men in the jungles know of him," Fronek said, "and are staying clear." Occasionally Fronek would tell his story to his fellow workers. If he had not managed to stagger through the door, he said, "I would have been murdered, too."

In August of 1938, Fronek's story caught the attention of Chicago police, perhaps as a result of the renewed attention stirred up by Ness's raid on Kingsbury Run. The Chicago authorities sent word to their coun-terparts in Cleveland. Detectives Peter Merylo and Emil Musil were dis-patched to escort Fronek back to the city to give an account of his "night of horror." Word of Fronek's saga spread quickly, drawing headlines across the country. "Clue to Torso Slayings Found," read one. "Nomad of the Road Thinks He Was Slated to Be Butcher's Victim," declared another. It is a measure of the intense interest in the story, at a time of "urgent diplomatic efforts" leading to the Munich agreement, that pho-tos of a dazed-looking Fronek were featured on the nation's front pages as prominently as those of Adolf Hitler and Neville Chamberlain.

Fronek, too, had been at the center of urgent diplomatic efforts. A Chicago newspaper reported that the "middle-aged stevedore and some-time hobo" had at first been unwilling to return to the scene of his es-cape, claiming that he was afraid of losing his job. At length Merylo and Musil persuaded him to cooperate, promising that they would only need him for one day. Reluctantly, Fronek allowed himself to be bundled into a car, and the three men set off for the airport.

On the way, Fronek had an abrupt change of heart. When the car stopped at a traffic light, he suddenly threw the door open and bolted. The detectives exchanged an incredulous look before jumping out of the car to pursue on foot. The sight of the two men chasing the "bedraggled dockworker" along Lake Shore Drive soon drew a great deal of attention. By the time Merylo and Musil corralled Fronek, they found themselves surrounded by Chicago police officers, some of whom "fingered their revolvers and wanted to know if there was a kidnapping going on." The Cleveland detectives had some explaining to do before they were allowed to continue.

Touching down in Cleveland, Merylo and Musil were eager to get straight to work. Merylo had told the newspapers that Fronek's story, although decidedly "weird," fit the general blueprint of the butcher's crimes and seemed to confirm the long-held notion of a killer who preyed opportunistically on transients. If Fronek could bring police to the "house of horrors" in which he had encountered the doctor, the killer might finally be unmasked.

Despite his efforts to slip away in Chicago, Fronek now appeared ready to cooperate, warming to the attention as reporters clamored for a quote. "I'll never forget that fellow," he told them. "He had the queerest eyes I've ever seen in a human being. They didn't seem to have any color."

For all of that, Fronek's confidence had faltered by the time he reached the Third Precinct. As detectives drove him through the neighborhood, his memory of the night in question appeared to desert him. Though he quickly narrowed the search area to a five-block radius, Fronek seemed unable to pinpoint the killer's lair.

Suddenly, as the cruiser rolled past the St. Alexis Hospital, Fronek straightened, as if catching a familiar scent. The doctor's office was close by, he insisted. Hoping to jog his memory, Fronek's escorts parked the car and continued the search on foot, accompanied by "a small army of detectives." Once or twice Fronek paused meaningfully and stared at a particular building, his face twisted with the effort of concentration, but then he would turn and continue walking. Behind him, the officers followed patiently, their expressions fixed and determined.

As the afternoon wore on, however, hopes began to fade. Soon, as previously agreed, Merylo would be forced to put Fronek on a plane back to Chicago so that he wouldn't lose his job, and another promising lead would go cold. Though Fronek offered to return and continue his efforts as soon as possible, the sense of disappointment was palpable. "Tip on Torso Killer in Cleveland is Dud," declared a national headline.

The episode put Ness in an uncomfortable bind. Though Fronek's time in Cleveland had been worryingly brief, Merylo and the other investigators had been instructed to carve out time for an interview with Ness, who spent a full hour questioning the dockworker behind closed doors. Expectations were high as Ness sat down with "the one who got away," but nothing came of it apart from a strangely ambiguous statement in the *Plain Dealer*. "Director Ness said he did not think the story was related to the series of murders here," the paper reported. "Police, however, will continue to search the area on the possibility that a fantastic tale will lead to the fantastic slayer."

Many theories would surface to explain Ness's curiously muted response to Fronek's tale. Some said that the transient's story did not fit into the established timeline of the murders. Others claimed that the "butcher's lair" must almost certainly be located closer to Kingsbury Run and the center of the city. It bears mentioning that Merylo, who rarely discounted a lead of any sort, also expressed reservations about Fronek's story. Merylo told reporters that he felt confident Fronek had related an honest account of his experience, but the detective remained unconvinced of a connection with the torso slayer's "death den." It marked a rare moment of accord between Merylo and Ness.

It is possible, however, that Ness had a more concrete reason to take issue with Fronek's story, perhaps because it failed to align with his own recent efforts, and offered no confirmation of his suspicions of Frank Sweeney. Hard on the heels of the shantytown raids, Ness had authorized an aggressive house-to-house search of the neighborhoods on the periphery of Kingsbury Run, an area covering roughly ten square miles. The effort expanded on searches carried out during the "murder quilt" investigation, taking questionable liberties with due process. A fire warden accompanied each search party so that police could enter the homes under the pretext of conducting a safety inspection, thereby skirting the need for a warrant. Six teams of men put the ambitious plan into action, including Detectives Merylo, Zalewski, May, and Musil, all veterans of the investigation. Ness launched the effort on Monday, August 22, four days after the shantytown raid, operating under a press blackout. Over the course of several days, the search teams entered every single building in the Roaring Third and beyond—every house, every shop, every restaurant—but they failed to uncover any sign of the butcher's "murder laboratory."

The timing of the house-to-house search may explain Ness's oddly discordant response to Fronek, who arrived just a few days later. Perhaps Ness believed that his men had already ruled out the neighborhood in which Fronek claimed to have encountered the mad doctor, or possibly he simply refused to put stock in the confused recollections of the former hobo. Or perhaps, as many have suggested, a deal had been struck with Frank Sweeney's powerful family, and Ness could not bring himself to discard it before the ink had dried.

It raises the question, however, of exactly what occurred during Ness's one-hour meeting with Fronek at city hall. "I'll never forget that fellow," Fronek told the press that day. Is it possible that Ness spent a full hour questioning Fronek without showing a photograph of Frank Sweeney? If so, one can only conclude that Fronek failed to provide a positive identification. One possible explanation is that Sweeney's appearance had changed in the four years since Fronek's encounter. The events Fronek described took place in the winter of 1934, prior to Jackass Hill. The man who deposited the remains found at Jackass Hill had been powerful enough to carry a heavy burden down the steep, sixty-foot slope without drag marks—"strong as an ox" was the frequent description. In the months following his latest stretch at the Soldiers' and Sailors' Home, however, Sweeney would be described as "delicate," as well as "fat and soft." Had he gone to seed after four years of heavy drinking and prescription drug abuse, to such an extent that Fronek could not make a positive identification of a more recent photograph, or did Ness simply have the wrong man? Either way, when Fronek left city hall that day, Ness would have experienced much the same frustration that he had felt after the face-off at the Hotel Cleveland. Frank Sweeney remained an exasperating enigma, and Ness had nothing he could take to court.

Ness's oddly muffled statement to the press about Fronek highlighted a glaring contradiction in the public persona he had crafted. The city had come to expect a safety director who kicked down doors and collared bad guys, but Ness's larger agenda, his slate of reforms, rested on his ability to succeed as a bureaucrat. The issue came to a crisis in the first moments of the "murder quilt" investigation. Even as the drama at East 9th Street played out across the front pages, Ness was laboring mightily to phase in a "revolutionary experiment in American policing," replacing the entrenched system of call boxes and beat cops with a centralized dispatch station and a new fleet of police cars and motorcycles. "Ness expects virtually to make a relic of the old-fashioned beat patrolman," readers of a United Press report were told, marking a complete break from what he called "the methods of 1890." These remarks appeared on August 17, the day after the discovery of the bodies at the East 9th Street dump. Ness and his revolution were relegated to the back pages.

He knew that his window of opportunity might soon close. Mayor Burton, who would again be up for reelection the following year, had begun to make noises about seeking higher office, which meant that Ness's fourth year as safety director could well be his last. His sledgehammer approach to the Kingsbury Run investigation at the end of August had been a sincere effort to put a stop to the murders, but it was also a bid to regain momentum for his reforms. Had he apprehended the killer—or, better still, had he been photographed snapping handcuffs on the butcher's wrists—he likely would have been able to push his agenda through with ease. Instead, for the first time, his ears were ringing with the unfamiliar sound of criticism from a hostile press and an utterly demoralized constituency. He had taken a mighty swing with his axe handle and missed the target completely.

Matters declined sharply in the weeks ahead. In September, at a city council finance meeting, Ness managed to get into a shouting match when a councilman queried a vaguely worded $17,000 provision in the safety department's budget. As it happened, this was the provision that funded the Unknowns, leading Ness to conclude, mistakenly, that his secret team of investigators had come under attack. Amid raised voices and the thumping of tables, Ness lashed out. "We've saved the citizens a lot of money in our safety work," he insisted. "We're engaging in a complete reorganization of the police department. All that requires extra help." Ness emerged with his budget intact, but it had become clear that he could no longer count on unconditional support. The days of the Unknowns were numbered.

Meanwhile, newspapers across the country took note of a grim anniversary: three years had passed since the discovery of the two bodies on Jackass Hill. "Facing the ominous date, police were forced to recognize that the torso killer has established an all-time record in American crime history," reported a widely circulated King Features article. This wasn't true by any measure, as the United States had produced at least a dozen far more prolific killers by this time, but the butcher's "terrifying procession of unsolved murders" commanded special attention. The article's headline summed up the increasingly pessimistic mood: "Wait 13th Torso Murder as Anniversary Nears."

On the actual anniversary, Ness found himself dealing with a more personal crisis. During the third week in September, the news of his impending divorce became public. Pressed for comment, Ness insisted that the decision had been amicable. "We just agreed a mistake had been made and set about in a sensible way to correct it," he told a reporter. Philip Porter, who had covered the safety director since the beginning, speculated that the long hours had taken an inevitable toll. "He did not talk about it," Porter wrote in a later memoir, but it also seemed obvious that Ness's carousing played its part. "Women were attracted to him," Porter said, "and during his bachelor period, he never lacked for gals who were charmed by his boyishness." This was a diplomatic assessment because the same could have been said of Ness as a married man, and it was clear that his attentions to other women had not passed unnoticed at home. "Eliot Ness was one of the most attractive men I have ever seen or known," a female friend once remarked. "He wasn't handsome or flashy, but women were drawn to him. Women threw themselves at Eliot. That was his trouble."

For a time, Ness threw himself into the bachelor life with a verve that many found unsettling. "Eliot was a gay, convivial soul, who liked nothing better than to sit around till all hours, drinking with friends, or dancing," Porter recalled. "It seemed to unwind him to visit night clubs and hotel dance spots." He became so much a fixture of the city's nightlife that two of these dance spots—the Bronze Room at the Hotel Cleveland and the Vogue Room at the Hollenden—reserved a table for his exclusive use. His drinking now appeared to be gathering force. "He was not a heavy drinker," Porter insisted, "but he could keep at it for long periods without giving any appearance of being swacked."

Perhaps so, but he was swacked much of the time. "I would have two drinks," a barroom companion would say, "and he would have twenty-two. He would drink 'em like water." He could often be seen bending an elbow in nightclubs favored by racketeers and mob figures. He made a point of sitting with his back to the wall at these places, in the tradition of an Old West gunslinger, keeping his eye on the door. "It wasn't that he was afraid," a friend remarked. "I suppose it was just the prudent thing to do, all things considered. We'd kid him about it and accuse him of seeing too many movies, but he'd just smile."

Somehow Ness maintained his punishing work schedule from early morning to late evening, but his off-hours activities grew more and more erratic. On any given night, he might hop aboard a lake cruiser with a group of card players, drinking and smoking cigars as the boat headed to Detroit, returning just in time to clock in at city hall the next morning. Another night might find him shooting a .22 rifle at tin cans along the shoreline. This behavior left him vulnerable to "backbiting by his enemies," Philip Porter admitted. "They spread the word that Ness was a lush; so how could a man who was on the sauce all the time be so all-fired virtuous?"

Frank Sweeney remained under close observation in the closing months of 1938. If there was a bright spot for Ness in this unsettled period, it was that he could take consolation in the fact that there had been no further outrages. Some investigators dared to hope that the shantytown raid, for all the surrounding controversy, might have put an end to the killings after all. The police effort pressed ahead as energetically as before, however, while hundreds of tip letters flowed into Central Station, many of them addressed to Sergeant Hogan. "I'm getting to be pretty popular," Hogan observed dryly. "We've never yet received a tip that has helped us in our investigation, but we're still hoping that we will."

In mid-October, a tip came in the most unexpected form imaginable: as a "flash report" on Walter Winchell's Sunday night radio broadcast. Suddenly and without warning, America's brightest spotlight turned to Kingsbury Run. Over the course of eight years, Winchell's clipped, urgent delivery style, together with his trademark mix of news and gossip items, had made him a national institution, opening his broadcast each week with the words "Good evening, Mr. and Mrs. America from border to border and coast to coast and all the ships at sea. Let's go to press." Winchell was then at the peak of his fame and influence, with a newspaper column syndicated in more than two thousand newspapers worldwide.

On Sunday, October 16, a radio audience of some twenty million people listened in as Winchell delivered his latest breaking news item, punctuated by the urgent beeping of a telegraph sounder:

> Attention, Cleveland, Ohio. The unsolved torso murders, more than a dozen of them in Cleveland, may one day result in the apprehension of one of Cleveland's outstanding citizens. This is the legend brought to New York by a newspaper publisher whose name I promised to withhold. His editors are familiar with the rumors that a fanatic, a medical man with great skill,

is allegedly responsible for the gruesome crimes in which all
the murdered were dismembered. The Jekyll-and-Hyde doctor
is better described as having a typical movie villain look.

In Cleveland, the lead investigators were utterly blindsided.
Winchell had said just enough to demonstrate that he had a legitimate
tip, and his imprimatur gave substance to the vaporous rumors first
raised in the "Hunt Ex-Doctor" story six months earlier. Most listeners
believed that if Winchell said it, it must be true.

Winchell might well have received information pointing to Frank
Sweeney, especially if the unnamed newspaper publisher was Louis B.
Seltzer of the *Press*, who had ponied up the money for Ness and the
butcher squad. If so, a terse denial from Robert Chamberlin, issued in
time for the following morning's *Plain Dealer*, appeared designed to
quash any inquiries in that direction. "There is only the routine investigation going on," Chamberlin stated. "I know of no doctor who is to be
arrested." Technically this would have been true even if Winchell had
been referring to Sweeney; in the absence of hard evidence, there were
no plans to arrest this particular "outstanding citizen." Sergeant Hogan
and Detective Merylo also expressed doubt about Winchell's information, though neither of them was privy to the interrogation of Sweeney.
"We had no such suspect in our books," Merylo insisted later, "although
we had questioned plenty of doctors."

Though they were quick to tamp down the public's expectations, the
detectives performed due diligence with Winchell's report. Eventually
they traced the story to a steel worker in Indianapolis who had spoken
with authorities there. "The information looks pretty good," an Indianapolis detective was quoted as saying. "The steel worker named a Cleveland doctor. I think the Cleveland police will make some arrests pretty
soon." How this information made its way to Winchell remains a matter
of speculation. Winchell himself declined to elaborate, and by the end of
the year, many of the Cleveland investigators had come to regard the tip
as another dead end.

By that time, a second, equally perplexing development had emerged. Exactly fifty years had passed since Jack the Ripper's "Autumn of Terror" in the Whitechapel district of East London. The bloody saga began on August 31, 1888, with the murder of Mary Ann Nichols, the first in the initial wave of victims now known as the "canonical five." Many articles appeared in 1938 to mark this somber anniversary, and almost all of them noted the similarities between London's "surgically skilled maniac," notorious for killing prostitutes, and Cleveland's phantom killer of Kingsbury Run, whose list of indigent victims included two women also alleged to have been prostitutes. The Cleveland killer "enjoys demonstrating a dissecting technique acquired as a doctor, hunter, nurse or butcher," noted one commentator. "This same surgical cunning marked the horrible trail 'Jack the Ripper' left behind him in Whitechapel."

Up to this point, one element of the Ripper crimes had been conspicuous by its absence. Like the Cleveland police half a century later, the detectives at Scotland Yard in 1888 had been deluged with tip letters, most of which were easily discarded. The London investigators also received a huge number of letters purporting to have been written by the killer himself, three of which commanded special attention. One of them, headed with the phrase "From hell," came attached to a box containing half of a human kidney, and an explanation that the killer had "fried and ate" the rest. Two others, known as the "Dear Boss" letter and the "Saucy Jack" postcard, were signed with the chilling name that has passed into history: Jack the Ripper. The authenticity of these letters has been a subject of furious debate from the moment they appeared, but they took an immediate hold of the public imagination, shaping the contours of the drama and seemingly giving voice to an otherwise faceless madman.

On December 29, 1938, Detectives Merylo and Zalewski were summoned to the office of a Cleveland postal inspector, who handed over a piece of mail addressed to George Matowitz, the chief of police. The letter had arrived without an envelope, typed onto a sheet of paper that was folded and addressed in ink on the opposite side, and fastened with Christmas seals. It read:

> *Chief of Police Matowitz,*
> *You can rest easy now as I have come out to sunny California for the winter. I felt bad operating on those people but science must advance. I shall soon astond [sic] the medical profession—a man with only a D.C.*
>
> *What did their lives mean in comparison to hundreds of sick and disease twisted bodies? Just laboratory guinea pigs found on any public street. No one missed them when I failed. My last case was successful. I now know the feeling of Pasteur, Thoreau and other pioneers.*
>
> *Right now I have a volunteer who will absolutely prove my theory. They call me mad and a butcherer [sic] but the "truth will out."*
>
> *I have failed but once here. The body has not been found and never will be, but the head, minus features is buried in a gully on Century Boulevard, between Western and Crenshaw. I feel it my duty to dispose of the bodies as I do. It is God's will not to let them suffer.*

X

Many were skeptical from the first. The letter appeared too good to be true, with its fevered portrait of a maniacal DC, or doctor of chiropractic, conducting experiments in the manner of a latter-day Frankenstein. The phrasings and misspellings, too, carried echoes of Jack the Ripper's "From hell" letter, suggesting that the writer might have taken inspiration from the spate of publicity surrounding the Whitechapel anniversary. Even so, detectives in Cleveland and Los Angeles mobilized a coordinated effort. Within days, California police began searching a mile-long stretch of Century Boulevard but found no sign of a "head minus features." Merylo remained hopeful. "There are certain things in that letter that make me believe its writer knows plenty about the torso cases," he said. "For instance, he tells of killing somebody out there and severing the head. Then he buries the head 'minus features.' Several of the heads we found here were disfigured with lye." The letter, he insisted, provided "a very precious clue—the best tip we've had."

This smacked of wishful thinking on Merylo's part since there was nothing in the letter that could not have been gleaned from close attention to the press coverage. Within a year, following an exhaustive probe of the matter, even Merylo had come to regard the letter as a hoax.

By that time, the drama had taken a fateful turn, beginning on July 7, 1939, with a stark headline that touched off a firestorm. It read: "Bricklayer Confesses Torso Murders."

15

THE HOT SEAT

I was neat, clean, shaved and sober, and I didn't care who knew it. I was everything the well-dressed private detective ought to be.

Raymond Chandler, *The Big Sleep*

Lawrence J. Lyons, whose friends called him "Pat," was a private detective at a time when such men were called gumshoes and keyhole peepers. For several years, he had steady work from Ray T. Miller, a former Cuyahoga County prosecutor and onetime mayor of Cleveland. "Sometimes business was good and sometimes it was bad," a reporter said of him, "but he always managed to get along." Occasionally he butted heads with the Cleveland police. Once, while investigating a gambling parlor, he found himself hauled before a judge on the nebulous charge of "being a suspicious person." Lyons received a thirty-day jail sentence, but the matter appears to have been dropped before he served any time.

In the summer of 1938, Lyons had an idea. "I think I can do something with those torso murders," he said. He came to believe, he later explained, that all of the killings had probably been committed at the same spot, and that it must be a "very peculiar place indeed" if twelve or thirteen murders could be committed there, and the bodies hidden for days or weeks at a time without discovery. "It must be soundproof; it must be easily cleaned; it must have storage facilities, probably refrigerated," he said. "There can't be very many such places in the Kingsbury Run area, so it should be easy to find."

This was not an original idea, and as several other investigators had learned to their sorrow, the place was not easy to find. After a few months of futile effort, Lyons took his plan to Ray T. Miller, his former patron, looking to get official backing. Miller, now chairman of the Cuyahoga County Democratic Party, liked what he heard. Miller might well have seen political advantages in the endeavor, especially if Lyons happened to succeed. This may explain why he neglected to consult Eliot Ness or anyone else in the current Republican administration, and turned instead to a Democratic colleague, Cuyahoga County Sheriff Martin O'Donnell.

Up to this point Sheriff O'Donnell had kept the torso investigation at arm's length, citing jurisdictional issues. "If Sheriff O'Donnell and his staff had ever done any crime detecting," a reporter noted, "they had kept it a secret." As he listened to Lyons's plan, however, O'Donnell decided to take the plunge. "The solution of the murders was of such importance that I told him to go ahead," the sheriff later said. Taking a cue from his colleagues at the Cleveland Police Department, who were using fire wardens as cover for their search efforts, the sheriff brought Lyons aboard as a real estate appraiser.

For a time, Lyons carried out his search for the butcher's den with the assistance of two of O'Donnell's deputies, covering much of the same ground as Ness's house-to-house campaign. The county officials had no better luck than their city counterparts, however, and Lyons soon turned his energies to another channel. "We knew we had to change the pace," he said. "We looked for friends of Mrs. Polillo and Edward Andrassy."

Again, this was a trail that many others had already blazed, but the shift in focus appeared to bring results. Lyons soon discovered that both Polillo and Andrassy had frequented a grubby saloon at the corner of East 20th and Central Avenue. Better still, Rose Wallace had also been a regular. In fact, Lyons learned, Wallace had often been seen in the company of Polillo. Then, according to an account in the *Plain Dealer*, the detective and his deputies caught a break: "The proprietor of a fruit store told them one day of a man who loved knives and had threatened friends and acquaintances with them. This was Frank Dolezal."

Frank Dolezal, a fifty-two-year-old Slavic immigrant who worked as a bricklayer, was also a regular patron of the saloon at East 20th Street. Further digging revealed that the "short, ruddy-faced bachelor" had many attributes that neatly slotted in with the killer's profile. Though he now had a place on East 22nd Street, Dolezal had previously lived in an apartment on Central Avenue just a few steps away from the White Front Meat Market, where Mrs. Polillo's remains had been found, and the Scovill Rag & Paper Company, with its "murder quilt" connection. Although he had no police record, Dolezal was known for his volcanic temper. Other witnesses soon confirmed the fruit vendor's account of threats made with knives.

There was more: Dolezal had once worked in a slaughterhouse, Lyons learned. The detective also heard whispers that Dolezal was homosexual, or at least that he sometimes picked up strange men in Public Square and took them home. "Then we found out that Mrs. Polillo had lived with Dolezal at times in the past," Lyons said, and that he may also have been seen in the company of at least one other torso victim. "We found that he had visited Mrs. Wallace," Lyons revealed.

The detective also learned that Dolezal had moved out of his old Central Avenue apartment in August of 1938, around the time of Ness's house-to-house sweep. Lyons and the two deputies found the building and talked their way into Dolezal's former apartment. In the bathroom, they discovered dark stains on the floor and in the bathtub. Lyons took scrapings and passed them on to his brother Gerald, who happened to be a chemist. The initial results came back positive for blood. It seemed incredible, even to Lyons, that this seedy four-room apartment might prove to be the long-sought "murder laboratory," as it met none of the criteria that he himself had anticipated. It had no soundproofing, the cleaning efforts appeared slapdash at best, and there were no refrigerated storage facilities apart from an ordinary icebox. "If Dolezal is the torso murderer and if his apartment is the place at which most of the murders were committed, the joke is on me," Lyons said. "His place would be the last I'd pick at which many murders could be committed without bringing the police on the run."

Still, Lyons believed he had the notorious butcher in his sights. Soon, his confidence got the better of him. One night at a saloon, worse for drink and looking to impress his fellow barflies, Lyons hauled out a gold badge and announced that he was hard at work on the torso murders. To back up his claim, he popped open a briefcase and began showing photos and newspaper clippings. To Helen Merrills, the bar's proprietor, he sounded like a crackpot. After a few minutes, she picked up the phone and put in a call to Peter Merylo.

Merylo often got tips to the effect that a drunk was mouthing off about the torso killings, and his first instinct was to put Lyons on his list of potential suspects. Soon, Sheriff O'Donnell became aware that Merylo, the tireless bulldog, had begun sniffing around at the edges of the investigation he had authorized. O'Donnell moved fast, undoubtedly worried that Merylo and the Cleveland police would jump his claim on Frank Dolezal. "We decided to make the arrest that night," he said. On the evening of July 5, 1939, deputies of the Cuyahoga County Sheriff's Department placed Dolezal under arrest.

The sheriff and other county officers grilled Dolezal for roughly forty-eight hours straight at the county jail. Details of the interrogation were kept deliberately vague, though it became known later that the prisoner had only limited food and water, and almost no periods of rest. Finally, on the evening of Friday, July 7, Sheriff O'Donnell called an emergency press conference. Frank Dolezal, the sheriff announced, had signed a confession to the murder of Florence Polillo. Then, as shouted questions filled the air, O'Donnell stood back. Flashguns popped as the city got its first look at the prisoner.

Dolezal appeared slight, ragged, and deeply shaken in a blue, sweat-stained shirt and dark work pants, unkempt and unshaven after his two-day ordeal. "Although muscular and strong from years as a brick-layer," the *Plain Dealer* noted, his appearance belied the long-held belief that the killer must be a large and powerful man. Dolezal stood barely five feet eight inches tall and weighed only 157 pounds, far smaller than anyone had imagined.

Many would comment on the peculiar, unfocused quality of his eyes. "He seemed just as normal as you or I, but his eyes seemed to stare right through you," a neighbor would remark. "They were like Svengali's eyes in the movies." This comment appeared to echo Walter Winchell's description of a suspect with "a typical movie villain look," but the resemblance ended there. Dolezal was neither a "medical man with great skill" nor "one of Cleveland's outstanding citizens." In photographs, at least, no suggestion of an evil mastermind could be seen in his dazed expression. He looked like a man who had caught sight of a falling piano.

"Imagine everyone's surprise," Philip Porter wrote. "O'Donnell had stepped in where the Cleveland police had failed, and in so doing cast discredit on Eliot Ness, Mayor Burton and all the detectives."

As he took questions from the press, Sheriff O'Donnell admitted that he was not entirely satisfied with the details of the prisoner's statement. "There are some discrepancies between what Dolezal says he did and what are known facts in the Polillo case," he explained. "We want to get a confession that will hold up in court before we place any charges."

Until he obtained "the kind of confession we want," the sheriff declined to release a copy of Dolezal's signed statement. Instead, O'Donnell offered a summary of the prisoner's shifting statements over the two-day interrogation, leading finally to an admission that he and Polillo had come to blows over money: "Yes, I hit her with my fist. She fell into the bathroom and hit her head against the bathtub. I thought she was dead. I put her in the bathtub. Then I took the knife—the small one, not the large one—and cut off her head. Then I cut off her legs. Then her arms."

Having finally admitted to the killing, O'Donnell said, the prisoner filled in the rest of the details. Once Dolezal finished the dismemberment, he gathered up some of the body parts, along with a couple of items of Polillo's clothing, and carried them to the spot where they were found the following day. Next, at roughly four in the morning, he walked three miles to the shore of Lake Erie and threw the remaining body parts, including the head, into the water. Later, he returned several times to be sure the remains hadn't washed ashore. All of this occurred, Dolezal said, in the early morning hours of Saturday, January 25, 1936.

Before calling the press conference, O'Donnell had bundled Dolezal into a car and driven him to his old Central Avenue neighborhood. Dolezal got out, the sheriff reported, and pointed to the spot behind the White Front Meat Market where Polillo's remains were found. Next, O'Donnell drove the prisoner to the lakeshore, where Dolezal described tossing away the remaining body parts. Dolezal expressed reluctance to return to his Central Avenue apartment, the *Press* would report, for fear of "seeing Mrs. Polillo's ghost."

Incriminating details came to light as the sheriff's men searched Dolezal's current apartment. Four butcher's knives were seized as evidence, two of them bearing suspicious stains. Some reports maintain that deputies found the heads and shoulders from several female mannequins. There was also a scrapbook from which several photos had been torn out, O'Donnell said, but Dolezal refused to talk about the missing images. At his previous apartment on Central Avenue, workmen pulled out the bathtub where the suspicious stains had been found. Additional discolorations were seen on the floor and walls. Neighbors there spoke of seeing the suspect in the building with a host of familiar figures—not only Polillo, but also Rose Wallace, Edward Andrassy and an unidentified sailor.

These reports of Dolezal with other torso victims had come to assume extraordinary importance. Nationwide headlines now claimed that Dolezal had confessed to all of the Kingsbury Run slayings, but in fact he had admitted only to the murder of Florence Polillo. "He flies off the handle when those other murders are mentioned," O'Donnell said. This placed the sheriff's men in a delicate position. "Does the confession of Frank Dolezal that he killed and dismembered Florence Polillo solve all the torso murders?" asked a *Plain Dealer* editorial. "Or will he admit responsibility for only the one crime, leaving the other eleven in the category of unsolved killings?" Sheriff O'Donnell believed he had cracked the case wide open, and expressed confidence that there would soon be concrete evidence to link Dolezal to the other crimes.

Corroborating evidence came to hand the following day, it seemed. Lillian Jones, a twenty-two-year-old prostitute, stepped forward to say that Dolezal had attacked her just a short time earlier. "I was in Dolezal's room a week ago when he came at me with a knife," Jones said. "I jumped out of a second story window to get away from him. The heel of one of my shoes was broken when I landed." No other injuries were reported, but she displayed the broken heel to O'Donnell, who appeared satisfied. The sheriff declared that Jones's story "strengthens my suspicions that Dolezal was connected with other torso murders."

O'Donnell had a lot riding on it. As the glare of the national spotlight turned on the county sheriff, the political underpinnings of his actions were laid bare. "It looked as if O'Donnell had pulled a marvelous coup, and that the political repercussions would be colossal," wrote Philip Porter. "If the case stood up in court, his re-election would be assured and the City Hall Republicans, represented by Burton and Ness, would be in the dog house."

For O'Donnell, this would be a welcome reversal. The sheriff had a grudge against Ness that stretched back three years to the Harvard Club raid. O'Donnell had been the mayor of a nearby suburb at the time, and he was widely seen as a figure in the mold of the much-maligned Sheriff Sulzmann, who had declined to lend assistance that night. When Sulzmann left office later that year, O'Donnell was elected to succeed him. "Like his predecessor," observed the *Plain Dealer*, "O'Donnell hides comfortably behind a 'home rule' fiction." Soon, there would be a concerted effort to oust him over his failure to shut down "such festering and infectious sores as the Harvard and Thomas Clubs," which had been allowed to reopen under the sheriff's benign neglect. With fresh elections looming, O'Donnell's fellow Democrats saw him as a liability.

Now, suddenly, O'Donnell had turned the entire situation on its head. "Sheriff O'Donnell and his staff have performed a major task in crime detection," observed the *Plain Dealer*, while Ness and the Cleveland police, "at work on the torso cases steadily for many months, seem to have victory snatched from under their noses." Even *Time* magazine weighed in, reporting that O'Donnell "had triumphed over Sleuth Eliot Ness, famed G-Man who 'got' Al Capone."

Publicly, Ness struck a magnanimous, if guarded tone. "The sheriff is to be commended for his intensive investigation," he said. "The leads he has uncovered will, of course, be followed up to see what possible connection the Polillo case may have with any others. My department and I stand ready to make available to the sheriff any facilities that he might feel would be of assistance."

Ness could say nothing more, at least for the moment. Dolezal's confession had placed him in an impossibly cruel bind. He still believed that Frank Sweeney, who remained under close watch, was almost certainly the real torso killer. If Dolezal's confession held up, and especially if the bricklayer proved to have committed the other crimes, Ness would face a harsh reckoning. He would be forced to admit that he had bungled the investigation, and the backlash might well torch his career. "It looks as though," said Jack Raper in the *Press*, "the 'great G-man' myth with which the people of Cleveland have been entertained for several years is on its way to the scrap heap."

Actually, it was worse than that. Up to this point, Ness's record had been spotless, giving his political opponents no ammunition to challenge him. The only exception, as journalist Ralph Kelly observed, had come two years earlier, when Congressman Martin L. Sweeney "campaigned vigorously for his democratic colleagues on the Ness-Burton failure to solve the torso murders." At the time, the congressman's strategy fell flat. Now, riding the crest of this breakthrough, "Sweeney may be a candidate himself this year." This would have put Ness and Mayor Burton on treacherous ground. If word of Ness's pursuit of the congressman's cousin got out during a heated mayoral campaign, Ness's efforts would be reduced to a smear campaign against a rival. At best, if Dolezal proved to be guilty, Ness had wasted his time chasing the wrong man. At worst, he had done so for political gain, making him no better than any of the corrupt officials he had targeted as safety director.

For the moment, Ness could do little but wait to see how the Dolezal investigation played out. In this climate of uncertainty, friends wondered how badly he wanted another term as safety director. Lately the job had become a wearying slog over familiar ground—rooting out more dirty cops, prosecuting more racketeers, quelling another round of unrest at a steelworks. Ness remained passionate about his reforms, but budget constraints had him wondering if he could push them forward. Even the latest staging of the Anvil Revue, with its satirical songs and sketches, had been dismissive of Ness's recent efforts, describing him as someone "who hasn't been exactly a dismal failure." In the audience, sitting nearby, Congressman Sweeney gave an appreciative cackle.

In his off-hours, Ness's behavior grew ever more erratic. For the better part of a decade, in both Chicago and Cleveland, he had presented himself as the straightest of straight arrows. Now, in the months following his divorce, he seemed to have regressed into a sozzled frat boy, with a growing penchant for elaborate practical jokes. One night, he planted recording devices at a party to eavesdrop on private conversations, and later played back the results at top volume. The victims were not pleased. On other occasions, he arranged for scuffles to break out at nightclubs, using confederates to stage fights that sometimes resulted in gunfire, just to see how his companions would react. Incredibly, he decided it would be amusing to pull this stunt on Martin Davey, the governor of Ohio, who made a dash for the rear exit. "I was in on it," said another friend, Dan Moore, who recalled the episode more than fifty years later. "That's just the way Eliot was at that stage of his life—a fun-loving guy." It might have seemed like harmless fun to Ness, but many of his friends found his behavior cruel and wildly inappropriate. "He'd do things like invite a seven-foot-tall woman to a party," Moore recalled, "and pair her up on a blind date with the shortest man in the room, just for laughs." Every so often, Ness would find that he was the only one laughing. Philip Porter recalled a singularly tasteless prank at the height of the butcher investigation when Ness arrived early to a social gathering in order to plant a fake leg beneath a sofa. Later, he arranged for party guests to uncover this grisly "evidence" of the butcher's presence.

Porter is silent as to whether anyone appreciated this bit of merriment; perhaps one had to have been there.

Ness had a fellow conspirator egging him on for many of these pranks. By the time his divorce became final in the early months of 1939, Ness had taken up with someone new, an artist and model named Evaline McAndrew. "Evaline may have already been in the picture when Eliot and Edna separated," George Condon suggested in a later memoir. It would have been fast work in any case; there would be many raised eyebrows when Ness informed a few close friends of their wedding later that year. "I hesitated to announce the marriage," he said, "because I'm too busy and I wanted to avoid a lot of entertainment." Entertainment seemed to find him in any case. For a time, the couple seemed determined to become Cleveland's answer to Scott and Zelda Fitzgerald, throwing boozy, high-spirited dance parties, at least one of which ended with the new Mrs. Ness peeling off her dress and plunging into Lake Erie.

Reporters were told that Evaline had found work as a fashion illustrator at Higbee's, a local department store, before the couple married quietly in Chicago. "The director and his wife have known each other for a number of years," wrote Ness's friend Clayton Fritchey, "the bride being a friend of Mr. Ness's family in Chicago." The *Plain Dealer* added that Mrs. Ness planned to stay on at Higbee's, given that the job would not interfere with her duties as a housewife. "The director's bride is a slender, attractive, friendly person, a smart girl and an unusual one," readers learned. "For example, she was reported as two years older than she is, and she isn't going to sue. She is 25."

Actually, the reporters had it right the first time: Evaline was twenty-seven. It was a minor point, but by this time concealment had become a habit. Ness worried that the real details of their courtship, if they came out, would cloud his reputation for moral probity. He and Evaline had both been married when they first shared a dalliance, having met on a train while Ness attended to some out-of-town traffic business. Far from being a family friend, Evaline had probably not met Ness's relatives when they tied the knot. The marriage took place in Greenup, Kentucky, a town Ness came to know during his time in nearby Cincinnati, and not in Chicago, as reporters were told.

Like Edna, Evaline had dark hair and sharp, striking features, but the resemblance ended there. Edna had been quiet and spent much of her time at home; Evaline liked the limelight, and drew attention with daring dresses and exotic turbans. "She wasn't beautiful, but she was wonderful-looking," a friend said of her, and she seemed to thrive on the high life. She could often be seen buzzing around the lake in a speed-boat, picking up her husband at the East 9th Street pier after work for a night on the town. At dance clubs, bandleaders struck up one of the couple's favorite tunes as they walked in. "We'd go out at night and have a good time, but there wouldn't be talk about his job," Evaline would re-call. "He always kept his emotions controlled. In fact, Eliot was probably the most controlled man I ever knew."

It may be closer to the truth to say that Ness wanted a distrac-tion from his troubles at city hall, especially as the drama over Frank Dolezal's confession built to a crisis in the second week of July. Coroner Gerber had now gone on record to say that the hunt for the torso killer was over, but Detective Merylo wasn't buying it. "I had been working on this case for years," he would recall, whereas Sheriff O'Donnell and his team "had been in it only a few weeks." More to the point, Merylo had already vetted Dolezal thoroughly and had eliminated him as a suspect. "I thoroughly questioned Frank Dolezal on two occasions," the detective reported. "I had questioned the women and the men who were his com-panions. I had him under surveillance a long, long time." In fact, Merylo had first questioned Dolezal in November of 1936, just a few weeks after Chief Matowitz put him on the case. The bricklayer must have been among the first of the hundreds of suspects who came across Merylo's radar. Although the detective generally had little use for anyone he saw as a "sex degenerate," he bore no ill will toward Dolezal. "The kids liked him," Merylo said. "The neighbors liked him, too."

Merylo would have found it galling that the press began treating him as an also-ran. One paper gave an overview of his three-year effort with Zalewski, casting up their many arrests and convictions as a sort of consolation prize. "They have this record of law enforcement to show for their efforts," the writer noted, "whatever may be their disappointment at not having wrung a confession from Frank Dolezal." Pressed for comment, Merylo took a neutral tone, telling a reporter that "while the sheriff's action upset his plans, he did not want to get into any controversy with him." This was far from true. Merylo dearly wanted a clash with O'Donnell, but Chief Matowitz urged him to bide his time.

Merylo wouldn't have long to wait. The confession, as Philip Porter noted, "had a slight odor of bad fiction about it from the start." Several sources pointed out that Dolezal could not have disposed of Polillo's remains at the lakeshore, as he had claimed. The city had been in the grip of a bitter cold snap at the time, and the surface of the lake had frozen solid to a considerable distance from the shore. Sheriff O'Donnell, who admitted to inconsistencies in Dolezal's statement, did not seem overly troubled. By Saturday, July 8, Dolezal had conveniently jettisoned the earlier story in favor of a fresh one. He now maintained, according to the sheriff, that he had gotten rid of the head while on his way to work at the American Steel and Wire Company. He explained that he had stopped by the railroad bridge at East 37th Street and set fire to the head after dousing it with a gallon of coal oil. "I can take you to the spot," he said, but a search produced no results. Later, when it emerged that Dolezal had never actually worked at American Steel and Wire, the prisoner obligingly produced a third scenario. This time, he claimed that he had disposed of the head while working for the Works Progress Administration, but a time card at the WPA office showed that he'd been elsewhere on the day in question.

A further round of interrogation the following day kicked up another layer of confusion: Dolezal now backed away from his admission of killing Florence Polillo. "He said it once, and we have his signed confession on that," O'Donnell maintained. "But I would like to get him to say it again." Now, apparently, Dolezal would admit only to inviting Polillo for drinks in his apartment. "When we get to the point of the killing," the sheriff said, "he shuts up."

Matters took a troubling turn on Monday, July 10, with an announcement that Dolezal had made two unsuccessful suicide attempts during the night. In spite of careful precautions, Sheriff O'Donnell insisted, Dolezal had somehow used his shirt to fashion a noose, so as to hang himself from a hook in his cell. A jailer rushed in and pulled him down, reporters were told, tearing the prisoner's shirt in the process. Four hours later, under suicide watch, Dolezal managed to make a second attempt, this time using his shoelaces in place of his shirt. The laces weren't strong enough to bear his weight, reporters were told, and a pair of deputies found him in a daze lying on the floor of the cell a short time later. Apparently the two failures had discouraged a third attempt: "I won't do it again," he reportedly told his jailers.

Even in the face of this alarming development, Sheriff O'Donnell would not be deterred from his plan to administer a lie detector test later that afternoon. "There are lots of loopholes in his story," O'Donnell said, "and we want to close them all up." By this time, several fresh loopholes had appeared. Skeptics now wondered why Polillo's clothing had not been found near the White Front Meat Market, if Dolezal had tossed it away as he claimed. Others pointed to Dolezal's statement that Polillo's death had occurred in the early hours of Saturday, January 25, one day prior to the discovery of the remains on Sunday morning. This presented a conflict with the findings of Coroner Pearse, who stated at the time that Polillo's death had occurred two to four days before discovery. Even Dolezal's experience of working at a slaughterhouse had now been called into doubt. Initially he had spoken of working as a "sticker," which was taken to mean that he participated in the slaughter of animals, but he now insisted that he worked only as a "stamper," someone who affixes labels to products. As the threads began to unravel, Peter Merylo gave a discreet tug from behind the scenes, supplying information that exposed ever-larger holes in Dolezal's statements. "This was my first experience where a man is making a confession to a murder," he later wrote, "and does not know the details of the crime which he is alleged to have committed."

O'Donnell hoped that the lie detector test would bring clarity. Unlike Ness, the sheriff did not have Leonarde Keeler and John Larson at his beck and call. There was only one lie detector in the region at this time, and it would be operated by a recent law school graduate. In all, the interrogation stretched out over five and a half hours. Incredibly, in all that time, Dolezal was never asked to confirm or deny his role in any of the other torso slayings. Instead, the interrogation focused exclusively on the Polillo murder, and the initial results appeared to show that Dolezal had been telling the truth when he admitted to the crime.

Questions about the validity of the procedure surfaced even before the prisoner entered the room. Reporters had been shocked by Dolezal's appearance that day, as deputies bundled him into a car before the examination. "One of his eyes was black and swollen," wrote William Miller in the *Press*. "Dolezal also complained that his 'ribs hurt.'" According to Miller, when a reporter ventured to ask Dolezal what was wrong with his ribs, a county detective yanked him away. "You ought to have your jaw punched," Sheriff O'Donnell told him. Later, the sheriff would tell a skeptical pool of reporters that Dolezal had injured himself during his suicide attempts. Observers now openly questioned whether the lie detector results had any value, amid concerns over coercion and physical violence while in custody. "Is Frank Dolezal the torso murderer?" asked the *Press*. "Or is he a harmless psychopath who has been forced into admitting a crime he did not commit?"

O'Donnell forged ahead. On Tuesday, July 11, a pair of psychiatrists examined Dolezal for ninety minutes and declared him to be sane, preempting the prospect of an insanity plea. Later that afternoon, Dolezal was formally arraigned on a first-degree murder charge. It would not have been easy to make the charge stick, given that Dolezal had explicitly stated that he acted in self-defense. As it happened, the arraignment would be overturned the following day amid protests that the prisoner had been denied counsel. By this time Dolezal had been held without charge for several days, spurring protest from the American Civil Liberties Union. "It would appear," wrote one critic, "that Cleveland has resorted to barbarism and has disregarded the hard-won rights of us all."

A great deal now hinged on the dark stains found in Dolezal's apartment, which the chemist Gerald Lyons, brother of private detective Pat

Lyons, had identified as blood. On July 13, a pathologist at Western Reserve University delivered his independent findings. "The tests I made on six samples that I obtained myself were negative," he announced. "They were just plain dirt." The news landed with a hollow thud. Not only had the sheriff's department failed to link Dolezal to any of the other torso murders, but now the evidence in the Polillo case looked to be crumbling. Dolezal, when finally granted access to an attorney, issued another repudiation of his confession. "He denies the killing," the lawyer reported. "He denies he is the torso murderer. He says he was in a daze when he made the confession." The *Plain Dealer*, reminding readers of the rumored beatings, pointed out that the confession could only be admitted into evidence if it had been made without threat of harm. "Otherwise," the writer noted, "it is considered a worthless piece of paper."

O'Donnell now found himself swimming against a tide of scorn. "Ordinarily you would suppose that a police officer, having made an arrest in a crime so bizarre and so famous, would be loudly acclaimed as a hero," Philip Porter wrote. "Instead, the prevailing opinion around town is that the 'solution' is not worth a nickel." Meanwhile, Dolezal remained in the county jail, the sole resident of his cell block, under round-the-clock suicide watch. He reportedly spent much of his time praying, clutching a string of rosary beads. Amid doubts that sufficient evidence remained for an indictment, a small notice in all three papers announced that a proposed grand jury hearing had been postponed.

As coverage dwindled, the city's attention turned elsewhere. News broke on August 24 that Nazi Germany had signed a treaty of nonaggression with the Soviet Union, the Molotov-Ribbentrop Pact, signaling dark times ahead. "Will Hitler actually move against Poland," asked that morning's *Plain Dealer*, "if he knows that it will mean war with Britain and France?"

Just before two that afternoon, a pair of deputies assigned to keep watch over Frank Dolezal were called away to show some visitors out of the building. According to the official report, Dolezal was left alone for no more than three minutes. When the deputies returned, they found the prisoner gasping and struggling for breath, having fashioned a makeshift noose from cleaning rags and attached it to a coat hook on the wall of his cell.

Sheriff O'Donnell appeared within moments, in response to frantic calls for help. "We found Dolezal hanging limply against the wall with a rag wrapped around his neck," the sheriff would tell reporters. The officers cut the prisoner free and summoned medical personnel who administered oxygen and a shot of insulin, to no avail. Within minutes, Dolezal was pronounced dead.

The news spread fast. By three, barely an hour later, Joseph Sweeney and James Hogan of the Cleveland police detective bureau, two men closely associated with the Kingsbury Run effort, arrived at the county jail to launch an investigation. Ness and Matowitz had sent two of their best. By the end of the day, O'Donnell would be hustled over to the Central Police Station to give a statement, along with Archie Burns, the assistant chief jailer. "What kind of jail are you running here, anyway?" asked Dolezal's lawyer. "I had a hunch something like this would happen before he ever came to trial."

Many were skeptical of the sheriff's account of the tragedy. Dolezal, who stood five feet eight inches tall, was said to have hanged himself from a hook only five feet seven inches from the floor. Although not impossible, it would have required considerable contortions, as well as a complete suppression of any reflexive survival instinct, to commit suicide in these circumstances. Moreover, he was said to have done it in only three minutes.

Coroner Gerber's autopsy raised more concerns. The findings showed that Dolezal had been left strangling for a period far longer than the sheriff's report had claimed—perhaps as long as fifteen minutes, rather than three—and that the prisoner had six broken ribs, three on each side. Dolezal's complaint of pain in his ribs on the day of his lie detector test now assumed new importance. "When and how did Frank Dolezal receive six rib fractures?" asked the *Plain Dealer*. Dolezal's lawyer asserted that the findings "should convince anyone that he was manhandled while he was a prisoner."

After some initial reluctance, Coroner Gerber bowed to pressure and convened an inquest the following morning. The level of hostility "was almost a solid wall," Detective Merylo would say. "We have nothing to hide," Sheriff O'Donnell claimed, insisting that Dolezal had never been mistreated, and that his injuries must have occurred either before his arrest or as a result of his two earlier suicide attempts. Others contradicted him, testifying that the prisoner had repeatedly complained of being gagged, blindfolded, and beaten senseless. At one stage, the proceeding grew so contentious that it nearly erupted into a brawl.

One piece of information stood out. Some eight weeks earlier, the twenty-two-year-old prostitute Lillian Jones had come forward to claim that Dolezal attacked her with a knife, prompting a daring leap from a second-story window. Now, as the inquest unfolded, Jones retracted her story. She had now admitted to Detective Merylo that she had fabricated the tale under pressure from the private detective Pat Lyons. Lyons had told her, she claimed, that "we will get it out of him, knock it out of him, he will never get out of there alive." Her sister Ruby had also overheard Lyons bragging about the case, and supplied additional testimony at Gerber's inquest: "Sure, we've got the right man," she quoted Lyons as saying. "He'll get the hot seat. He'll never live to walk out of County Jail." Lyons went on to say, according to Ruby Jones, that Dolezal would be beaten to "make him say he's the man, whether he did it or not." A thirty-six-page document was prepared on the strength of Lillian Jones's retraction of her accusations against Dolezal. Gerber declined to accept the report as testimony, arguing that it technically had no bearing on the inquest.

In a climate now thick with pessimism and distrust, Gerber issued his final report on September 5. It managed to tread a cautious middle ground between blame and absolution, letting O'Donnell off the hook with a finding that Dolezal had, in fact, committed suicide. Although Gerber now maintained that the prisoner's injuries had been inflicted while in custody, he declined to specify whether they had come as a result of beatings or prior suicide attempts. Gerber stated explicitly, however, that Dolezal had been left alone, in extremis, for a longer period than initially claimed, and that he might have survived if aid had been administered sooner. Privately, he offered a less-forgiving verdict on the affair. "As far as I am concerned, he wasn't even a suspect," Gerber would say. "He was just unfortunate to live in the neighborhood where these things occurred, and maybe he talked too much."

Five months later, on Thursday, February 1, 1940, Pat Lyons got into an automobile accident and found himself arrested on a charge of "special intoxication." There was a certain irony in it. The collapse of the case against Frank Dolezal had largely extinguished the political fortunes of Mayor Burton's insurgent challengers, including Congressman Sweeney, who chose not to enter the mayoral race. Burton had been comfortably reelected in the fall campaign, leaving Ness free to resume the crackdown on "tipsy driving" that had ensnared Pat Lyons.

Peter Merylo made a point of being present in the courtroom the following day as the private detective paid his fine, and afterward, the two men held an informal postmortem on the Dolezal affair. Merylo seized the occasion to offer some advice. "You've got the wrong technique," he told Lyons, referring to the barroom chatter that directed the private detective to Dolezal. "Don't believe everything drunks tell you." Lyons ruefully agreed, worrying that he himself might be "washed up with any more investigations." Merylo wasn't in a mood to be sympathetic. "Furthermore," he told Lyons, "I hope you know that you bungled up everything when you arrested Dolezal?" Lyons considered the matter for a moment. "I guess I did," he said.

Three days later, a special request crossed Detective Merylo's desk, asking him to interview a suspect in the Kingsbury Run case. Merylo didn't give it much thought. By this time, he had received hundreds of similar interview requests, and he saw little reason to treat this one any differently. He took note of the suspect's name and made the necessary arrangements. The suspect's name was Frank Sweeney.

It does not appear as if the name held any special significance for Merylo or his partner, Martin Zalewski. "Dr. Sweeney was referred to us by Superintendent Cowles of the Scientific Bureau of Investigation for a further check-up," Merylo noted in his report, "as it was believed that Dr. Sweeney might be a good suspect in the Torso Murders." At the time, Sweeney was still a resident of the Soldiers' and Sailors' Home in Sandusky. Cleveland police had been notified, in accordance with the notation in his file, that he had left the facility that week to visit his sister in Cleveland.

Merylo and Zalewski interviewed Frank Sweeney on February 5, 1940. Sweeney struck the detectives as something of an eccentric, with a "slight ego complex." During questioning, Merylo recalled, the doctor paced back and forth "as though he were dictating a business letter." Although Sweeney was a large man, weighing perhaps 220 pounds, Merylo judged him to be rather "delicate," and not the type of person who could "mix with transients around railroad tracks and swamps." Neither of the detectives seems to have given him serious consideration as a suspect. Although he displayed a great many familiar characteristics—as a broken-down, mentally disturbed, binge-drinking disgraced physician—the two detectives had turned their energies to a different channel by this time. Merylo, in particular, was doing a great deal of fieldwork in Pennsylvania, in New Castle and McKees Rocks, where suspicious remains had recently been found. Over time, Merylo had drifted away from the notion that the killer operated a secret "murder laboratory" somewhere near Kingsbury Run. Instead, he came to believe that the torso slayer moved from place to place by rail, instead of operating exclusively in Cleveland, and that he used empty freight cars to perform his butchery. Possibly, by the time Merylo interviewed Frank Sweeney, the detective had become so attuned to the notion that the Cleveland and Pennsylvania crimes were linked that he dismissed a relatively sedentary figure, like Sweeney, who did not fit this hypothesis. His report makes it clear that Sweeney raised no serious suspicions. "After our conversation," Merylo concluded, "it is our opinion that Dr. Sweeney had no connection with the Torso Murders."

Merylo's statement is remarkable for what it does not say. Detectives Merylo and Zalewski clearly had no idea that they were interviewing Ness's prime suspect. Nearly two years had passed since the interrogation at the Hotel Cleveland, but even now, Ness continued to keep his secret investigation entirely walled off from his own detective bureau, declining to share potentially vital information with the men officially assigned to solve the case. Some have excused Ness's secrecy for the simple reason that there had been no further outrages in Cleveland since August of 1938, when the two sets of remains were discovered at the East 9th Street dump. If, in February of 1940, Ness simply wanted to send a message to Sweeney, clearly demonstrating that there had been no letup in surveillance, Merylo was as good a messenger as any, and better than most. Perhaps Ness saw value in getting a fresh perspective, putting his prime suspect in a room with Merylo, the department's indefatigable bulldog, just to see what happened. If so, Merylo had been sent in with one hand tied behind his back, a disservice to a dedicated veteran who had given so much to the effort.

If Ness still regarded Sweeney as a person of interest in February of 1940, it raises disturbing questions about his failure to intervene as the tragedy of Frank Dolezal unfolded the previous year—especially if Ness still believed, definitively, that Sweeney was the killer. Although Ness's name is largely absent from the official records of the Dolezal investigation, it is clear that he kept tabs on the unfolding events, and that he remained alert to developments after Dolezal's death. In the spring of 1940, a few days after Merylo's interview with Frank Sweeney, the detective fielded another special request when Ness asked for a summary report on the Dolezal case. One reason for the safety director's interest would have seemed obvious to everyone at the time. Dolezal's brother Charles had initiated legal action against Sheriff O'Donnell and others on charges that included false arrest and mistreatment of the prisoner. Though Ness had no administrative role in the running of the county sheriff's office, and had often found himself hampered by "home rule" issues, he still had a professional stake in the lawsuit.

It is significant, however, that Ness asked for a briefing from Merylo, "the torso detective," rather than Joseph Sweeney or James Hogan, the two detectives sent to investigate on the day of Dolezal's death. This suggests that Ness was more interested in the viability of Dolezal as a suspect rather than the circumstances of his death. Publicly, Ness had done nothing to intercede in the Dolezal case, choosing instead to step back and let the unhappy chain of events play out to its tragic conclusion. Some have cited jurisdictional issues, but at the Harvard Club and elsewhere, Ness had shown himself willing to override inconvenient restrictions of this type. It beggars belief, if Ness truly believed he had identified Frank Sweeney as the torso killer, that he and the butcher squad stood idly by during Dolezal's long ordeal and kept silent at the time of his death. A quiet word behind the scenes might have prevented or at least mitigated this disaster. No bargain of silence with Congressman Sweeney, no matter how dire the potential consequences, could have justified Ness in washing his hands of the matter. One must conclude that during the summer of 1939, more than a year after his interrogation of Sweeney, Ness was willing to entertain the possibility that Frank Dolezal had some role in the series of crimes.

Even if Ness believed that Frank Sweeney was the true butcher, as the continued surveillance and interrogation suggests, it would not necessarily have excluded Dolezal's involvement. If Ness thought it possible that Dolezal actually killed Florence Polillo, the crime to which he initially confessed, it might have opened the door to a new, overarching theory of the case. Perhaps more than one killer had carried out the crimes, in spite of Coroner Gerber's multiple statements to the contrary. Instead of a single series of crimes carried out by a single killer, perhaps the crimes should be viewed as two or more separate groupings, carried out by two or more killers, independent of each other. Ness might have weighed up the possibility that Dolezal had killed Polillo, and perhaps even some or all of the other female victims, and that Sweeney had done away with Andrassy and the other male victims. The possibility might, to Ness's way of thinking, have brought clarity to the otherwise contradictory sexual element of the crimes. Ness's terse statement in response to Dolezal's arrest allows for this possibility: "The leads [the sheriff] has uncovered will, of course, be followed up to see what possible connection the Polillo case may have with any others."

In the days ahead, Ness continued to weigh up information from Detective Merylo, even if the detective's theories did not support his suspicions of Frank Sweeney. In May of 1940, Robert Chamberlin and David Cowles, Ness's closest associates, were in McKees Rocks, Pennsylvania, assisting Merylo in his efforts to prove that the killer was still active, and using freight cars to perform his butchery. If the words of a Pennsylvania colleague are accurate, Chamberlin and Cowles were willing to consider the notion that these latest crimes had been committed "by the same person who killed a number of humans in a like manner in and around Cleveland." That person could not have been Frank Sweeney.

Ness had made no public comment on Dolezal's death in custody, but he continued to monitor the progress of the lawsuit brought by the victim's brother. In the end, the legal maneuvering would drag on for more than a year before a quiet announcement that the case had been "settled and dismissed at defendants' cost." The exact details remained vague, perhaps owing to the sudden death of Sheriff O'Donnell, who succumbed to a heart attack in June of 1941.

Sheriff O'Donnell's death did not bring the matter to a close. Frank Dolezal's story remains an ugly chapter in the city's history and a subject of enduring debate. More than sixty years later, at the start of a new century, there would be an unsettling coda to the story when a group of researchers uncovered photographs of Frank Dolezal's autopsy. The images revealed a troubling, unexpected detail: "a deep, piano-wire-thin scar" around the dead man's neck, very unlike the mark one would expect to see as the result of a noose fashioned from old cleaning rags. "I'm no pathologist," one of the researchers remarked, "but I don't see how a noose made of rags could have made that mark." All of the parties concerned readily acknowledge that no definitive conclusions can be drawn from the images, or from the lengthy transcript of the coroner's inquest that surfaced a short time later, but the debate continues even now. The implications are staggering, even at a remove of many decades, raising difficult questions of complicity and high-level cover-ups, and throwing yet another shadow across the sad legacy of Frank Dolezal.

Perhaps Eliot Ness was aware of these unanswered questions when he requested the report from Detective Merylo in the early months of 1940. If so, his continued silence becomes even less defensible, and may serve to illustrate the wounds inflicted by his pursuit of Frank Sweeney. Ness's career had been laid on a foundation of moral rectitude. He was a clean cop who took down dirty cops. Dolezal had been held without charge, subjected to strong-arm tactics, and denied his right to counsel. One would have expected Ness's voice to be the loudest in railing against these abuses of power.

At the time of Dolezal's arrest, however, Ness could no longer claim the moral high ground. He had surrendered that right the moment he snatched Frank Sweeney off the street. His suspect, too, had been held without charge, subjected to strong-arm tactics, and denied his right to counsel. It is too much to say that Ness was no better than the men who tormented Dolezal. Frank Sweeney, at least, had lived to walk away from his interrogation. But Ness had paid a price. He had abused his power and left himself vulnerable to the machinations of political enemies. Now, the Boy Scout had a dirty secret.

Because of Frank Sweeney, Eliot Ness was no longer untouchable.

16

THERE GOES ELIOT NESS

I have never regretted anything more in my life.

Eliot Ness, March 6, 1942

It was nearly five o'clock on a cold Tuesday morning, March 3, 1942, but Eliot Ness was just heading home, driving his Cadillac along Buckley Boulevard after a long night of drinking at the Vogue Room. Evaline sat in the passenger seat, woozy but still in high spirits. The couple had moved to a four-story boathouse in the elegant Clifton Park neighborhood soon after their marriage, and the roads near the lakeshore were slippery.

The Nesses' marriage was also headed for a slippery patch. "Eliot started drifting back to his carefree lifestyle," said a friend, diplomatically. "Something had to give." Evaline was less circumspect. Her husband, she later remarked, "screwed everything in a skirt." Unlike Edna, Evaline would not be content to sit at home by herself. She often went out and found her own excitement, leading to angry repercussions at home. "She was an interesting, generous, creative person when she was sober," a relative would note. "And she was very unpleasant and confrontational when she was drunk."

She and her husband were often drunk, separately and together, and this undoubtedly played a role on that frigid March morning when their Cadillac drifted across the center line and slammed into an on-coming car. It was a jarring impact, but not catastrophic. Ness's head bounced off the steering wheel, loosening a couple of teeth. Evaline's shoulder struck the dashboard and she fell back, dazed. Ness reached over to assure himself that she wasn't seriously hurt, then got out to check on the other driver. Robert Sims, a twenty-one-year-old machinist, sat sideways in the driver's seat, with the door open and his feet planted on the running board. He'd banged his head, he said, and his knee hurt.

What happened next remains obscure. Later, Ness would admit that he had been drinking, but he insisted that alcohol had not been a factor in the accident. "I had several drinks during dinner," he said. "Then we went to the hotel room of one of my friends and chatted with him about his farm and other matters for a couple of hours. I had nothing to drink in the room. When we left the hotel we started for home. It was very slip-pery and the thing just happened like *that*—" Ness snapped his fingers to emphasize the point.

After speaking with Sims at the scene of the accident, Ness ex-plained, they made arrangements to go to a hospital. "I had told Mr. Sims we would follow him," he said, "but Mrs. Ness said she was feeling better and would rather go home. After I got home I immediately called the hospital and talked to someone." Ness had wanted to check on Sims, he said, but he declined to give his name because the man at the other end of the line—a policeman, as it turned out—had not identified him-self. "I didn't know who he was," Ness insisted.

By the time Ness offered this carefully parsed version of the events, two days had passed. The crash and its aftermath had hit the headlines as "L'Affaire Ness," amid a swirl of accusations. Critics charged that Ness had left the scene of the accident and failed to identify himself in hope of hushing the matter up, and that he might never have come forward if someone hadn't noticed his distinctive license plate: "EN-3." Robert Sims had suffered a broken kneecap, and his father complained to reporters that he'd had to contact the Cleveland Automobile Club to learn who was driving the other car. Ness, for his part, maintained that he had identified himself to Sims at the scene, but hurried back to his own car out of concern for Evaline. "My first thought was for my wife, because I thought she was the most seriously injured," he said. "She had had the wind knocked out of her." Ness also suggested, at one stage, that instead of leaving the scene, he'd simply gone to move his car off the road, only to find that Sims had headed to the hospital with a passing motorist in the meantime. He continued to insist that he'd done right by Sims, but he acknowledged his lapse in judgment. "Obviously I was trying to avoid publicity," he admitted.

Ness's tardy explanation did nothing to silence his detractors. As safety director he had repeatedly urged his traffic squad to "quit coddling tipsy drivers," as evidenced by the charges against private detective Pat Lyons. Now he faced a bracing comeuppance. "The hero had been toppled from his pedestal," wrote journalist George Condon. "Sir Galahad a hit-skip driver?" His political rivals smelled blood, and Evaline saw his spirits plummet. "I don't think he could stand the criticism," she said, "especially when it came to his job. That's why he tried to avoid the publicity. It certainly didn't reflect well on him."

In truth, a backlash had been building for some time. Though Ness still worked as hard as ever, his anti-corruption crusade had lost focus. "When it seemed to Ness that the Police Department had rounded into trustworthy shape," Condon observed, "he directed his attack towards other targets." There were many triumphs in these years, including an audacious campaign to take down the city's notorious Mayfield Road Mob, the city's premier mafia faction at the time, but Ness also occupied himself with efforts that seemed trivial by comparison. He expended a great deal of energy railing against slot machines and pinball parlors. At one stage, he initiated charges against a member of the Cleveland library board for soliciting bribes from book binderies, resulting in a five-day trial and two-to-twenty in the Ohio Penitentiary. Ness, the man who once smashed up Al Capone's breweries, was now going after shady librarians.

By this time, Ness no longer had Mayor Burton watching his back, which emboldened his critics. Burton had won a US Senate seat in the 1940 elections, leaving the city's law director to serve out the remainder of his term. Some of Ness's friends at the newspapers had seen an opportunity in this, banding together to push Ness to declare himself as a candidate for mayor in 1941. Ness doesn't seem to have given any serious consideration to entering the race. Evaline would recall that her husband and his friend Frank Lausche, a Democratic municipal court judge, often bantered with each other over the issue. "Eliot would tell Frank that he ought to run for mayor and Frank would insist that Eliot run," she said.

It might have been a joke to Ness, but not to Lausche. In the end, Judge Lausche secured the Democratic nomination and won the election easily. Next, he upended generations of political convention by retaining Ness as safety director rather than handing the job over to a fellow Democrat. The decision sent waves of resentment through the Democratic vanguard. Ray T. Miller, the party boss who had helped to set the Dolezal affair in motion, complained loudly and promised to go to FBI Director J. Edgar Hoover for "a real G-man" if only Lausche would fire Ness.

Although Ness had now survived two changes of administration, his political rivals were gaining strength. Soon, the budget axe fell on Ness's funding for the Unknowns. He gathered the team in his office to deliver the bad news, but as Arnold Sagalyn would recall, the men appeared unfazed. With the country mobilizing for war, many of the Unknowns had made plans to join the military intelligence services, "where they were desperate for people with such skills."

By this time, Ness had also begun feeling his way into wartime service, intent on doing his bit after Pearl Harbor. He started locally, as the head of an Industrial Safety Committee charged with protecting the city's important manufacturing plants from spies and saboteurs. His actions drew a fresh round of disparagement from J. Edgar Hoover, who accused Ness of "attempting to usurp the functions of accredited law enforcement agencies."

Harold Burton, the newly minted senator, reached out from Washington to offer Ness a post with the Social Protection Division, clamping down on vice around military bases. In time, Ness would head up a campaign to curb social diseases among enlisted men. "It was a kind of police work," as Philip Porter noted, "and must have seemed challenging to Ness." Although only a part-time consultancy at first, Ness's frequent trips to Washington drew more unfavorable comment at home. "I am wondering whatever became of Eliot Ness," a *Press* reporter wrote at one stage. "You know, he's the safety director, if he's still supposed to be on my beat, I think you should know that it has been more than four weeks since I've seen him. Maybe we should turn in a missing-person report on him."

Ness's car crash in March of 1942 brought the criticism to a new and more insistent pitch. Though Mayor Lausche declared the accident "a closed matter," the storm surrounding "L'Affaire Ness" made it clear that his days as safety director were numbered. Ness had already laid the groundwork for a graceful departure with his work in Washington. On April 23, 1942—less than two months after the accident—he handed in his resignation. He told Mayor Lausche that it had been an honor to serve as safety director, but he now felt obliged to "fulfill my duty to the nation." In six years, Ness had seldom passed a reporter without stopping to offer a quote, but that day, he slipped away from city hall without comment.

As word of his departure spread, the critics fell silent. "As Ness enters full-time federal service, an era has ended here," Philip Porter wrote. "He was always several jumps ahead of the chair-warmers and connivers in city government, and even to this day they can't figure him out, but have spent a good deal of their time criticizing him." Ness had never been "content to put Al Capone behind bars," the *News* added. "Apparently, he will not rest until every enemy of the people has been brought to justice."

One enemy of the people appeared to have slipped through his grasp. The mad butcher of Kingsbury Run had been silent for quite some time; no further remains had been discovered in Cleveland since the two victims at the East 9th Street dump, more than three years earlier. Merylo and Zalewski were working as hard as ever, but people didn't talk about the murders as much, as one resident recalled, and the climate of fear had subsided. Those who did raise the subject approached it with caution, as if fearful of poking a sleeping bear. Many had come to believe that Frank Dolezal must have had something to do with it after all since the crimes appeared to have stopped following his arrest. Coroner Gerber disagreed. "The arrest of Dolezal didn't stop the murders," he would say, "they had already stopped."

Not everyone agreed, especially if police found themselves confronting a set of suggestive features at a crime scene. On June 28, 1942— just two months after Ness's resignation—three young boys playing in Kingsbury Run came across a battered steamer trunk resting in a clump of weeds. Inside they found the torso of a young African American woman. Police rushed to the scene and quickly discovered the victim's head and arms a short distance away. The legs would be recovered later. Soon, investigators identified the dead woman as a nineteen-year-old prostitute named Marie Wilson.

Earlier in the day, a fourteen-year-old girl had seen a tall, muscular African American man climb out of a cab at the edge of the Run, struggling with a heavy trunk. Police tracked down the cab driver, who identified his fare as Willie Johnson, a thirty-six-year-old laborer with an extensive criminal record. Arrested at his rooming house, Johnson told police a remarkable story. He had knocked Wilson unconscious, he said, after she attacked him with a knife. Next, apparently satisfied the situation had been properly handled, he went to bed. When he awoke, as the *Press* related, he was "mystified to find her lying in pieces all over the floor." After further questioning and a viewing of the dismembered remains at the morgue, Johnson broke down and admitted to the killing.

For a brief time, investigators believed they might forge a link to the earlier torso slayings. Witnesses claimed that Johnson had known Rose Wallace, and may in fact have been the last man seen in her company, and that he also enjoyed an acquaintance with Florence Polillo. Johnson angrily denied any connection, and the effort soon petered out in the light of various inconsistencies, notably the fact that the dismemberment had been performed crudely with a saw, rather than a scalpel-like blade, and showed none of the butcher's familiar technique.

Marie Wilson's murder case came to trial in December. Johnson received a guilty verdict, which at that time carried an automatic sentence of death. In March of 1944, as the date of execution neared, Coroner Gerber drove to the death row penitentiary in Columbus with *News* writer Howard Beaufait. The two hoped that Johnson, in his final hours, might shed some light on the torso murders, or perhaps even reveal himself as the butcher. Instead, Johnson denied killing Marie Wilson, the crime for which he'd been convicted and sentenced. He now claimed that a mysterious stranger had given him twenty-five dollars to carry the remains to Kingsbury Run, but the story convinced no one. Johnson went to the electric chair on March 10, 1944, still protesting his innocence. "Johnson," Gerber would declare, "wasn't the torso murderer."

By that time, Detective Merylo had been taken off the case. Chief Matowitz could no longer justify a full-time "torso detective," as there had been no verifiable developments since 1938. Merylo's single-minded focus on the case had driven him to remarkable extremes by this time. He had even taken to posing as a hobo and wandering through homeless encampments, blending in as well as he could and even sleeping rough, while a partner kept watch from a nearby place of concealment. Merylo was now convinced "beyond a doubt" that the butcher had carried his killing spree into neighboring Pennsylvania. "I think it's safe to say," he told a reporter at one stage, "that the Mad Butcher's victims now total twenty-three." In spite of his reassignment, Merylo showed no sign of letting up. "I will continue on this investigation, regardless of what my other assignments may be," he wrote in his final report. "I will continue to work on my days off and my vacations as I did in the past."

Even now, the name of Frank Sweeney was never mentioned. Ness's resignation had made no difference; he and his inner circle maintained their silence with a fervor appropriate to the Manhattan Project. In years to come, however, some of the men who had been in the room during Sweeney's interrogation would make oblique reference to the affair. John Larson, who had administered one of the two lie detector examinations, later claimed that Ness assured him the matter had been settled. Larson reported that "arrangements were made" and that the suspect "was

placed in a special hospital where he has supposedly been for years."
Others would report that Sweeney ended up "confined as a mental patient" in Michigan. Royal Grossman, the court psychiatrist, is said to
have claimed that Ness himself arranged for the committal. The suggestion of a bargain with the family of Congressman Sweeney, preventing
any details from reaching the public, always loomed in the background.
"The suspect tested had very powerful contacts," Larson said.

Decades later, members of Detective Merylo's family would recall
his bitterness when he became aware, sometime during his final years
on the force, of a suspect with a connection to a politically influential
family. Merylo was told to "leave it alone," his relatives recalled, because
the suspect had been institutionalized. It cannot be said for certain that
this was Frank Sweeney, whom Merylo had interviewed in 1940, but it
is clear that the detective placed no confidence in this suspect's committal as a final solution to the mystery. Long after his retirement from
the force in 1944, Merylo continued his investigation, now working as a
private detective. So long as the butcher remained "at large, and alive,"
Merylo said, "I will never give up my work on these torso murders."

As the Second World War came to a close, Ness found himself at loose
ends. His work with the Social Protection Division brought him a great
deal of distinction, but it proved difficult to translate his achievements
there into peacetime success. His résumé now included a curious
pamphlet—*What About Girls?* by Eliot Ness—which warned against the
dangers of venereal disease. His discomfort is evident on every page.
"He always had trouble with the word 'whore' and—this is so typical of
him—he would look for ways to avoid saying it," his friend Dan Moore
would recall. "One time, he came up with 'women who have a low
threshold of sexual approachability' to describe them."

In November of 1945, as he wrapped up his wartime service and
returned to Cleveland, Ness's second marriage also came to end. Once
again, the circumstances excited a great deal of gossip. Some of these rumors centered on Evaline's wandering eye, which seemed occasionally to
come to rest on other women. She saw no reason to deny any whispers.

Years later, after she had found success as an author and illustrator of children's books, she would tell a friend of an artist's model who played a role in the dissolution of the marriage. "In order to have that beauty I saw in her, I had to have her," she said. "So I left Eliot to be with her."

Two months later, the rumor mill sprang to life again as Ness announced his third marriage. His new wife was a Cleveland artist named Elisabeth Anderson Seaver, known as Betty, whose divorce from her husband Hugh had been finalized just two weeks earlier. Once again, Ness put a light gloss on the circumstances surrounding his divorce and speedy remarriage. "We talked about a big wedding, with all our friends and family members there for a big celebration, but we both decided that we didn't want all the fuss," he said. "We're just eager to get on with our lives."

For all the murmuring behind his back, Ness appeared to have gotten it right this time. He had known Betty socially since the days of the Great Lakes Exposition, where she had created the twelve-foot sculptures of "Beauty" and "Protection" that flanked the symphony shell amphitheater. By all accounts, the marriage was happy, and Ness finally seemed ready for a more traditional home life and career path. For years, friends had taken note of his relatively modest salary as safety director and wondered why he didn't go after a more lucrative position in the private sector. "Someday I may take one of those jobs," he had remarked in 1938. Now, through his connections in the business community, he sought to establish himself as an up-and-coming executive. In January of 1946, the month of his marriage to Betty, *Fortune* magazine ran a flattering profile titled "There Goes Eliot Ness," reporting his recent elevation to chairman of the board of directors at Ohio's Diebold Inc., best known at the time as makers of locks, safes, and business equipment. "I may fall flat on my face," Ness remarked, "but I'm sure having fun."

Soon, he fell flat on his face. He began juggling his position at Diebold with other, riskier positions elsewhere, including a partnership in an export company alongside his friend Dan Moore. It quickly became clear that Ness was in over his head. "I don't hold it against Eliot," Moore would say. "He had no instinct for it and it was obvious to everyone except

Eliot." In the years following, as George Condon would write, his business dealings became "a checkerboard that challenges analysis."

Condon and other friends were all the more mystified, in the summer of 1947, when Ness declared himself a candidate in the upcoming Cleveland mayoral race. "I am so situated financially that I do not have to worry about a livelihood," he declared. "I have some ideas about public service—and I want to try them." He chose his moment poorly. All agreed that he could have sailed into office in 1941, at the peak of his popularity in Cleveland, but the war years had altered the landscape. To many, Ness appeared to be a figure from the distant past, while others remembered "L'Affaire Ness" and his other missteps all too well. Still, his old friends at city hall considered him their best option. "The Republicans were desperate for a candidate to run against Mayor Tom Burke, who seemed unbeatable by anyone but Superman, and possibly not by him," Philip Porter recalled. In the end, the "Vote Yes for Eliot Ness" campaign failed to gather any real momentum. "His day had passed," Porter said. "Burke clobbered him."

Attempting to be magnanimous, Ness appeared at a victory party at Burke's home to offer his congratulations, and accepted perhaps one too many glasses of celebratory champagne. At one stage, he raised his glass and offered a double-edged toast: "Who'd want an honest politician anyway?" He might have thought it funny, but this was a singularly tactless thing to say of Burke, who had been at his side at the Harvard Club.

"From then on, it was downhill all the way for Eliot," Porter recalled. "Like Alexander the Great, he'd reached his peak too young, and after being safety director, had no more worlds to conquer." Worse, his bid for mayor took him out of the running for fresh opportunities in police administration, where political aspirations were seen as a liability. "Eliot abandoned something that he was best in the world at doing," as Moore said, "and he suffered the consequences."

When a change of management ended his tenure at Diebold, Ness found himself scrambling for work of any kind. About a year after losing the mayor's race, he appeared in the office of a campaign associate. "I'd regard it as a favor," he is reported to have said, "if you could put me on the payroll for about sixty dollars a week." At one stage, he took a job in a bookstore. "He was still a fairly young man, but he simply ran out of gas," a friend said. "He didn't know which way to turn."

Mercifully, he found stability at home. "There wasn't a dull moment in my life married to him," Betty would say. "I loved every minute of it." Both Ness and his new wife wanted children. Though they would have been considered older parents at the time—she was thirty-nine at the time of their marriage, and Ness was forty-three—they began proceedings to adopt a three-year-old son, Robert Eliot Ness. "Parenthood was a new experience for Eliot and he enjoyed it immensely," a friend said, but he expressed frustration at being on the road much of the time, chasing various business opportunities. "He wanted to spend more time with Betty and Bobby, and they missed him, too."

One night in late 1955, Ness found himself in New York City with a business associate named Joseph Phelps. He and Phelps had recently become officers in the North Ridge Industrial Corporation, where efforts were under way to develop a new, fraud-proof watermarking process for checks and other business documents. The company's president believed that Ness's background in law enforcement would help to establish legitimacy to the enterprise, and assist in winning over potential investors.

At the bar at the Waldorf Astoria, Phelps ran through his sales pitch for an old childhood friend, Oscar Fraley, a United Press sportswriter. Fraley soon made it clear that he was in no position to take a flier on the new company, but the two old friends kept talking. "Ness sat listening while Phelps and I enjoyed one of those good old 'long-time-no-see' bull sessions," Fraley would recall. For several hours, Ness appeared content to sit and drink. Later, the party moved upstairs to their hotel room, where Ness occasionally dozed off on a nearby couch. Sometime after midnight, Phelps tried to bring Ness into the conversation. "You'll have to get Eliot to tell you about his experience as a prohibition agent in Chicago," Phelps said. "He's the guy who dried up Al Capone. Maybe you never heard of him, but it's real gangbuster stuff; killings, raids and the works. It was plenty dangerous."

Fraley's expression, as he gazed at the "mild man with the easy manner," must have seemed incredulous. Ness met his gaze and smiled. "It was dangerous," he said. Encouraged by alcohol and a receptive audience, Ness began talking. With Fraley urging him on, Ness seemed uncharacteristically eager to revisit his "deadly days in Chicago." At one stage, Ness kicked off his shoes and settled himself on the floor, recalling incidents he hadn't thought about in twenty years. "Eliot could talk with entertaining ease," Fraley recalled. "The next thing I knew it was 6 a.m."

Ness appeared sheepish over having spoken at such length. "Let's knock this off and get some breakfast," he said, getting to his feet.

Fraley had been utterly enthralled. "Someday, you should write a book," he said. "You might make some money with it."

Ness paused in the midst of tying a shoelace and looked up. Fraley could hear bitterness in his voice as he replied, "I could use it."

Six months passed before the two crossed paths again. By this time, it was clear that Ness's latest business venture was going sour. As a cost-cutting measure, North Ridge Industrial would shortly relocate from Cleveland to Coudersport, a small town in northern Pennsylvania. Perhaps the uncertainty over his future put Ness in a more receptive frame of mind when Fraley asked if he'd given any thought to writing a book about his Chicago experiences. "Well," Ness answered, "why don't you write it?"

Ness didn't think anything would come of it, but he saw no reason not to play along when Fraley began sounding out interest from publishers. Fraley asked Ness to send along his notebooks, letters, and other source material so that he could begin pulling together some sample chapters. Ness also sat down and knocked out some twenty pages of firsthand recollections. It was a strange, awkwardly written document, betraying Ness's discomfort. If he hoped to make the book exciting, Fraley told him, Ness would have to let go of his "fetish" for honesty. Ness struggled to find a balance between storytelling and colorless adherence to fact. He did a creditable job describing a standoff with armed hoods, but he could not resist including a long and excruciatingly dull account of his "Law Enforcement Theory."

Even so, Ness sounded enthusiastic as he sent his pages off to Fraley. "If you find parts sketchy on which you would like more detail," Ness told him, "please drop me a note." Fraley wanted a great deal more. The two men spent time working together in Coudersport, where Ness strained to recall specifics. "Eliot knuckled his brow, stamped about the room and berated himself as he groped for names, places and incidents half forgotten," Fraley recalled.

Smoothing over the gaps in Ness's memory, Fraley pressed ahead with sample chapters to show to potential publishers, making use of invented dialogue and heavily embellished action. When Ness expressed concern over the exaggerations, Fraley tried to reassure him. "Don't get scared if we stray from the facts once in a while," he wrote. "We've got to make a real gang-buster out of this thing and after all, we have literary license."

This did nothing to quiet Ness's fears. "I remember him saying that he was a little upset that Fraley insisted on making his Chicago days sound much more thrilling than they really were," a Coudersport friend would say. "That bugged Eliot." His discomfort grew when Fraley secured a contract from the first publisher who saw the sample pages. "He was actually surprised that the publishing world was interested in his story," another friend reported.

Fraley and Ness now felt pressure to produce a complete manuscript that lived up to the exaggerated promise of the sample chapters. While trying to marshal his facts, Ness gave a talk to the Coudersport Rotary Club. Afterward, as the meeting broke up, one of the club members expressed incredulity to a friend: "Who the heck does he think he's kidding with a story like that?" Only then did he realize that hovering nearby was Ness, who offered a smile to show that he took no offense.

As the project moved forward, however, Ness grew ever more hesitant. "I don't believe Eliot actually wanted the book to be published," a friend would say. "He was many times on the verge of chucking the whole project because the book made him out to be a hero, which he honestly didn't consider himself to be." It might have pleased his friends to recall him as a reluctant paladin, but Ness was far from blameless. Occasionally he would quote a remark of Fraley's, to justify the book's excesses: "If you want it to be interesting, you have to embellish a little."

In the end, as several of his friends would recall, Ness desperately needed the money. "The last time I saw Eliot," David Cowles would recall, "he didn't have two pair of shoes to wear." The North Ridge Industrial Corporation was unraveling fast, amid charges of gross mismanagement by associates in whom Ness had placed his trust. The move to Coudersport saw him running up debt and bouncing checks, and he came to see the book as a lifeline. A friend recalled his giddy pleasure, as the publication date approached, at receiving a call from New York. "They just told me Hollywood is nibbling on the book idea!" Ness announced.

In March of 1957, it became clear that North Ridge Industrial would soon run completely off the rails, and it looked as if Ness and others would have to seek redress in court. The following month, he reviewed page proofs of the book, having tried to comb out some of the more extreme elaborations. Betty had a hand in excising an anecdote involving a raid on a brothel. Apparently she disapproved of a scene in which the rear doors of a paddy wagon flew open while rounding a corner, scattering women with "a low threshold of sexual approachability" onto the street. Ness didn't much care for Fraley's working title, but in the absence of a better suggestion, it went to press as *The Untouchables*.

On May 16, an uncommonly humid day in Coudersport, Ness and his friend Joseph Phelps, who had introduced him to Oscar Fraley, were conducting a grim review of company financial statements. When Phelps complained of a headache, the two men agreed to take a break and meet later at Ness's house to continue. Ness headed home, stopping along the way to pick up a bottle of gin. He paid with money from his advance for *The Untouchables*. He also had two paychecks from the North Ridge Industrial Corporation in his wallet, but in the company's current state of decline, the checks had become worthless.

Ness and his family now lived on the bottom level of a small, two-story house on Coudersport's 3rd Street, near the Allegheny River. When Ness arrived at the house, he found Betty outside, bent low over her flower beds. Bobby, now ten years old, sat in the living room. He looked up as Ness came through the door, and later said that his father appeared uncomfortable, perhaps in pain. Ness dabbed at his forehead with a handkerchief and went to the kitchen for a glass of water.

After a moment, Betty heard the sound of glass shattering. She raised her head. Now she could hear water running in the sink. She got to her feet, brushing off her hands as she took a step toward the house. "Eliot?" she called.

Moments later, neighbors heard her scream. A doctor arrived within minutes, but there was nothing to be done. Ness was dead of a heart attack at the age of fifty-five. In some versions of this sad scene, Betty's sobs were briefly interrupted by the sound of a heavy package thudding to the floor through the mail chute—the latest proofs of *The Untouchables*.

"And, what the hell," as Fraley had him say in those pages, "nobody lives forever!"

17

THE AMERICAN SWEENEY

Enclosed a few items for your, Personal Perusal.
                    Frank Sweeney to Eliot Ness, February 14, 1954

The Untouchables hit bookstores in September of 1957, with a hastily added epilogue to inform readers that "Eliot Ness did not see the finished product." He could not have dreamed, as George Condon would say, "that it would be the vehicle that would make him an international celebrity, through television."

It happened fast. In April 1959, the story would be dramatized as a two-part episode of *Desilu Playhouse*, with the commandingly rugged Robert Stack in the lead role. The "two-part tingler" offered a gritty retelling of the pursuit of Capone, with journalist Walter Winchell providing clipped, urgent narration that lent an air of newsreel credibility. A promotional tagline promised "the true story of FBI man Eliot Ness's savage war on gangland's greatest empire!"

Soon there would be complaints of excessive violence and anti-Italian stereotyping, culminating in a million-dollar lawsuit filed on behalf of the Capone family. By this time, however, the program's high ratings had spawned a weekly series. By week two, any resemblance to real life had gone down in a hail of bullets. Even some of the former Untouchables objected. "There wasn't any shooting during our raids,"

Barney Cloonan remarked. "Nobody got killed or even wounded." J. Edgar Hoover, undoubtedly aggravated by the early misidentification of Ness as an FBI agent, had staff members make notes on the program each week, looking out for further misrepresentations.

Betty Ness also kept an eye on the program. She had moved back to Cleveland to work in a clothing boutique after her husband's death, facing a struggle to support herself and her son, and she now sought advice to ensure that she received an equitable share of the profits. "People are of the opinion that a lot of money has rolled in because of the book and the programs," she said, "but it hasn't." She praised the television show publicly, but admitted that she and Bobby often laughed at the portrayal of Ness as a man with iron fists and a quick trigger finger. Her husband "did not like haphazard killing," she insisted, and had hesitated even to go fishing. Still, she must have appreciated the revisionist view of his marital history. There would be no mention of Edna or Evaline—only Betty, introduced as Ness's plucky fiancée in the Chicago-era pilot.

By the time the series finished in 1963, it had become necessary to remind people that it was based on a real person. "I was a fan of the Untouchables," one reader told a television columnist, "and I would like to know if there really was an Eliot Ness." Robert Stack himself occasionally addressed this question, and every so often he would display Ness's signature on a bounced check that had come into his possession. "Here's a guy who could have been wealthy if he would have accepted the bribes he was offered," Stack said. "But he stood for something greater, and what kind of thanks did he get? He couldn't even cover a ten-dollar check. I consider Ness a hero."

"Had Eliot lived a little longer, he might have cashed in," Philip Porter would write in later years. Perhaps so, but it seems equally likely that Ness's discomfort over the show's excesses might have had a chilling effect, with the soft-spoken, mild-mannered original serving as a reality check on the granite-jawed TV hero.

One thing is certain. If Ness had lived, there would have been a second collaboration with Oscar Fraley, a sequel to *The Untouchables* set in Cleveland. Fraley laid the groundwork when Ness appeared to be growing despondent over the first book, framing the idea as a chance to set the record straight on his accomplishments as safety director. Ness warmed to the idea. The two men took long walks during which Ness told stories about fighting corruption in the police department, going up against the mob, and ferreting out union racketeers. These details were much fresher in Ness's memory and, as Fraley recalled, he felt more comfortable taking the credit for events in Cleveland, where he had called the shots. His work on crime prevention, in particular, had been on his mind in his final days. Just a few days before his death, he spoke at a gathering in Coudersport about his work with youth gangs in the Tremont area of Cleveland, where he'd helped to launch an innovative "save the kids" campaign for juvenile delinquents.

At one stage, Ness spoke to Fraley about Kingsbury Run. It was perhaps the only time he ever spoke at length on the topic to anyone outside of his inner circle, and even now he remained guarded in his approach, apparently using the Gaylord Sundheim alias to describe Sweeney. In time, this material would find its way into Fraley's 4 Against the Mob, a half-baked follow-up to The Untouchables, published in 1961, which one reviewer dismissed as "another delightful bit of whimsy." The padding was all too obvious this time out, given that Ness had not been around to flesh out the details, and never more so than in the book's cursory treatment of Kingsbury Run. "The killings were so fiendish and gory," Fraley remarked at one point, "that Ness absolutely refused to discuss them with his pretty wife Betty." In Fraley's telling, the reign of the torso killer ended with the suspect's death in a mental institution, two years after his committal. "The case of the 'Mad Butcher of Kingsbury Run' still is marked unsolved on the Cleveland police blotter," he concluded. "But Ness always was certain that Gaylord Sundheim was the man."

Frank Sweeney was still alive when Fraley's book appeared. In 1961, Sweeney was well along in his odyssey through veterans' hospitals and mental facilities, which finally ended with his death of heart failure in July of 1964, at the age of seventy. Sweeney had become fixated on Ness in the final years of life, and he undoubtedly followed Ness's rebirth as a television icon with amused contempt. On occasion, Sweeney's obsession with Ness took the form of angry letters to high-ranking officials. In 1953, a rambling four-page letter crossed the desk of J. Edgar Hoover to lodge a complaint about the spread of "Nessisms," a subject that Sweeney appeared to have raised with the director previously. "May I call your attention to this fact," Sweeney wrote, "that the condition continues to prevail and that a basic principle of our individual freedoms is not at Stake, but, being Prostituted." Sweeney closed by urging Hoover to give the matter close attention, as he saw no reason "to tolerate his Weak-ness."

Sweeney trained most of his energy on Ness himself, showering him with "venomous, jeering" postcards and incoherent letters. A small handful of Sweeney's communications, mostly postcards, are preserved in Ness's scrapbooks at the Western Reserve Historical Society in Cleveland. Even the shortest of Sweeney's messages presents a challenge to comprehension, rising up from a blast furnace of inkblots, erratic spellings, scattershot punctuation, and frenetic underlining. The printing is only fitfully legible, and even then, the meaning remains obscured by odd phrasings, cryptic allusions, and laborious attempts at humor.

Through the fog, one hears a steady thrum of seething contempt. One postcard, addressed to "Eliot-Am-Big-U-ous Ness," displays an ad for pansy seeds, undoubtedly referencing the derogatory use of the term "pansy" as an aspersion on Ness's manhood. Another card, addressed to "Eliot (Esophogotic) Ness," features a man in a comically large hat sticking out his tongue. The printed phrase "post card" is embellished with blue ink to indicate that a "mental-defective Post Card-ed this." A third message, to "Eliot Direct-um Ness," seizes on the phallic potential of a soaring 151-foot bell tower with a message that reads, in part, "In-das-Freudiology-this-organ-has-the-eminence-of-a-reamer." Carrying the bell tower image to an extreme, Sweeney adds: "Be seein of ya some-time in US Court-of-Peals." Other cards feature an image of two men behind bars and an advertisement for a collection of stories called *Handbook for Poisoners*, while a rambling, incoherent letter makes reference to "Phony Pschotization" and declares, "I trust that we shall meet again Amongst more favorable 'Federal issues'?"

In each case, Sweeney seems to have taken special care with his sign-off. On one card he identifies himself as "The-Sweeney Boy," while another reads: "F.E. Sweeney-M.D. / Paranoidal-Nemesis / The-Better-Half-Legal-Exaction / Will-Up-On-You-One Day?" At times he appears to be posturing as the villain of a penny dreadful, and never more so than when he makes reference to Sweeney Todd, perhaps best known at the time as the subject of a 1936 film called *The Demon Barber of Fleet Street*. The grisly tale had also featured in recent radio and stage dramas, all centered on the legend of the barber who slit his customers' throats, sent them tumbling through a trap door, and then cooked their remains into meat pies. One can only imagine Ness's thoughts at receiving a post-card signed: "Good-Cheer, The-American Sweeney."

It is tempting to read an admission of guilt here. The messages pre-served in Ness's papers were sent from a veterans' facility in Dayton, Ohio, in the mid-1950s. They clearly show a fury that remained undimmed more than a decade after the long ordeal at the Hotel Cleveland. The frequent references to legal action and psychological evaluation tend to support the notion that Ness had a hand in arranging at least some of Sweeney's en-forced stays in mental institutions. There is nothing, however, that rises to the level of a confession. Perhaps, as a defense attorney would surely have argued, these bizarre communications were nothing more than an angry rebuke over a misplaced accusation. In all of this seemingly uncontrolled ranting, the self-described "mental-defective" never crossed the line. He never gave Ness anything that would stand up in court.

Publicly, Ness made no mention of this barrage of messages, but in Fraley's telling, the nagging regularity of their arrival filled Betty with terror: "Don't worry about it," Ness was quoted as saying. "The guy who is writing these is well out of the way and you don't have to worry about him."

He could not have been quite so sanguine. Sweeney, the man he believed to be the butcher, was thumbing his nose at him.

Even after his death, Ness's former colleagues honored his silence with an almost religious fervor. More than ten years would elapse before Marilyn Bardsley, the true crime writer and researcher, narrowed in on the real name behind the Gaylord Sundheim alias. Even then, the principal figures in the drama remained wary, and the information only emerged by slow degrees. In the early 1970s, Bardsley contacted Dr. Royal Grossman, the psychiatrist who had been present during the Hotel Cleveland interrogation. Now in his eighties, Grossman confirmed the long-standing rumors of what had occurred in the hotel suite but would not identify the suspect. Bardsley then reached out to David Cowles, who verified Grossman's account but also declined to provide a name.

Further digging led Bardsley to a reformed burglar named Al Archaki, who told a story of meeting an affable, well-dressed stranger in a downtown nightclub in 1934. Archaki recalled that his new acquaintance flashed a roll of bills while offering to buy him a drink. "Do you live around here?" the stranger asked. "Do you have a wife?" There did not appear to be anything menacing in the stranger's curiosity, but Archaki felt no inclination to pursue the acquaintance. After a while, Archaki took his leave.

Three years later, while serving a prison term in Mansfield, Ohio, Archaki took part in a work release program at the Soldiers' and Sailors' Home in Sandusky. There, in the mess hall, he came across a man he recognized as the affable stranger from Cleveland, who now identified himself as a doctor. The two men renewed their acquaintance and quickly settled into a mutually beneficial relationship. Archaki supplied the doctor with alcohol, and in return, the doctor gave his new friend prescriptions for "barbitals."

Over time, Archaki noticed a disturbing pattern: the doctor's occasional absences from the Soldiers' and Sailors' Home appeared to coincide with the Kingsbury Run murders in Cleveland. His name, Bardsley learned, was Francis Edward Sweeney. Bardsley confirmed the identity with Royal Grossman, and then placed a second call to David Cowles, whose angry response—"Who gave you that name?"—demonstrates that he remained committed to his promise of silence.

"None of this, of course, irrefutably puts the Butcher's knife in Francis Sweeney's hand," writes Professor James Jessen Badal, "especially in the legal sense." Badal, an author long renowned as Cleveland's "Scholar of Evil," has written extensively on Kingsbury Run and other notable crimes, confirming and expanding upon Marilyn Bardsley's efforts.

A turning point for Badal came in August of 2012. He had just delivered a talk on the Kingsbury Run murders, he recalls, when a stranger approached and handed him a photograph. The yellowing image showed a grouping of six young doctors in white coats, apparently partners in a medical practice at 5026 Broadway Avenue, within sight of St. Alexis Hospital, in a once-thriving Central European neighborhood on the city's east side. At the center of the photograph sat a young Frank Sweeney.

For Badal, Sweeney's presence in the photo was a "proverbial jaw-dropper," throwing a sharpened focus on one of the enduring mysteries of Kingsbury Run. The neighborhood centered around the St. Alexis Hospital, where Frank Sweeney served his medical internship, was also the scene of the drama surrounding Emil Fronek, the hobo now known as "the one who got away." Fronek claimed that he would "never forget that fellow," but four years later he proved unable to locate the "house of horror" in which he'd nearly lost his life, much to the distress of Peter Merylo and the other detectives. Now, seventy-four years later, the photograph in James Badal's hands placed Frank Sweeney at the scene of Fronek's ordeal. If, as Badal believes, the photo reveals the exact location of the butcher's long-sought "murder laboratory," it also forges the most solid connection yet between the murders and Frank Sweeney.

The building had long since been demolished, but Badal soon established several important details. "It was not an office building in the accepted sense of the term at all," he explained, "it was a large, two-story house, a former residential structure whose first floor had been remodeled to serve as a small medical facility complete with waiting room, examination room, even a room for minor surgery. The second floor, however, could still serve as a living space." These details appear to conform with Emil Fronek's hazy recollection of what had occurred at the scene. Additionally, the building was bracketed by railroad tracks, supporting Fronek's description of having stumbled from the house to take refuge in an empty boxcar. At the same time, the unconverted second-floor living space affords a possible explanation to the puzzle of where Sweeney spent his time in the years following his divorce, a period in which he vanishes from city records. It also bears noting that Jackass Hill, the stagnant "murder pool," and other key locales would have been only a short distance away.

It remains puzzling, however, that Fronek did not recognize the building afterward, though a number of possible explanations suggest themselves. A separate, one-story rectangular building stood directly in front of the house, blocking at least one viewing angle and obscuring others. The awkward positioning of this structure, which abutted one side of the house and extended sharply toward the street, could well have confused Fronek, assuming he ever saw the building from that angle. The house stood on a corner, raising the possibility that Fronek approached it in 1934 from a different side, or that his view was blocked by the protruding structure. Badal theorizes that this smaller building, which housed a delicatessen, might have provided the plate of meat and potatoes served to Fronek by the mysterious doctor, which otherwise appeared to have been conjured from nowhere.

A second, perhaps even more crucial point centers on a funeral parlor that stood a few yards away. Years later, David Cowles would make mention of "an undertaker who buried all of the indigent bodies," whose business stood near St. Alexis Hospital. Cowles explained that Ness's suspect, whom he still resolutely declined to name, would regularly "go over there and would amputate." This cryptic statement slots in neatly with what is known about the medical practice at 5026 Broadway. An establishment called the Raus Funeral Home operated virtually next door, within sight of St. Alexis. The Raus family also maintained a second building nearby, reserved for corpses of the city's indigent population. Perhaps Cowles meant to state that the suspect had secured permission to practice surgical techniques on unclaimed bodies, but he offered no clarification. Instead, he went on to add a bewildering additional detail, stating that the doctor's amputations were performed "exactly the same way he would do with unknown bodies in the war." This startling re-

mark suggests that Ness's team had acquired heretofore unknown details of the suspect's military service, and uncovered evidence that the
bodies of fallen soldiers had been subjected to butchery of the type seen
at Kingsbury Run. Here again, Cowles offered no clarification. The exact
nature of these procedures remains frustratingly unknown, and there
is no indication of how the information came to light. It bears repeating,
however, that Frank Sweeney served overseas with a medical supply
unit during the First World War.

Today, Professor Badal is certain that the cumulative effect of these
details has made it possible "to pinpoint the exact location of the Butcher's long-sought-for 'secret laboratory.'" He also believes that the proximity of the Raus Funeral Home may clear up the confounding questions
that linger over the East 9th Street dump site, where two sets of remains
were discovered in the days following the standoff at the Hotel Cleveland. One of those victims, the anatomist Wingate Todd asserted, had
been embalmed. If Dr. Todd's claim was correct, perhaps these remains
came from the Raus mortuary or its adjunct facility. If Sweeney was
responsible, however, he somehow managed to transfer the remains to
the dump at a time when he would have been under close watch. Possibly the butcher squad's surveillance wasn't as rigorous as claimed, or
perhaps Sweeney shook off his shadows as he had once done with young
Arnold Sagalyn. It can't be proved either way, but the notion that these
remains were placed boldly within sight of city hall as a taunt to Ness
has become one of the enduring themes of the saga.

Another perplexing question remains. If David Cowles knew about
the building at 5026 Broadway, it stands to reason that Eliot Ness also
knew. It cannot have escaped the notice of either man that Fronek's tale
meshed perfectly with their suspicions of Frank Sweeney. And yet, after spending a full hour questioning Fronek behind closed doors, Ness
emerged to say that "he did not think the story was related to the series
of murders here." Even allowing for Ness's concerns over the lack of
hard evidence, his statement seems pointedly dismissive. *Move along;
there's nothing to see here.* He might just as easily have offered an open-
ended comment to the effect that inquiries would continue, given that

Fronek had promised to return at a future date. Badal sees the heavy hand of Congressman Martin Sweeney in this. "The curtain of silence," he writes, "had already begun to descend."

Perhaps this would have been true in 1938, when Ness made the comment, but the men at the center of this drama seemed fully prepared to carry the secret to the grave, long after the political constraints of the moment had faded. Cowles and Grossman only grudgingly confirmed the identity of the suspect once the ex-convict Al Archaki had spilled the beans. Even then, Cowles declined to give the name during his 1983 comments on the murders. "I won't mention any names," he said. "A relative of his was a congressman." This degree of concealment remains difficult to explain. There are limits to the power of a congressman, especially one who, by 1983, had been dead for more than twenty years.

The answer may rest with Harold Burton. At every stage of his tenure as mayor, Burton had his eye fixed on higher office. As early as 1936, when Burton campaigned so vigorously to bring the Republican National Convention to Cleveland, his name was briefly circulated as "dark horse material" in the event of a deadlock, "for either first or second place on the Republican ticket." By the time Ness handed in his resignation as safety director in 1942, Burton had been elected to the United States Senate. Three years later, in October of 1945, Burton took a seat on the Supreme Court of the United States.

As mayor, Burton would not have taken an active role in the day-to-day operations of Ness's butcher squad, but he could not have been ignorant of their workings. Burton himself directed Ness to take personal charge of the Kingsbury Run investigation in September of 1936. It stands to reason that Ness briefed him on their progress. By the same token, Ness was known to have sought Burton's advice—both legally and politically—before taking actions that might have negative consequences, as he had done before mobilizing his assault on the Harvard Club, where he had no legal authority.

There is no way to know if Ness consulted the mayor before he snatched up Frank Sweeney and grilled him for days on end at the Hotel Cleveland. Either way, Burton's fingerprints would have been all over it. There can be no question that the mayor would have been caught up in any legal or political reprisals that resulted from a public airing of the matter. Congressman Martin Sweeney, who once referred to Ness as Burton's "alter ego," would have enjoyed slinging mud at his long-time political adversary, and Burton's elevation to the Supreme Court could only have served to add luster to the prospect. There is no reason to imagine that Congressman Sweeney, a gleefully vitriolic critic of FDR, his own party's sitting president, would have backed away from a clash with a Republican Supreme Court justice. At best, this would have embarrassed Burton, but it could also have seriously undermined the reputation of a man now sworn to uphold equal justice under law. Ness would have done everything in his power to avoid drawing Burton into a potential scandal.

On hearing of Ness's death in 1957, Justice Burton sent a heartfelt note to Betty: "I have lost a great and good friend," Burton wrote. "The nation has lost a valuable citizen." By that time, Burton had begun to manifest the onset of Parkinson's disease, which would force his resignation from the Supreme Court the following year. Burton's illness would have left Cowles and the others all the more determined to spare him the repercussions of the Sweeney affair.

No single explanation can account for the icy depth of the silence that Ness imposed on himself and his colleagues, but concern for Burton's reputation would have been prominent on the list. When Ness resigned as safety director, Burton wrote to thank him for the "high standard of integrity" he had brought to the job. "I hope," Burton added, "you feel that the sustained effort you put into this work has been worthwhile." No effort in Ness's career was more sustained than this bargain of silence, and it came at a cost. The Kingsbury Run murders have shadowed his legacy as the case he couldn't crack, the mass murderer he failed to bring to justice. At the end of his life, however, even as his convictions about Sweeney hardened into certainty, he could take satisfaction in having defanged the serpent, even though his suspect never faced a judge. Al Capone had gone to prison on relatively minor charges, and though many found it disappointing at the time, this pragmatic solution ended his criminal reign. Perhaps Ness came to believe that a similar consolation could be taken in this instance, but he left few hints. His public statements were few and far between, and once he left office in Cleveland, he made no comment on the case whatsoever—with one notable exception.

In 1947, at the height of his ill-fated mayoral campaign, Ness spent a great deal of time making the rounds of civic groups and garden clubs, gamely answering questions on topics such as public transportation charters and water filtration plants. At every stop, he leaned hard on his efforts to make Cleveland a safer city during his time at city hall. "This work," he said, "probably is the most important I have ever done."

He appeared momentarily thrown, at the height of the campaigning, when a reporter came forward with a question about the torso slayings, suggesting that the unsolved case weighed heavily on his record. Ness paused, clearly uncomfortable, and chose his words carefully. "That case," he answered at last, "has been solved."

He would say nothing more.

EPILOGUE

Eliot-Am-Big-U-ous Ness

That case has been solved.

Eliot Ness

Was Frank Sweeney the butcher, or did Eliot Ness get it wrong?

The passage of time, together with Ness's impenetrable wall of silence, makes it unlikely that the question can ever be answered to the satisfaction of all. It remains a subject of lively debate, especially among true crime specialists. "We will never know for sure," writes Steven Nickel. "Ness's 'solution' must remain another enigma in the Torso case." John Stark Bellamy II sees "little reason to think that Ness was right," and suggests instead that there might have been several different killers at work: "There is virtually no evidence—other than the medical monomania of Sam Gerber and like-minded theorists—to indicate that the so-called Kingsbury Run Torso victims were murdered by one individual." Even after the revelations of the 5026 Broadway photo, James Badal stops short of declaring the matter closed. "I'm still not at that point, not 100 percent," he says, but he adds, "I'm much more comfortable now saying I believe Sweeney was indeed the killer." Badal admits that the evidence is circumstantial and concludes that "short of sworn testimony about a deathbed confession or some yet-to-be-discovered personal diary or letter, there is no way to tie Francis Sweeney—or anyone else—directly to the crimes."

And yet, as his longtime collaborator Mark Wade Stone adds: "Everything we find out points to him. Nothing has so far pointed away."

I could cheerfully argue either side of this equation, owing to the fact that nagging questions hang over every phase of the investigation: Were the findings of Coroners Pearse and Gerber accurate? Were they consistent? Did all of the Cleveland victims die by the same hand? Were the Pennsylvania crimes tied to the Cleveland series? Was Archaki telling the truth? Was Fronek? Could Gerber really have failed to detect signs of embalming in the East 9th Street remains? If so, what else did he miss? Was the killer a "sex degenerate" or a "thrill-killer" or something else entirely? Each factor in this equation is a variable, making it impossible to solve for X.

Each of these individual questions folds into a larger one: Did Ness truly believe that Sweeney was the guy? I put the question to James Badal late one night as we sat together in a bar near Kingsbury Run. His answer was quick and steely: "He *knew* it."

There have been times over the past several years when I fell prey to the impulse, common among true crime enthusiasts, to try to shed fresh light on the puzzle. I spent the better part of a month chasing a fleeting reference to Gaylord Sundheim through World War I documents at the Library of Congress. I also fell down a fairly deep rabbit hole when I discovered a "Dr. Manzella" in connection with the 1933 murder of "Iron Mike" Malloy in New York, a case that has passed into legend as "The Murder Trust." It will be recalled that a record of payments to an unknown "Dr. Manzella" appeared among the effects of Florence Polillo, but I could find no connection between the two. For a time, I became obsessed with a pair of small but seemingly significant variations between Walter Winchell's radio broadcast and his newspaper column, the latter describing the unnamed suspect as "a socially-registered physician" with "that menacing Barrymore look in his left eye." I logged a great many hours chasing after names in the *Cleveland Blue Book*, and comparing photos of Frank Sweeney's slightly unfocused gaze to those of John and Lionel Barrymore. I regret nothing.

I'd love to be able to talk it all over with my grandfather Fred, who made so many jokes at Ness's expense with his merry band at the Anvil Revue. It turns out that Fred got to know a great many Cleveland newspapermen in those days, and several of them were lead reporters during the Kingsbury Run years. As a child, according to my father, I had Thanksgiving dinners with a fair number of them. "You wouldn't remember," my father told me. "You'd have been under the table with your Matchbox cars." I'd probably be just as happy not knowing this, I admit. I still have some of those cars, including an Eliot Ness–style Ford Coupe, but I'd gladly trade it for an hour or two with Clayton Fritchey or Philip Porter.

I often wonder what Fred really thought of Ness, which invariably sends me back to some advice he once gave me, toward the end of his life. We were talking about a book I was writing at the time, a biography of an author I'd admired since the age of eleven. "Prepare yourself," he said. "You may not like this guy so much after spending all this time with him."

I still like Ness just fine, even after spending all this time with him, but I suspect Fred would have told me that he was a loudmouth, fond of tooting his own horn. Maybe so, but if I've learned anything, it's that Ness could keep his mouth shut when it counted.

Still, people seem to enjoy cutting him down to size. "The real Eliot Ness," one account notes, "was named after the novelist George Eliot, had almost nothing to do with the conviction and imprisonment of Al Capone, once ran for mayor of Cleveland (losing by a two-to-one margin), and died a semidrunk in 1957." That seems a little reductive to me, but the backlash persists because the attention paid to Ness comes at the expense of the men who built the tax case against Capone—men like George E. Q. Johnson, Elmer Irey, and Frank Wilson. It is appropriate that Ness should be judged for his excesses, but there have, in fact, been any number of efforts to give the Treasury men their due. In 1949, eight years before *The Untouchables* came to be written, a movie called *The Undercover Man* opened in theaters across America, based on an article published in *Collier's* by Treasury Agent Frank Wilson. The film, billed as the "shocking bullet-by-bullet story of America's secret war on the mobs," tracks the efforts of a Treasury agent named Frank Warren, played by Glenn Ford, as he builds a tax evasion case against a powerful crime figure known as the Big Fellow. It turns out, as the story unfolds, that Warren is the kind of bookkeeper who can take a punch, and who coolly empties his revolver at an oncoming sedan, leaping out of the way at the last instant. Perhaps the comparison is unfair, as Wilson's name was changed, but if Ness is to be lambasted for going Hollywood, it should at least be acknowledged that he wasn't the only one, or even the first. Maybe it would be closer to the truth to say that he had better writers.

Ness would not have recognized himself in any of his recent portrayals, either as a bulletproof hero or a feckless drunk, and in paying so much attention to what he did in Chicago, we lose sight of the miracle he wrought in Cleveland. "Ness restored a sense of hope and pride to a beleaguered community," Clayton Fritchey wrote on the day of Ness's resignation. "Today, policemen no longer have to tip their hats when they pass a gangster on the streets."

Even in his final days, friends who knew nothing of his earlier life took note of an inflexible sense of honor. "I have never known an individual who lived by a stricter code," said William Ayres, a colleague of the Coudersport days. "They say all men have a price. Well, whatever his price was, it was so high that nobody could pay it."

Ness's own view was more straightforward. "Hell, I'm just like anyone else," he once said, "no braver nor any more timid. There were things which I had to do."

He paused and gave a smile as he added: "I did them."

ACKNOWLEDGMENTS

This book would not have been possible without the assistance of the following institutions and their knowledgeable research assistants: The Library Research Center of the Western Reserve Historical Society, with special thanks to Ann K. Sindelar and Vicki Catozza; the Harold H. Burton Papers, Manuscript Division, Library of Congress, with special thanks to Thomas Mann and his League of Extraordinary Gentlemen; the Michael Schwartz Library, Special Collections, Cleveland State University, with special thanks to William Barrow and Elizabeth Piwkowski; the Cleveland Police Historical Society and Museum, with special thanks to Mazie Adams; the Cleveland Public Library, with special thanks to Brian Meggitt; the historical archives of the Bureau of Alcohol, Tobacco, Firearms and Explosives; the Harold Washington Library Center of the Chicago Public Library; the National Archives and Records Administration of College Park, Maryland; and the National Law Enforcement Museum of Washington, DC.

In addition, I am grateful to the following individuals for lending their talents and unflagging support: James Badal, Rebecca McFarland, Marilyn Bardsley, Arnold Sagalyn, Charles Spicer, Andrew Martin, Sarah Grill, Hector DeJean, Susanna Einstein, Patterson Smith, Harlan Coben, Jeff Abbott, Sonny Wareham, Linda Rutledge, the

Allen Appels (père et fils), Larry Kahaner, John McKeon, and Marc Smolonsky.

Special thanks always to Alison Corbett, till a' the seas gang dry.

And a lasting debt of gratitude to Jon Lellenberg (1946–2021), my dear friend and frequent collaborator.

NOTES

Many of the sources for the quotes and historical details in these pages are specified in context, and a number of them appear in multiple works. The notes below will assist readers in locating important sources that will not otherwise be clear. In cases where the bibliography includes more than one work by a particular author, a more specific reference is given. (Unless otherwise specified, the notation of "Badal" refers to *In the Wake of the Butcher*, by James Jessen Badal, and the notation of "Collins" refers to Eliot Ness and the Mad Butcher, by Max Allan Collins and A. Brad Schwartz.) In addition, most chapter headings are followed by a summary of general background sources.

The following abbreviations are used throughout:

AI—author interview
AP—Associated Press
CHE—*Chicago Herald and Examiner*
CN—*Cleveland News*
CP—*Cleveland Press*
CPD—*Plain Dealer*
CPHS—Cleveland Police Historical Society archives
CT—*Chicago Tribune*
ENCPL—Eliot Ness Clippings, 1935–1973, Cleveland Public Library

ENP&S—Eliot Ness Papers and Scrapbooks, Microfilm Collections, Western Reserve Historical Society

ENMS—Eliot Ness Manuscript, original summary document written by Ness as background for his memoir, *The Untouchables*, from the Eliot Ness Papers and Scrapbooks, Microfilm Collections, Western Reserve Historical Society

HHB—Harold H. Burton Papers, Manuscript Division, Library of Congress

INS—International News Service

LPUCB—John Larson Papers, University of California Berkeley

NYT—*New York Times*

UP—United Press

SPAU—Sagalyn Papers, American University Special Collections

WP—*Washington Post*

WRHS—Western Reserve Historical Society

Prologue: The Last of the Good Guys

1. "egg-tossing vandal"—CPD, 3/16/36
1. "Eight Agents Caught Capone"—AP, 6/14/31
1. enraged Capone swinging a baseball bat—ENP&S, reel no. 1
2. "veteran policemen were cynical"—Porter, pp. 97–98
2. "Cleveland coasted downhill"—Miller, p. 136
2. "tip their hats"—CP, 4/27/42; Condon, p. 244
2. "remote director . . . I am going to be out"—Heimel, p. 153; Nickel, p. 27; Perry, p. 126
3. "He is about 5 feet 11½ inches tall"—CP, 12/11/35
3. "There was never anybody like him"—Condon, p. 243
3. "a real-life 'Murders in the Rue Morgue'"—CN, 09/12/36
3. "Same Manner as Jack the Ripper"—UP, 09/20/38
4. "Ten times in Cleveland"—CP, 07/10/37
4. "I want to see this psycho caught"—Bellamy, p. 134
5. "background and incidents of the Capone case"—Eliot Ness letter to Oscar Fraley, ENMS
8. "I'm the youngest safety director"—Carl D. Friebolin Papers, WRHS
9. "almost unknown creature, a master criminal"—Martin, p. 95
9. "One of these days"—CPD, 6/18/61

1: The Lady in the Lake

Background: Badal, pp. 22–28; Bellamy, pp. 15–19; Collins, pp. 9–19; Martin, pp. 61–62; Cleveland newspapers and AP reports, 09/03/34–09/23/34

13. "Nothing to depress or demoralize"—Van Tassell, p. 381

14. "The Dark City"—CP, 12/14/34

14. "no one ever complained"—CPD, 10/29/34

15. "slaked lime for quick lime"—CPD, 09/07/34

15. "prankishly inclined"; "There is no question"—CP, 09/05/34

15. "Hacked Body of Woman Found"—CP, 09/05/34

16. "fitted roughly"; "It was the coroner's theory"—CPD, 09/07/34

17. "expertly dismembered"—CP, 09/04/34

18. "waving"; "Badly frightened, she ran home"—CP, 09/06–07/34

18. "Heavy storms"—CP, 09/04/34

19. "but so close to being perfect"—Bellamy, p. 18

19–20. "He is Eliot Ness"; "I am just finding . . . Our job was more spectacular"—CPD, 09/21/34

2: Chicago Has Fallen

Background: Bair, pp. 10–129; Bergreen, pp. 343–54; Collins: *Scarface and the Untouchable*, pp. 35–43, 67–71, 349–65; Eig, pp. 209–46; Heimel, pp. 19–114, Nickel, pp. 30–45; Okrent, pp. 227–74, 321–69; Perry, pp. 9–109; Slocum, pp. 15–33

21. "Eliot Ness really was two men"—*Coronet* magazine, July 1961

21–22. "His speech sounds candid"; "He is in short, an enigma"—CPD, 09/14/36; Heimel, p. 100

22. "Some people considered him arrogant"; "Elegant Mess"—Heimel, pp. 21–22

22–23. "something big"; "I'm so proud . . . I didn't see him all that much"—Heimel, pp. 16–19; Perry, p. 3; NP&S, reel no. 2

23. "We used to tease him"—Heimel, p. 21

23. "courageous federal operative"—AP, 01/07/32

23. "like trying to dry up"; "Wield Mop"—Perry, p. 24; AP, 12/27/28

24. "hadn't worked day and night"; "The enrollment first"—Heimel, pp. 22–23

24. "The trouble with the Prohibition Law"—ENMS, p. 22

25. "I don't think I could stand the monotony"—CHE, 06/15/31

25. "a tidal wave of beer"—CT, 06/15/31

25. "We're big business"; "a smile and a gun"—Eig, p. 81

25. "Together with his ruthlessness . . . Under that patent leather hair"; "giving the public"—Heimel, pp. 17, 97

26. "They talk to me . . . and so do they"—Eig, p. 272

26. "The skies were black"—Slocum, p. 19

26. "Chicago . . . has fallen"—Perry, p. 25

26. "Corruption was apparently a continuous problem"—ENMS, p. 1

26. "wouldn't be much competition"—Porter, p. 106

26. "popping photographers' flash . . . on unsuspecting Chicago"—Slocum, p. 20

27. "One time two truckloads . . . He was on the take"—Bergreen, p. 347

27. "He bent a few rules"—Heimel, p. 97; Perry, p. 4

27. "murderous fusillade"—AP, 02/14/29

28. "the law-abiding people of Chicago"—ENMS, p. 9

28. "oldest Special Agent"; "reputation for honesty . . . fearlessness in raids"—Perry, p. 51

29. "domino effect"; "a lot to learn, kid"—Heimel, p. 51

29. "not paying enough income tax"—ENMS, p. 9

29. "Go out and actually prove"—NYT, 06/18/31

29. "I was allowed to pick a number of agents . . . general qualities I desired"—ENMS, p. 9; Ness and Fraley, *The Untouchables*, p. 26

30. "consuming liquor not in the line of duty"—Perry, p. 101

30. "knees shook like jelly"—*Los Angeles Times*, 10/04/62

31. "Our first move . . . first observation . . . cleaning barrels"—ENMS, pp. 10–12

32. "At last we felt we had a Capone brewery . . . If this group of 12 . . . as we would design a football play"—ENMS, pp. 10–12

33–34. "we would drive the truck through the doors . . . There was no brewery . . . on the necks of five operators"—ENMS, pp. 12–14

34. "We seized some 45 trucks"—ENMS, p. 14

35. "We'd go in blazing"—Heimel, p. 81

35. "Well . . . looks like we're dished again"—Perry, p. 93

35–36. "to look good for his wife . . . we learned a great deal"—ENMS pp. 16–18

36. "We always travelled with sawed-off shot guns in our pockets"—ENMS, p. 7

36. "As my investigation of the Capone mob went on . . . He immediately threw it back"—ENMS, pp. 18–19

37. "wang slashed off"—Bergreen, p. 349

37. "flashy new car . . . I found a gun . . . meant for us"—ENMS, p. 7; Perry, p. 40

37. "Capone was brought to the bar of justice"—ENMS, p. 21

38. "all the praise . . . should be shared"—AP, 06/14/31

38. "No soldier on the battlefield"—Perry, p. 90

38. "men on the firing line"—AP, 06/14/31

38. "The 'Untouchables' . . . are waiting for further orders"—NYT, 06/18/31

39. "Did you ever think"—Perry, p. 98

3: Jackass Hill

Background: Badal, pp. 29–43; Bellamy, pp. 45–48; Collins, pp. 21–24; Martin, pp. 56–62; Nickel, pp. 11–21; Cleveland newspapers and AP reports, 08/15/35–10/12/35

41. "city within a city"—"The Cleveland Union Station," souvenir pamphlet, 06/28/30

41. "from an overgrown country town to a real metropolis"—Condon, p. 197

42. "rookeries and dives"—"The Cleveland Union Station," souvenir pamphlet, 06/28/30

42. "If you enjoy feeling your flesh creep"—CP, 09/11/36

42. "some trouble in a saloon . . . headless and limbless form"; "torso murder"—CPD, 01/27/1874; CL, 11/13/1905

43. "a dead man with no head"—Nickel, p. 15

43. "neatly positioned"; "a snaky thing"—Martin, p. 56

43. "You find the head?"—Nickel, p. 15

44–45. "murder of passion"; "headless and otherwise mutilated"—CPD, 09/24/35–09/25/35

45–46. "I saw the head"; "This man's death"; "It's a hell of a job"—Badal, pp. 32–35

46. "some unknown chemical"—CT, 09/25/35; Martin, p. 56

47. "saturated with oil"—Badal, p. 36

47. "Andrassy was the type of fellow"—Martin, p. 58

49. "Italian and Greek vendettas"—Martin, p. 59

49. "stabbed an Italian"; "Edward lived in continual fear"—Badal, p. 38; Bellamy, p. 47

50. "female doctor"—Martin, p. 60

51. "prostitutes, pimps, hobos . . . they wondered if Andrassy"—Martin, pp. 57–59

51. "He was anything but"—Badal, p. 48

51–52. "a 'nationality case'"; "Eddie seemed very nervous"—Martin, pp. 60, 68

54. "flood of tear gas"—UP, 09/30/35

54. "The gang was rounded up by Eliot Ness"—AP, 09/26/35

55. "bad feeling about this one"—Nickel, p. 17; Bellamy, p. 48

4: Snorky's Last Ride

Background: Bair, pp. 130–248; Bergreen, pp. 404–13, 432–510; Collins: *Scarface and the Untouchable*, pp. 483–501; Eig, pp. 318–77; Heimel, pp. 15–17, 115–37; Nickel, pp. 42–45; Chicago newspapers and AP reports, 04/25/30–09/14/34

56. "I was now . . . becoming known as a 'gangbuster'"—ENMS, p. 15
56. "I'm no Italian"—Bair, p. 10
57. "extremely undignified"; "So 'Untouchables' it was"—NYT, 06/18/31
58. "Al's Nemesis Boasts Ph.B."—CHE, 06/15/31
59. "colorless work"; "overthrow the Capone dynasty"—AP, 06/19/31
59. "satrap of Chicago"—Bergreen, p. 273
60. "hoped everybody was satisfied"—AP, 06/19/31
60. "impossible to bargain"—Eig, p. 341
60. "Judge Wilkerson has set"—NYT, 09/11/31
60. "the especial thorn"—*Chicago Daily News*, 09/23/31
61. "Worried? . . . who wouldn't be?"—Bair, p. 230
61. "Capone's boys have a complete list"; "bring me his entire panel of jurors"—Bergreen, pp. 438–42
61. "Eliot Ness . . . may take the stand"—AP, 07/29/31
62. "tillers of the fruitful soil"; "chap who supplied the drapes"—Runyon, pp. 227–35
62. "Is it conceivable"—Bergreen, p. 477
62. "much of an income"—Eig, p. 276
63. "Well, Snorky"; "I'll kill 'im!"—Heimel, p. 166; Ness and Fraley, *The Untouchables*, p. 204; Nickel, p. 43
64. "it was found that a truck . . . the fruit of the racket"—ENMS, p. 15
64. "gale of oratory"—Runyon, p. 245
65. "I'm not through fighting"—AP, 10/17/31
65. "airtight"; "new booze conspiracy"—Perry, p. 100
66. "I just wish"—Heimel, p. 20
66. "the end of Al Capone"—Bergreen, pp. 507–08
66. "Mussolini was passin'"—CT, 05/04/32
67. "Keep your eyes open"—Ness and Fraley, *The Untouchables*, p. 251
67. "For one thing, it'll be hot"—Bergreen, pp. 507–08
67–68. "Well, I'm on my way"; "strange idea"—Heimel, p. 17
68. "ain't too stiff a rap"—Bergreen, p. 501
69. "fed up . . . everybody knows—now"—CPD, 04/01/36

5: Capone Nemesis Gets Big Job

Background: Collins, pp. 24–38; Condon, pp. 230–44; Heimel, pp. 141–78; Nickel, pp. 23–29, 47–48; Porter, pp. 94–98; Cleveland newspapers and AP reports, 04/13/34–01/02/36

73. "municipal side glance"—Condon, p. 231

74. "Boss is using his influence"; "I do not think"—Bergreen, p. 594; Perry, pp. 107–09; *Smithsonian*, October 2014

75. "passing through a rather unsettled period"; "Those mountain men"—Heimel, p. 144

76. "ambitious for Eliot Ness"—CN, 07/14/38

77. "was not one to blow his own horn"—Porter, p. 96

77. "dear to the hearts of reporters"—CPD, 12/11/35

77. "Had he done so"—Heimel, p. 148

78. "boodling and incompetence"—Porter, p. 87

78. "as good a time"—CPD, 12/28/33

78. "I don't know"; "still a potent figure"; "consorting on terms"—CPD, 07/02/35–07/04/35

79. "won't hurt us a bit"—CPD, 07/04/35

79. "came like a breath of spring"—Porter, p. 94

79. "I'd hate to lose him"—CPD, 11/20/35

80. "just the kind of guy Burton needs"—Porter, p. 97

80. "Ness was the boy . . . local mobs don't alarm him too much"—CPD, 12/11/35

80. "How elections are won"; "qualifications of this marvel"—CPD, 12/11/35–12/12/35

81. "I will accept the position"—CP, 12/08/35

81. "We were beginning to be tagged"—CPD, 12/13/35

81. "Racketeering here is rampant"—Perry, pp. 130–31

82. this group of "Unknowns"—Heimel, pp. 185–89; Nickel, pp. 96–97

83. "mild-mannered, collegiate-looking"; "I am greatly honored"—AP, 12/11/35; CP, 12/11/35

83. "mingled anxiety and high expectations"—CPD, 12/09/35

83–84. "safety directors come and safety directors go"; "32 and single"—CPD, 12/12/35

85. "plain and fancy gambling"—CPD, 04/14/36

85. "attracting the attention"; "They're jittery anyway"—CPD, 12/14/35

85. "I've served under five safety directors"—Perry, p. 126

85–86. "A quarter century of political favoritism . . . cleaning out the Augean stables"—Porter, p. 98; CPD, 12/22/35

6: Woman Slain, Head Sought in Coal Bins

Background: Badal, pp. 50–61; Bellamy, pp. 67–72; Collins, pp. 47–48; Martin, pp. 61–67; Nickel, pp. 51–55; Cleveland newspapers, 01/26/36–02/20/36

87. "meat shop burglars"—CP, 01/27/36

90. "white girls"—Badal, p. 52

91. "No surgeon . . . manipulate a knife"—CP, 09/06/34

92–93. "twirling his night stick"; "similar to 12,000 others"—CPD, 03/05/41; *Canton Repository*, 07/09/39

93–94. "a police character"; "immoral purposes"; "any sex desires"—Bellamy, p. 68; Martin, p. 64; *Official Detective Stories*, November 1937

94, 96. "She never gave us any trouble"; "mean stuff"; "She usually ironed"—CP, 01/27/36

96. "very dirty looking"; "cut her all up"; "nice looking"—Badal, p. 56–57; Martin, p. 66

97. "Captain Swing"—CP, 02/07/36

97–98. "drinking quite hard . . . took all of her clothes and went away"—Martin, p. 65

99. "wrenched"—Badal, p. 59

99. "shed little light"—ENP&S, reel no. 2

100. "howling, yelling, whistling youngsters"—CN, 04/04/36

100. "decently operated police department"—CPD, 12/22/35

101. "a personable gentleman"; "a glamor and a glow"—Condon, p. 231

101. "My order should not be construed"—CPD, 09/02/36

101. "that ancient nest of intrigue"—CPD, 12/22/35

102. "additional prestige"; "sulphurous language"; "every man on the force"—CN, 12/15/35; CP, 04/11/40; CPD, 12/15/35

102–3. "In any city . . . crooked, lazy, and drunk!"; "double-entry booking"—Condon, p. 236

103. "New York . . . has its Eliot Ness"—CPD, 02/08/36

7: "Let's Go"

Background: Collins, pp. 35–48; Condon, pp. 233–35; Heimel, pp. 160–65; Nickel, pp. 48–51; Perry, pp. 132–41; Porter, pp. 100–101; SPAU, Box 1; CPD magazine, 02/04/2001; Cleveland newspapers and AP reports, 01/01/36–02/05/36

104. "I lost my shirt"—ENCPL

104. "Long before there was a Las Vegas"—*Cleveland Magazine*, August 1987

105. "Have my body cremated"—CPD, 02/03/91

105. "debatable whether gambling is morally wrong"—Condon, p. 236

105. "Choke Crime By its Purse"—CPD, 01/23/36

106. "telling Sheriff Sulzmann"—CP, 01/11/36

106. "as Irish as the keeper of the Blarney Stone"—Perry, p. 147

106. "Anyone who knows Frank"—CPD, 06/25/57

106. "It was a public joke"—CPD, 02/04/2001

107–8. "how large a sucker"; "state of siege"; "The hell with that"—CP, 01/11/36

109. "brazen defiance"—CPD, 01/11/36

109–10. "If an arrest is made"; "Prosecutor Cullitan is at the Harvard Club"—CP, 01/11/36

111. "I found the boys just coming off duty"—CP, 01/11/36

111. "I would be unable to exaggerate . . . 'we must go where you go'"—CPD, 01/14/36

112. "an issue no less important"—CPD, 01/11/36

112. "the holster's enough"—Heimel, p. 177

112–13. "Let's have a light here . . . Let's go"—CPD, 01/11/36

113. "I'm Eliot Ness . . . We'll back them up"—Nickel, p. 50; CPD, 02/04/2001

114–15. "Say, who do you"; "haymaker"; "happened so fast"—CP, 01/11/36; CPD, 01/11/36–01/14/36

115. "Don't try to slug me"—CP, 01/11/36

116. "Gee . . . awful lot"—CPD, 01/11/36

116. "blinked in surprise and pleasure"—Condon, p. 235

116. "Our objective"—CN, 01/11/36

117. "manhood had been impugned"—Gentry, p. 187

118. "cordially disposed"; "There is no advice"—Heimel, p. 187; *Smithsonian*, October 2014

8: The Tattooed Man

Background: Badal, pp. 62–70; Bellamy, pp. 89–94; Collins, pp. 60–61; Heimel, pp. 167–82; Martin, pp. 68–69; Nickel, pp. 59–69; Vacha, pp. 45–114; SPAU, Box 1; Cleveland newspapers, 06/02/36–08/30/36

119. "We see the pants all rolled up"—CPD, 06/06/36

122. "The hand which removed . . . is the same hand"—CPD, 06/06/36

123. "a crazed killer with a flair for butchery"—Bellamy, p. 92

124. "maniac with a lust to kill . . . That's a maniac's trick!"—CPD, 06/07/36

124. "a madman whose god is the guillotine"—CN, 07/23/36

126. "in an effort to aid in identification"—CP, 06/06/36

126. "how that man can sell newspapers!"—Bellamy, p. 94

126. "thought it imperative to enter"—CPD, 06/07/36

127. "most misjudged man"—CPD, 07/31/36

127. "A falling domino pattern began to develop"—Porter, p. 98

128. "boyish face and enigmatic manner"—CPD, 07/26/36

128. "world's original mystery man"—CPD, 09/14/36

129. "new Untouchables . . . one hundred consecutive summer nights"—Condon, p. 237

129. "a diplomat, a marksman, a memory expert"—Condon, p. 237; CPD, 3/16/41; Nickel, p. 96

129. "Murder Room"—CPD, 06/15/37

130. "There is nothing . . . gold rush days"—CN, 10/02/40

130. "Need Ness"—Perry, p. 182

132–34. Great Lakes Exposition—AI; CN, 06/06/36; CP, 07/25/36; CPD, 06/05/36–06/010/36; Vacha, pp. 74–80

134. "It was so lifelike"—AI, David L. Stashower

9: Lake Torso

Background: Badal, pp. 71–87; Bellamy, pp. 117–20, 131–38; Collins, pp. 71–86; Martin, pp. 69–71; Nickel, pp. 72–80; Perry, pp. 170–74; Cleveland newspapers, 07/15/36–09/21/36

136. Barkley's wanderings—AP, 10/18/33; CPD, 10/21/33; *Arkansas Gazette*, 10/18/33

137. "innumerable worms . . . dog or other animal"—Badal, p. 73

137. "probable murder" by an unknown method—Badal, p. 73

139. "Fiend Beheads Living Victims"—CP, 07/24/36

141. "drunk detector . . . camera-eye squad"—ENP&S, reel no. 2

141. visit to the city by President Roosevelt—CPD, 08/15/36; CP, 08/15/36; Vacha, pp. 75–83

144. "oily, coffee-colored creek"—CN, 09/11/36

145. "some heavier instrument"; "probable murder by decapitation"—Badal, p. 81

145. "sex maniac of the sadistic type"—CN, 09/11/36; Badal, p. 81

148. "old shoes"; "We never see anything"—CPD, 09/13/36

149. "tourists"—Badal, p. 82

149–50. "blank wall of clewless mystery"; "very slight"—CP, 09/10/36; CN, 09/10/36

150. "Of all horrible nightmares"—CN, 09/12/36

150. "quagmire . . . beyond his experience"—James Badal interview by Sam Allard, https://www.clevescene.com/cleveland/scholar-of-evil-james-badal-clevelands-resident-torso-murders-historian/Content?oid=4345717

151. "He had to do something"; "I want to see this psycho caught"—Badal, p. 87; Bellamy, p. 134; Nickel, p. 82

10: Voodoo Doctors and Chicken Freaks

Background: Badal, pp. 117–33; Bellamy, pp. 136–37; Collins, pp. 89–95; Martin, pp. 71–77; Nickel, pp. 82–93, 103–4; Cleveland newspapers, 06/15/36–11/22/36

153. "Police Act on Order of Ness"—CP, 09/12/36

153. "This killer has great cunning"—Nickel, p. 126; Heimel, p. 196

153. "a concerted effort . . . groping"—ENP&S, reel no. 2

153. "a bit of decayed flesh . . . about a month ago"—CN, 09/15/36; CPD, 09/15/36; ENP&S, reel no. 2

154–55. "It is hoped"; "perversion or cannibalism"; "normal life"—CN, 09/14/36; CPD, 09/16/36; ENP&S, reel no. 2

155. "advance the theory"—ENP&S, reel no. 2

156. "we're right where we were"—Bellamy, p. 135.

156. "balky, often skeptical department"—CPD, 01/26/88

157. "It's not fun"—Badal, p. 34

157–58. "Another special detail?"; "If you don't find the killer"—Badal, pp. 90–91

158. "wonderful Sherlock Holmes"—Badal, p. 95

158. "hard worker . . . I'd hate to have Pete Merylo after me"—CPD, 10/12/75

159. "sex degenerate . . . blood flow"—Badal, p. 177

159. "You can't bring up Eliot Ness to Peter"—Badal, p. 93

160. "endless patience and determination"—CPD, 05/30/37

160. "With the Kingsbury amphitheater"—CPD, 05/30/37

160. "I always call their bluff"—AP, 09/15/38

161. "voodoo doctor"; "I'm pretty much alive"—CP, 09/14/36; CPD, 12/21/28

161. "nothing but junk"—Badal, p. 84

162. "every man was his own expert"—Badal, p. 94

162. "loco weed cigarettes"—CN, 09/06/36

162. "cut a lot of meat"—CN, 09/12/36

163. "keeps my head cool . . . second million"; "degenerate tendencies"—CPD, 10/16/36, 05/30/37

164. "people I never knew"—AP, 09/15/38

164. "retributive justice"; "evade capture with uncanny success"—CPD, 05/30/37

166. "The swamp is a handy place"; "blew up"; "Flynn returned to Cleveland"—CPD, 09/17/36; Badal, p. 100

167. "I was convinced beyond any doubt"—Badal, *Hell's Wasteland*, p. 42

168. "super-Amazon"; "Was you there, Charlie?"—Badal, pp. 94, 103

168. "As I've said before"—Heimel, p. 181

169. "I inherited a lot of information . . . The possibility of a different operator"—Nickel, p. 101

11: Steel and Bone

Background: Badal, pp. 108–21; Bellamy, pp. 145–68; Collins, pp. 106–132; Heimel, pp. 191–92; Martin, pp. 76–81; Nickel, pp. 98–107; Perry, 187–207; Cleveland newspapers, 03/07/37–10/18/37

173–74. Anvil Revue—Carl D. Friebolin Papers, WRHS

175. "his alter ego, the great G-man"—CPD, 03/06/37

175–76. "biggest task"; "No one belittles . . . oft-elected gentleman"—CPD, 03/06/37–03/07/37

176. "bad taste"—CPD, 01/22/36

177. "At first I thought"; "last two days"—CPD, 02/24/37

179. "anatomical landmarks"—Bellamy, p. 146; Martin, p. 79

179. "a little undeclared war"—CPD, 01/15/39

180. "not marked with the same skill"; "lake rolling"—CPD, 02/24/37

181. "Baby Farm"—CP, 02/24/37

181–82. "It is the theory of Detective Merylo"—CPD, 02/25/37

182. "Eight dismembered human bodies"—CP, 02/24/37

183–84. "swan boat"; "every five months"—CPD, 02/24/37

185. "I didn't know what it was"—CPD, 06/07/37, 04/11/38

185. "definite knife marks"—Badal, p. 118

186. "no more than a good guess"—Bellamy, p. 166

187. "ephemeral loyalties and peculiar friends"—Bellamy, p. 167

187. "boyfriend"—CP, 04/11/38

187. "disappeared in the same circumstances"—CPD, 04/11/38

187. "That's my mother"—Badal, p. 120

189. "Is this the city of Cleveland"—CPD, 06/10/37

189. "a couple of hundred rumor-carriers"—CPD, 06/06/37

190–91. "There is no doubt"; "signature every time"—CP, 07/06/37–07/07/37; CPD, 07/07/37

191. "flickering block of violet light"; "cutting people up"—CPD, 07/07/37

191–92. "inside story"; "We'll get him"—CP, 07/09/37; Nickel, p. 116

192–93. "Ness myth"; "Capone had an interest in it"—CPD, 09/26/37, 10/14/37

193. "How was it possible"; "solve this crime"—"Address of County Engineer John O. McWilliams," HHB, 10/06/37; CP, 09/07/37

193–94. "During the entire period"; "not to let Eliot Ness down"—ENP&S, reel no. 2

194. "kindly and unassuming"; "prepared for anything"—CP, ENP&S, reel no. 2

12: Do You Know This Room?

Background: Badal, pp. 44–48, 122–40; Bellamy, pp. 187–92, 213–18; Collins, pp. 147–152; Martin, pp. 81–84; Nickel, pp. 107–25; Cleveland newspapers and AP reports, 03/27/38–07/14/38

197. "Dad never stopped reading Cleveland papers"—CPD, 01/26/1988

198. "He used to get drunk and call Eliot . . . things that only the killer could know"—Bardsley, pp. 230–31

198. "Who gave you that name?"—Badal, p. 227

199. "Crude knife marks"—Badal, p. 134

200. "the fellow to see"—CPD, 07/31/36

200–201. "no statement"; "missing leg of the 10th victim"; "I refused to let Chamberlin"—CPD, 04/09/38–04/10/38

202. "Have you got a match, fellow?"—Badal, p. 45

204. "I don't think . . . all the same"—CP, 04/14/38

205. "NECROPHILIA, APHRODISIA, OR EROTOMANIA"—Bellamy, p. 295; Martin, p. 94

205. "Smoldering dissension"—CP, 04/14/38

206–7. "once-prominent Clevelander . . . with apparent sadistic tendencies"—CN, 04/09/38

207. "as neat a job of amputation"—CPD, 05/18/38

208. "going down and down and down with the booze"—Badal, *Though Murder Has No Tongue*, p. 134

208. "The suspect was a middle-aged man from a respectable family"—Sagalyn, p. 50

209. "a 'hot' suspect for the last two years"—CN, 04/09/38

209. "Yes, we are watching him . . . as well as two or three others"—CN, 04/09/38

210. "intensive work . . . the end of the chain of killings"—CPD, 04/09/38; Nickel, p. 126

210. "I won't mention any names"—Badal, p. 232

13: Gaylord Sundheim

Background: Alder, pp. 103–23; Badal, pp. 141–57, 217–59; Bellamy, pp. 243–49, 266–68; Collins, pp. 144–45, 155–66, 177–81, 256–60; Fraley, *4 Against the Mob*, pp. 126–37; Heimel, pp. 201–5, 219–25; LPUCB; Martin, pp. 86–89; Nickel, pp. 132–43, 202–4; Perry, pp. 213–26; SPAU, Box 1; Cleveland newspapers and AP reports, 05/31/38–09/13/38

215–16. "my white shadow"; "His maneuver exposed me"; "If he wants to try again"—Badal, p. 219; Sagalyn, p. 51

216. "in my file"; "No More Bodies"—Badal, p. 219

216–17. "dig here"; "to no avail"—Sagalyn, p. 52

217. "That's the man"—CPD, 02/17/91; *Des Moines Register*, 10/29/61

217. "This killer must be caught"—Martin, p. 88

217–18. "drinking heavy . . . played on him . . . week or two"—Badal, *Though Murder Has No Tongue*, pp. 134, 140

218. "must supplant brutality"—CP, 01/04/37

218. "does not exist in Cleveland"—CPD, 02/21/37

219. "We had Keeler come in"—Badal, *Though Murder Has No Tongue*, p. 140

219. "with the affection that a father would a son"—Alder, p. 243

220. "I think you did those killings!"—Fraley, *4 Against the Mob*, p. 135

220. "When Keeler got through"—Badal, p. 221

220. "disturbances indicative of guilt"—Alder, p. 161

222. "She lived incognito"—Heimel, p. 289; *Tampa Bay Times*, 10/08/2005

223. "coat sticking out"—CPD, 08/17/38

224–25. "Portions of it were dry"; "But the hunt will go on"—CN, 08/17/38; CPD, 08/17/38

225. "found the pelvis bones"—Badal, p. 145

226. "He's changing his technique . . . He's smart but he's gonna slip up"—Badal, p. 149; UP, 08/18/38

227. "matched the technique of the previous murders"—CN, 08/17/38

227. "subjected to lie detector tests"—CN, 05/31/38

228. "Where in this densely populated"—CPD, 08/18/38

229. "slayer's death house"—CPD, 08/25/38

232. "Ness refuses to get excited"—ENP&S, reel no. 3

232. "terrible hovels"—CN, 08/20/38

232–33. "target of investigation"; "live off refuse"—CP, 08/18/38; Badal, p. 154

235. "Burn it to the ground"—Perry, p. 225

14: Misguided Zeal

Background: Badal, pp. 235–42; Bellamy, pp. 246–49; Collins, pp. 183–92; Nickel, pp. 128–31; Perry, pp. 224–25; Cleveland newspapers, 08/13/38–08/30/38

236. "I remember the fire"—AI, David L. Stashower

236. "The net result"—CP, 08/26/38

237. "repeal your ordinances"—CPD, 08/23/38

237. "such men will have to stay"—CP, 08/18/38

237. "The torso killer—bah!"—Kerr, p. 69

238. "Misguided Zeal"—CP, 08/19/38

239. "schizoid personality; "He is considered incompetent"—Badal, p. 233

239. "first real clue"—INS, 08/28/38

239–42. Emil Fronek—AP, 08/29/38–08/30/39; CPD, 08/29/38–08/29/39; INS, 08/28/38–08/29/38; NYT, 08/29/38

244. "delicate . . . fat and soft"—Badal, p. 252

246. "We've saved the citizens a lot of money"—CPD, 09/20/38

246. "We just agreed a mistake had been made"—CPD, 09/21/38; Nickel, p. 145

246–47. "He did not talk about it . . . That was his trouble"—Heimel, p. 212; Porter, p. 102, Perry, pp. 4, 12

247. "Eliot was a gay, convivial soul"—Porter, p. 102

247. "two drinks . . . he would have twenty-two"—Perry, p. 287

247. "It wasn't that he was afraid"—Heimel, p. 211

248. "all-fired virtuous?"—Porter, p. 102

248. "I'm getting to be pretty popular"—CPD, 08/31/38

248. "Attention, Cleveland, Ohio"—"On Broadway with Walter Winchell" column, 10/20/38; Badal, p. 248

249. "There is only the routine investigation"—CPD, 10/17/38

249. "no such suspect"; "The information"; "arrests pretty soon"—Badal, p. 248

250. "This same surgical cunning"—*Kansas City Star*, 08/25/38

251. *"You can rest easy"*—*Los Angeles Times*, 01/06/39; Nickel, p. 147

251. "There are certain things"—AP, 01/08/39

252. "Bricklayer Confesses"—AP, 07/07/39

15: The Hot Seat

Background: Badal, pp. 186–207; Badal, *Though Murder Has No Tongue*, pp. 30–64; Bellamy, pp. 268–74; Collins, pp. 204–7, 229–50; Heimel, pp. 219–25; Martin, pp. 90–91; Nickel, pp. 155–68; SPAU, Box 1; Cleveland newspapers and AP reports, 05/03/39–10/12/39

253–54. "Sometimes business was good"; "should be easy to find"—CPD, 07/08/39

254. "If Sheriff O'Donnell . . . kept it a secret"—CPD, 07/16/39

254. "The solution of the murders"—CPD, 07/08/39

254. "We knew we had to change the pace"—AP, 07/09/39

255. "visited Mrs. Wallace"—CPD, 07/08/39

255–56. "If Dolezal . . . the joke is on me"—AP, 07/08/39

256. "We decided to make the arrest"—CPD, 07/08/39

257. "Svengali's eyes"—Badal, p. 186

257. "Imagine everyone's surprise"—CPD, 07/16/39

257. "There are some discrepancies . . . the kind of confession we want"—CPD, 07/08/39

257. "I hit her with my fist"—CPD, 07/08/39

258–59. "He flies off the handle"; "came at me with a knife"—AP, 07/09/39

259. "marvelous coup . . . in the dog house"—CPD, 07/16/39

260. "triumphed over Sleuth Eliot Ness"—*Time*, 07/17/39

260. "The sheriff is to be commended"—CPD, 07/08/39

260. "the Ness-Burton failure"—Nickel, p. 114

261. "hasn't been exactly a dismal failure"—Carl D. Friebolin Papers, WRHS

261. "I was in on it . . . a fun-loving guy"—Heimel, p. 206

262. "Evaline may have already"—*Cleveland Magazine*, August 1987

262. "I hesitated to announce"—CN, 10/26/39

262. "The director and his wife"; "The director's bride"—CPD, 10/27/39; ENP&S, reel no. 3

263. "She wasn't beautiful"—Perry, p. 190

263. "We'd go out at night"—Heimel, p. 211

263. "I had been working on this case for years . . . The neighbors liked him, too"—Badal, p. 192

264. "They have this record"—CPD, 07/09/39

264. "while the sheriff's action"; "slight odor"—CPD, 07/07/39, 07/16/39

264–65. "He said it once . . . loopholes"—CPD, 01/10/39

265. "This was my first experience"—Badal, p. 192

266. "One of his eyes"; "ought to have your jaw punched"—CP, 07/11/39

266. "Is Frank Dolezal the torso murderer?"—CP, 07/11/39

266. "Cleveland has resorted to barbarism"—Badal, *Though Murder Has No Tongue*, p. 46

267. "The tests I made"—AP, 07/14/39

267. "not worth a nickel"—CPD, 07/16/39

268. "What kind of jail are you running"—Badal, p. 198

269. "was almost a solid wall"—Badal, p. 201

269. "He'll get the hot seat"—CPD, 08/30/39

270. "wasn't even a suspect"—UP, 09/05/69

270. "wrong technique"; "I guess I did"—CPD, 02/03/40

270–71. "Dr. Sweeney was referred . . . no connection with the Torso Murders"—Badal, p. 252; Perry, p. 245

274. "a deep, piano-wire-thin scar"—Badal, p. 205

274. "I'm no pathologist"—Rebecca McFarland, quoted in Badal, p. 205

16: There Goes Eliot Ness

Background: Collins, 263–68, 275–80, 291–337, 355–75; Condon, pp. 240–42; *Coronet* magazine, July 1961; Heimel, pp. 229–31, 258–62; Jedick, pp. 45–57;

LPUCB; Nickel, pp. 180–81; Perry 1–4, 247–51, 289–95; Porter, pp. 103–4; SPAU, Box 1; Cleveland newspapers and AP reports, 03/12/41–11/30/52

276. "Eliot started drifting"—Heimel, p. 216

276. "screwed everything in a skirt"; "when she was sober"—Perry, pp. 231–35

277–78. "I had several drinks . . . My first thought . . . avoid publicity"—CP, 05/07/42

278. "Sir Galahad a hit-skip driver?"; "I don't think he could stand"—Condon, p. 240; Jedick, pp. 52–53

278. "When it seemed to Ness"—Condon, p. 239

279. "Eliot would tell Frank"—Jedick, p. 51

279. "a real G-man"—Condon, p. 241

279. "attempting to usurp"—McJimsey, vol. 32, p. 73

279–80. "It was a kind of police work"—Porter, p. 104

280. "whatever became of Eliot Ness"—CP, 5/22/40

280. "a closed matter"—CP, 03/09/42

280. "an era has ended here"—CPD, 04/29/42

281. "The arrest of Dolezal didn't stop the murders"—Badal, p. 199; Martin, p. 96; Nickel, p. 168

281. "mystified to find her lying in pieces"—Badal, p. 209

282. "Johnson . . . wasn't the torso murderer"—*Cleveland Magazine*, March 1984

282. "beyond a doubt . . . now total twenty-three"—Bellamy, pp. 293–94

282–83. "I will continue on this investigation . . . I will never give up"—Badal, p. 167

283. "low threshold of sexual approachability"—Heimel, p. 235

284. "In order to have that beauty"—Perry, p. 268

284. "We talked about a big wedding"—Heimel, p. 240

284. "Someday I may take"—*Reader's Digest*, February 1939

284. "I don't hold it against Eliot"—Heimel, p. 245

285. "I do not have to worry about a livelihood"—Condon, p. 242

285. "anyone but Superman . . . Burke clobbered him"—Porter, pp. 104

285. "Who'd want an honest politician"—Bergreen, p. 603

285. "downhill all the way"—Porter, pp. 104

285. "Eliot abandoned something"—Heimel, p. 254

285. "I'd regard it as a favor"—Condon, p. 243

286. "ran out of gas"—Perry, p. 287

286. "There wasn't a dull moment"; "Parenthood was a new experience"—Heimel, pp. 245, 281–83

287. "It was dangerous . . . why don't you write it?"—*Coronet* magazine, July 1961

288. "Don't get scared"—Tucker, p. 261

288. "actually surprised"; "Who the heck"—Heimel, p. 270

288. "verge of chucking the whole project"—Perry, p. 293

289. "The last time I saw Eliot"—CPHS, David Cowles interview

289. "Hollywood is nibbling"—Perry, p. 295

17: The American Sweeney

Background: Badal, pp. xi–xiv, 226–243; Bardsley, pp. 225–234; Collins, pp. 349–352; Coronet, "The Truth About Eliot Ness," July, 1961; Fraley, *4 Against the Mob*, pp. 126–137; Heimel, pp. 183–225; Perry, pp. 272–295; Tucker, pp. 256–265

291. "Enclosed a few items"—ENP&S, reel no. 3

291. "There wasn't any shooting"—Heimel, p. 280

292. "People are of the opinion"—CPD, 10/17/59

292. "cover a ten-dollar check"—Heimel, p. 282

292. "Had Eliot lived a little longer"—Porter, p. 105

294. "Nessisms . . . to tolerate his Weak-ness"—ENP&S, reel no. 3

295. "Don't worry about it"—Fraley, *4 Against the Mob*, p. 137

296. "Do you live around here?"; "barbitals"—Badal, p. 226

296–97. "None of this . . . especially in the legal sense"—Badal, p. 235

297. "proverbial jaw-dropper . . . serve as a living space"—Badal, pp. xii, 237–40

298–99. "an undertaker . . . and would amputate . . . pinpoint the exact location"—Badal, pp. xiv, 243

300. "The curtain of silence"; "I won't mention any names"—Badal, p. 238

300. "dark horse material"—CPD, 12/18/35

301. "a great and good friend"—Heimel, p. 277

301. "high standard of integrity . . . sustained effort"—ENP&S, reel no. 3

302. "probably is the most important"—ENP&S, reel no. 3

302. "That case . . . has been solved"—Perry, p. 281

Epilogue: Eliot-Am-Big-U-ous Ness

303. "We will never know for sure"—Nickel, p. 214

303. "little reason to think that Ness was right"—Bellamy, p. 267

303. "I'm still not at that point, not 100 percent"—*Cleveland Magazine*, 06/19/2014

305. "The real Eliot Ness"—Okrent, p. 136

306. "Ness restored a sense of hope . . . policemen no longer have to tip their hats"—Condon, p. 244

306. "all men have a price"—Heimel, p. 292

306. "Hell, I'm just like anyone else"—*Coronet* magazine, July 1961

SELECT BIBLIOGRAPHY

Books

Abbott, Karen. *Sin in the Second City: Madams, Ministers, Playboys, and the Battle for America's Soul.* New York: Random House, 2008.

Alder, Ken. *The Lie Detectors: The History of an American Obsession.* New York: Free Press, 2007.

Asbury, Herbert. *Gem of the Prairie: An Informal History of the Chicago Underworld.* Garden City, NY: Garden City Publishing Co. Inc., 1942.

Badal, James Jessen. *Hell's Wasteland: The Pennsylvania Torso Murders.* Kent, OH: Black Squirrel Books, 2013.

———. *In the Wake of the Butcher: Cleveland's Torso Murders*, revised edition. Kent, OH: Kent State University Press, 2014.

———. *Though Murder Has No Tongue: The Lost Victim of Cleveland's Mad Butcher.* Kent, OH: Black Squirrel Books, 2010.

Bair, Deirdre. *Al Capone: His Life, Legacy, and Legend.* New York: Nan A. Talese/Doubleday, 2016.

Bardsley, Marilyn J. *The American Sweeney Todd: Eliot Ness's Toughest Case.* Savannah, GA: DarkHorse MultiMedia Inc., 2017.

Bayer, Oliver Weld. *Cleveland Murders.* New York: Duell, Sloan and Pearce, 1947.

Bellamy, John Stark, II. *The Maniac in the Bushes and More Tales of Cleveland Woe.* Cleveland: Gray & Co, 1997.

Bendis, Brian Michael, and Marc Andreyko. *Torso: A True Crime Graphic Novel.* Orange, CA: Image Comics Inc., 2003.

Bergreen, Laurence. *Capone: The Man and the Era.* New York: Simon & Schuster, 1994.

Blum, Deborah. *The Poisoner's Handbook: Murder and the Birth of Forensic Medicine in Jazz Age New York.* New York: Penguin Press, 2010.

Brinkley, David. *Washington Goes to War.* New York: Knopf, 1988.

Burrough, Brian. *Public Enemies: America's Greatest Crime Wave and the Birth of the FBI.* New York: Penguin Press, 2004.

Bush, Lee O., Edward C. Chukayne, Russell Allon Hehr, and Richard F. Hershey. *Euclid Beach Park Is Closed for the Season.* Mentor, OH: Amusement Park Books Inc., 1978.

Capuzzo, Michael. *The Murder Room: The Heirs of Sherlock Holmes Gather to Solve the World's Most Perplexing Cold Cases.* New York: Gotham Books, 2010.

Cigliano, Jan. *Showplace of America: Cleveland's Euclid Avenue, 1850–1910.* Kent, OH: Kent State University Press, 1991.

Collins, Max Allan, and A. Brad Schwartz. *Eliot Ness and the Mad Butcher: Hunting America's Deadliest Unidentified Serial Killer at the Dawn of Modern Criminology.* New York: William Morrow, 2020.

———. *Scarface and the Untouchable: Al Capone, Eliot Ness, and the Battle for Chicago.* New York: William Morrow, 2018.

Condon, George E. *Cleveland: The Best Kept Secret.* Garden City, NY: Doubleday & Company Inc., 1967.

Douglas, John, and Mark Olshaker. *Mindhunter: Inside the FBI's Elite Serial Crime Unit.* New York: Scribner, 1995.

Eig, Jonathan. *Get Capone: The Secret Plot That Captured America's Most Wanted Gangster.* New York: Simon & Schuster, 2010.

Fraley, Oscar. *4 Against the Mob.* New York: Popular Library, 1961.

Grabowski, John J., and Diane Ewart Grabowski. *Cleveland Then and Now.* San Diego, CA: Thunder Bay Press, 2002.

Graysmith, Robert. *The Laughing Gorilla: A True Story of Police Corruption and Murder.* New York: Berkley Books, 2009.

Gentry, Curt. *J. Edgar Hoover: The Man and the Secrets.* New York: W. W. Norton, 1991.

Heimel, Paul W. *Eliot Ness: The Real Story,* second edition. Nashville, TN: Cumberland House, 2000.

James, Bill. *Popular Crime: Reflections on the Celebration of Violence.* New York: Scribner, 2011.

Jedick, Peter. *Cleveland: Where the East Coast Meets the Midwest.* Cleveland: Fine Line Litho, 1993.

Kerr, Daniel R. *Derelict Paradise: Homelessness and Urban Development in Cleveland, Ohio.* Amherst and Boston: University of Massachusetts Press, 2011.

Martin, John Bartlow. *Butcher's Dozen and Other Stories.* New York: Harper & Brothers, 1950.

McGill, Neil W., and William H. Perry. *Court Cases of Eliot Ness: The Cleveland Story of the Sleuth of the Century.* Fullerton, CA: Sultana Press, 1971.

McJimsey, George T., ed. *Documentary History of the Franklin D. Roosevelt Presidency.* 47 vols. Bethesda, MD: University Publications of America, 2001.

Messick, Hank. *The Silent Syndicate.* New York: Macmillan, 1967.

Miller, Carol Poh, and Robert Anthony Wheeler. *Cleveland: A Concise History, 1796–1996,* second edition. Bloomington: Indiana University Press, 1997.

Ness, Eliot, with Oscar Fraley. *The Untouchables.* New York: Barnes & Noble Books, 1996.

Ness, Eliot. *What About Girls?* New York: Public Affairs Committee, 1943.

Nickel, Steven. *Torso: The Story of Eliot Ness and the Search for a Psychopathic Killer.* Winston-Salem, NC: John F. Blair, 1989.

Okrent, Daniel. *Last Call: The Rise and Fall of Prohibition.* New York: Scribner, 2010.

Oliver, Willard M. *August Vollmer: The Father of American Policing.* Durham, NC: Carolina Academic Press, 2017.

Perry, Douglas. *Eliot Ness: The Rise and Fall of an American Hero.* New York: Viking, 2014.

Pezet, A. W., and Bradford Chambers. *Greatest Crimes of the Century.* Clinton, MA: The Colonial Press, 1954.

Porter, Philip W. *Cleveland: Confused City on a Seesaw.* Columbus: Ohio State University Press, 1976.

Rasmussen, William T. *Corroborating Evidence IV,* expanded fourth edition. Santa Fe, NM: Sunstone Press, 2012.

Ressler, Robert K., and Tom Shachtman. *Whoever Fights Monsters: My Twenty Years Hunting Serial Killers for the FBI.* New York: St. Martin's Press, 1992.

Rich, Bob. *A Touch of Cleveland History: Stories from the First 200 Years.* Cleveland: Gray & Company, 1995–1996.

Robsky, Paul, and Oscar Fraley. *The Last of the Untouchables.* New York: Popular Library, 1962.

Ruminski, Dan, and Alan Dutka. *Cleveland in the Gilded Age: A Stroll Down Millionaires' Row.* Charleston, SC: History Press, 2012.

Runyon, Damon. *Trials and Tribulations.* New York: International Polygonics Ltd., 1991.

Sagalyn, Arnold. *A Promise Fulfilled: The Memoir of Arnold Sagalyn.* Washington, DC: International Arts and Artists, 2010.

Schwarz, Ted. *Cleveland Curiosities.* Charleston, SC: History Press, 2010.

Seltzer, Louis B. *The Years Were Good.* Cleveland: World Publishing Company, 1956.

Slocum, William J. *The Tax Dodgers: The Inside of the T-Men's War with America's Political and Underworld Hoodlums.* New York: Greenberg, 1948.

Tucker, Kenneth. *Eliot Ness and the Untouchables: The Historical Reality and the Film and Television Depictions,* second edition. Jefferson, NC: McFarland & Company Inc., 2012.

Turzillo, Jane Ann. *Unsolved Murders & Disappearances in Northeast Ohio.* Charleston, SC: History Press, 2015.

Vacha, John. *Meet Me on Lake Erie, Dearie!: Cleveland's Great Lakes Exposition, 1936–1937.* Kent, OH: Kent State University Press, 2011.

Van Tassell, David D., and John J. Grabowski, eds. *The Encyclopedia of Cleveland History.* Bloomington: Indiana University Press, 1987.

Magazines and Journals

American History Illustrated. "The Real Eliot Ness" by Steven Nickel. October 1987.

The American Magazine. "America's Interesting People." May 1937.

Cleveland Magazine. "The Last American Hero" by George Condon. August 1987.

Coronet. "The Truth About Eliot Ness" by Oscar Fraley. July 1961.

Harper's Magazine. "The Cleveland Torso Murders" by John Bartlow Martin. November 1949.

International Journal of Humanities and Social Sciences. "The Last Boy Scout" by George E. Richard. September 2011.

Library Journal. "Evaline Ness" by Ann Durell. March 15, 1967.

Master Detective. "Ohio's Riddle of the 12 Headless Bodies" by James Farrington. September 1976.

Official Detective Stories. "$5,000 Reward: Who is Cleveland's Dread Butcher of Kingsbury Run?" November 15, 1937.

Reader's Digest. "Cleveland vs. the Crooks" by Stanley High (adapted from *Current History*). February 1939.

Smithsonian. "Eliot Ness vs. J. Edgar Hoover" by Erick Trickey. October 2014.

Time. "Cleveland's Butcher." July 17, 1939.

True Detective Mysteries. "25 Headless Bodies" by Aaron Green. January 1940.

INDEX

Donna Turner

DANIEL STASHOWER is a *New York Times* bestselling author, acclaimed biographer and narrative historian, and winner of the Edgar, Agatha, and Anthony Awards, as well as the Raymond Chandler Fulbright Fellowship in Detective Fiction. His work has appeared in *The New York Times, The Washington Post, Smithsonian Magazine, AARP: The Magazine, National Geographic Traveler,* and *American History,* as well as other publications. His books include *The Hour of Peril, Teller of Tales,* and *The Beautiful Cigar Girl.*